Networked Governance and Transatlantic Relations

I0003205

"This is a must-read pioneering work. It links our understanding of cutting-edge science and technology policy issues locally and regionally in the context of today's transatlantic diplomacy and recognizes the power of networks that cross national and physical boundaries."

—***Nanette S. Levinson***, *American University School of International Service*

"Paár-Jákli's work provides a fresh and compelling analysis of an underappreciated aspect of the transatlantic relationship. By highlighting the role of digital networks, the author introduces a dynamic new component in the evolving relationship between North America and Europe. The volume updates transatlantic relations in an interesting and thought-provoking fashion."

—***Alberta Sbragia***, *University of Pittsburgh*

In today's complex and interconnected world, scholars of international relations seek to better understand challenges spurred by intensified global communication and interaction. The complex connectedness of modern society and politics compels us to investigate the pattern of interconnections among actors who inhabit social and political spaces.

Gabriella Paár-Jákli's study aims to advance theory and practice by examining the networks used by specialists in North America and Europe to achieve their policy goals in the area of science and technology. Her book suggests that to overcome policy problems transnationally, three critical factors should be considered. First, as science and technology policy becomes increasingly critical to resolving global issues, it should be regarded as an integral element of the foreign policy process. Second, as liberal international relations theory argues, the increasing role of NGOs must be taken seriously alongside states as vital agents of policy reform. Third, as transatlantic relations remain center to maintaining the global order, they must be reconsidered. Paár-Jákli assesses the role of digital networks as facilitators of regional cooperation. Utilizing various techniques of social network analysis, her research indicates an active and structurally discernible network in cyberspace among transatlantic organizations, and demonstrates the role of virtual networks as facilitators of cooperative arrangements in transatlantic relations.

Paár-Jákli's original research uses social network analysis to investigate transatlantic cooperation, a new approach that will be noteworthy to network and transatlantic scholars as well as policy-makers.

Gabriella Paár-Jákli is an Assistant Professor of Political Science at Kent State University.

Routledge Advances in International Relations and Global Politics

For a full list of titles in this series, please visit www.routledge.com

87 **The Contested Politics of Mobility**
Borderzones and Irregularity
Edited by Vicki Squires

88 **Human Security, Law and the Prevention of Terrorism**
Andrej Zwitter

89 **Multilayered Migration Governance**
The Promise of Partnership
Edited by Rahel Kunz, Sandra Lavenex and Marion Panizzon

90 **Role Theory in International Relations**
Approaches and analyses
Edited by Sebastian Harnisch, Cornelia Frank & Hanns W. Maull

91 **Issue Salience in International Relations**
Edited by Kai Oppermann and Henrike Viehrig

92 **Corporate Risk and National Security Redefined**
Karen Lund Petersen

93 **Interrogating Democracy in World Politics**
Edited by Joe Hoover, Meera Sabaratnam and Laust Schouenborg

94 **Globalizing Resistance against War**
Theories of Resistance and the New Anti-War Movement
Tiina Seppälä

95 **The Politics of Self-Determination**
Beyond the Decolonisation Process
Kristina Roepstorff

96 **Sovereignty and the Responsibility to Protect**
The power of norms and the norms of the powerful
Theresa Reinold

97 **Anglo-American Relations**
Contemporary Perspectives
Edited by Alan P. Dobson and Steve Marsh

98 **The Emerging Politics of Antarctica**
Edited by Anne-Marie Brady

99 **Genocide, Ethnonationalism, and the United Nations**
Exploring the Causes of Mass Killing Since 1945
Hannibal Travis

100 **Caribbean Sovereignty, Development and Democracy in an Age of Globalization**
Edited by Linden Lewis

101 **Rethinking Foreign Policy**
Edited by Fredrik Bynander and Stefano Guzzini

102 **The Promise and Perils of Transnationalization**
NGO Activism and the Socialization of Women's Human Rights in Egypt and Iran
Benjamin Stachursky

103 **Peacebuilding and International Administration**
The cases of Bosnia and Herzegovina and Kosovo
Niels van Willigen

104 **The Politics of the Globalization of Law**
Getting from Rights to Justice
Edited by Alison Brysk

105 **The Arctic in International Politics**
Coming in from the Cold
Peter Hough

106 **Understanding Transatlantic Relations**
Whither the West?
Serena Simoni

107 **India in South Asia**
Domestic Identity Politics and Foreign Policy from Nehru to the BJP
Sinderpal Singh

108 **A Strategic Understanding of UN Economic Sanctions**
International Relations, Law and Development
Golnoosh Hakimdavar

109 **Politics and the Bomb**
The Role of Experts in the Creation of Cooperative Nuclear Non-Proliferation Agreements
Sara Z. Kutchesfahani

110 **Interpreting Global Security**
Mark Bevir, Oliver Daddow and Ian Hall

111 **Foreign Policy, Domestic Politics and International Relations**
The Case of Italy
Elisabetta Brighi

112 **The Scourge of Genocide**
Essays and Reflections

113 **Authority, Ascendancy, and Supremacy**
China, Russia, and the United States' Pursuit of Relevancy and Power
Gregory O. Hall

114 **The Politics of Arctic Sovereignty**
Oil, Ice and Inuit Governance
Jessica M. Shadian

115 **Small States and International Security**
Europe and Beyond
Edited by Clive Archer, Alyson J.K. Bailes and Anders Wivel

116 **Networked Governance and Transatlantic Relations**
Building Bridges through Science Diplomacy
Gabriella Paár-Jákli

Networked Governance and Transatlantic Relations

Building Bridges through Science Diplomacy

Gabriella Paár-Jákli

Routledge
Taylor & Francis Group
NEW YORK AND LONDON

First published 2014
by Routledge
711 Third Avenue, New York, NY 10017

and by Routledge
2 Park Square, Milton Park, Abingdon, Oxfordshire OX14 4RN

First issued in paperback 2016

Routledge is an imprint of the Taylor & Francis Group, an informa business

Library of Congress Cataloging-in-Publication Data

Paár-Jákli, Gabriella.
Networked governance and transatlantic relations : building bridges through science diplomacy / by Gabriella Paár-Jákli.
pages cm — (Routledge advances in international relations and global politics ; 116)
1. Science and state—International cooperation. 2. Technology and state—International cooperation. 3. Internet and international relations. 4. Technology and international relations. 5. Diplomacy—Technological innovations. 6. International relations—Computer networks. 7. Social media—Political aspects. 8. Non-governmental organizations. 9. European Union countries—Foreign relations—United States. 10. United States—Foreign relations—European Union countries. I. Title.
JZ1254.P33 2014
338.9'26—dc23
2013047669

ISBN13: 978-1-138-69641-9 (pbk)
ISBN13: 978-0-415-85417-7 (hbk)

Typeset in Sabon
By Apex CoVantage, LLC

To Laura and Olivia

Contents

Figures

Tables

Preface

> What is possible is not independent of what we believe to be possible. The possibility of such developments in the practical world depends upon their being grasped imaginatively by the people who make the practical world work.
>
> Neil MacCormick, 1993[1]

This book evolved from the many intriguing questions that have been at the center of my interest. One of these most compelling questions is perhaps best summarized by the title of John Avery's book Space-Age Science and Stone-Age Politics. As Avery explains, these two can constitute a rather dangerous mixture. The problem he demonstrates is that human knowledge reflected in science and technology has advanced much faster than our social and cultural evolution. In a way, Avery's research could appeal to traditional realists who are preoccupied with man's violent nature, because he argues that tribalism can indeed still be detected in human nature. Avery explains that humans have a tendency to feel loyalty toward their "own kinds," which typically refers to defensiveness and altruism toward a narrower kind of community (family, tribe, or nation), coupled with "intertribal aggression." He adds that this is due to the fact that in the larger part of our human history the idea of "survival of the fittest" prevailed. The resurfacing of inter-ethnic rivalries and motives for terrorist activities certainly demonstrate these kinds of—perhaps, but not necessarily, innate—primitive loyalties. As Avery interprets, this can cause dangerous divides and enhanced hostilities still present in our "space-age."[2] This need not be the case in the 21st century due partially to emerging common ethical and moral norms, values, and considerations. The level of interconnectedness and the complexity of a multitude of worldwide phenomena also require that we address these challenges collectively.

This book constitutes an initial step in uncovering how existing differences between European and American policy positions can be resolved via European and US-based knowledge network (KNET) initiatives. This project materializes through an investigation of the transatlantic partnership and pivotal leadership role that the United States and Europe can undertake in shaping global trends and overcoming challenges. The book investigates the knowledge-based structure of the transatlantic relationship as a core element of the international system, and reveals that it has the potential to be a primary catalyst in the resolution of transnational policy problems. This information makes it possible to configure alternative strategies to further transatlantic cooperation as well as identify future directions.

This research takes an interdisciplinary approach and draws on the works of scholars who point in the direction of the linked, yet fragmented, nature of an increasingly interconnected world. Through emphasizing the role of networks that are continuously being formed among diverse sets of transnational actors, they search for a global order. Taken as a whole, this book aims to contribute to understanding how networks, and network-based governance, can facilitate a more dynamic flow of reliable information and knowledge. Complex issues, such as energy security, distinctly require expert-knowledge and cooperation transnationally. Considering the increasing role of science and technology policy in all foreign policy decisions, the choice of this policy seems warranted as a focus of transatlantic cooperation.

Acknowledgments

This book is a product of the dissertation research I undertook as a graduate student at Kent State University; and it would not have been possible without the active cooperation and participation of a great many people, all essential. Support has come in numerous forms. Special thanks go to my adviser Steven Hook for all his guidance and advice on theoretically important issues. I also am indebted to my committee members: Andrew Barnes, Alberta Sbragia, Julie Mazzei, and John Logue, who is forever in my memories. I want to extend my special thanks to another committee member and an extraordinary interdisciplinary research collaborator, Ruoming Jin; his and his graduate student's, David Fuhry's, expertise in data-mining and network analysis was indispensable for my research method. I also wish to thank my colleagues at the annual conventions of the International Studies Association, especially Nanette Levinson and Derrick Cogburn, for the fruitful conversations and invaluable advice they have given me throughout these years. Diane Stone provided me with instrumental guidance with the knowledge network aspect of the research and the significance of their operations in governance processes and the global political economy; her approach has been inspirational. Additionally, I also am grateful to Cathy DuBois and Rick Schroath, who believed in me and encouraged me to pursue my PhD studies; their faith that a former policy-practitioner would succeed in the academia was an essential part of the process. Furthermore, I wish to thank Steven Brown for always being ready to talk and share ideas throughout the years—a rare example of the true "renaissance man" indeed. I also thank my colleague and friend, Katalin Csorba, for being a great research collaborator on Hungarian and EU science and technology policy and innovation, which has contributed to the development of this project as well. Last, but not least, I am also indebted to Natalja Mortensen, editor of this series at Routledge, and the anonymous reviewers for their insightful recommendations that made the final product stronger.

Without doubt, I owe tremendous debt to my family, my husband Tony, and my daughters Laura and Olivia. Thank you for being there for me and tolerating all my anxiety throughout the undeniably frustrating process of writing this book. In addition, I would like to thank my parents, who nurtured my intellectual curiosity, inspired me, and taught me that there is no such thing as impossible; we just have not tried hard enough. I am also grateful to Bonbon, our family shih-poo, for being my companion and reminding me every morning to go straight to my home office, where she settled suggestively next to my computer chair. I probably could not have done this without her either.

Gabriella Paár-Jákli
Kent, Ohio
November, 2013

NOTES

1. Neil MacCormick, "Beyond the Sovereign State," *The Modern Law Review* 56, no. 1 (1993): 1–18.
2. John Avery, *Space-Age Science and Stone-Age Politics*, e-book (Copenhagen: Danish Pugwash Group, 2005).

1 Introduction

> *Abstract systems depend on trust, yet they provide none of the moral rewards which can be obtained from personalized trust, or were often available in traditional settings from the moral frameworks within which everyday life was undertaken. Moreover, the wholesale penetration of abstract systems into daily life creates risks which the individual is not well placed to confront; high-consequence risks fall into this category. Greater interdependence, up to and including globally independent systems, means greater vulnerability when untoward events occur that affect those systems as a whole.*
>
> —Anthony Giddens, 1991[1]

While fundamental questions that have guided the work of international relations scholars, such as why people wage wars, what are the prospects for peace, or what conditions facilitate conflict and cooperation remain unchanged, human interaction takes place in a tremendously different global context in the 21st century. As the nature of security threats changes, scholars of international relations keep investigating the human capacity to resolve conflict and "to replace the institution of war with more effective, less brutal ways of seeking security."[2] In exploring alternative approaches, Fry emphasizes that global interdependence demands increased reliance on cross-cutting ties that have the potential to foster cooperation to help overcome global challenges.[3]

This book is centrally concerned with how transatlantic networks and the use of communication technology can enable the United States and the European Union to assume greater responsibility and a stronger leadership role in addressing global challenges.[4] The argument is that in our *increasingly complex and interconnected world, network-based solutions* of knowledge creation, dissemination, and the diffusion of best practices can enhance our capacity to define and address policy problems more efficiently. This research uses the transatlantic cooperative partnership as a case study and points out what we can learn from looking at EU–US relations and, within that, science and technology policy through the network perspective.

Ultimately, the insight we gain from the study should help us guide future policies that are crucial in transatlantic relations.

While this book is one of many that centers around transatlantic relations, its unique contribution lays in the *interdisciplinary investigation* of the prospects of these relations as they relate to the international system as a whole. As this research considers the *international system as a complex system* with interrelated ties, it pursues *structural analysis* and explores the structure of existing transatlantic network connections in general, and in the area of science and technology policy specifically.[5] This book premises that the architecture of networks matters and that structural and relational characteristics influence political outcomes. As Hanneman and Riddle explain, "the network approach emphasizes that power is inherently relational; it is also a consequence of patterns of relations," and as a result, it varies with divergent structural arrangements.[6] Structural positions in a relational network constrain, as well as provide, opportunities to network-members, which in turn determine how powerful or influential they become in their networks. Network positions influence the acquisition and distribution of resources, information in our case, within the network. Additionally, the book builds on the idea that the gathering and transmission of information represents a powerful political resource and can be regarded as an incentive to induce cooperative action among organizations, as well as a means to further legitimizing the organization itself.[7] Combining these suggestions with Lazer's proposition—that structural characteristics of a network influence information flow and relationships among network actors as well as impact systemic success—this study argues that the knowledge of network specifics, such as potentially significant and interesting groups of actors inside the network, should help uncover an innovative approach to successful transnational cooperation and policy-coordination.[8]

The policy choice, science and technology policy, here is not coincidental. Foreign policy decisions are increasingly driven by issues such as energy security and environmental problems, all of which require expert-knowledge and the cooperation of a diverse set of scientific disciplines. As the American Association for the Advancement of Science's (AAAS) new science diplomacy center states, science and scientific cooperation promote international understanding and prosperity:

> [m]any of our most pressing foreign policy challenges—energy, climate change, disease, desperate poverty and underdevelopment, and WMD proliferation—demand both technological and policy solutions. In these and other areas, U.S. national security depends on our willingness to share the costs and benefits of scientific progress with other nations.[9]

As no nation-state has the expertise or the resources to face these unique 21st-century challenges alone, foreign policy decision-makers need to focus on building a coherent strategy for science diplomacy.[10] In line with liberal international relations (IR)theory, this research assumes that the role of non-governmental organizations (NGOs) and transnational networks calls for an alternative approach to unravel patterns of cooperation in the 21st century. Recognizing the idea that some of these NGOs, such as think tanks and other independent expert organizations, can be regarded as "third party vetters of trust," this study puts an emphasis on the potential value of such epistemic community-like entities, or knowledge network (KNET) members in the international system.[11,12] This research is based on the insight that *networks* can be *regarded as new mechanisms of governance and that we can benefit from these networks' ability to systemize knowledge from a wide variety of sources as well as disseminate* it.[13] As this book stresses the role of networks that are more on the informal scale of institutions, and also investigates the power of shared ideas and communication through networking patterns, it raises question of legitimacy and discourse. As such, it aims to advocate for a dialogue and a theoretical synthesis between liberal institutionalism and social constructivist ideals. This book reflects the assumption that theories that reflect diverse approaches may capitalize on their complementarities.[14]

Guided by these premises, this book examines how virtual communication networks gather and disseminate both information and policy-specific knowledge that might foster inter-organizational trust. Following Giddens' underrated advice that, in the absence of "personalized trust," new ways of obtaining trust should be explored, this book investigates transatlantic relations through analyzing the complex web of interactions, or networks, among institutional web pages. Trust and social capital are vital elements of democratic governance at all levels; trust facilitates information exchange and a faster, more flexible adaptation to the changing environment.[15] Additionally, trust that "lubricates social life" and assists the creation of social capital is a prerequisite to addressing collective action problems in the international system.[16]

To support these ideas through empirical evidence, this research uses a case study: the cooperative partnership between the European Union and the United States. As the relevant literature points out, transatlantic cooperation is considered a vital element of the international system.[17] Yet, reflecting on the New Transatlantic Agenda of 1995, Pollack and Shaffer suggest that there is a *gap in the literature* on what constitutes the communicative *linchpin in transatlantic relations*.[18] As this book asserts, *the potential "linchpin" in transatlantic cooperative relations is the network of transatlantic think tanks, policy research institutions, academics, and research analysts along with other experts and professionals, and their virtual networking practices*. In light of these insights of the recently emergent network theoretical perspective, this book aims to find answers to specific questions. Does the network theoretical perspective bring us closer to uncovering the "linchpin" of US–EU cooperation? What role do knowledge networks and their hyperlinking communication practices play in fostering transatlantic relations?[19]

What strategic tools might be applied to develop more inclusive cooperative engagements? Can we support the claim, in line with liberal IR theory, that non-state actors play a significant role in transatlantic relations? What is the role of potential knowledge network members, such as academics, research, and policy institutions, and also think tanks in the virtual transatlantic networks? If the empirics of this research show that these actors emerge as brokers in the network, then their potential to integrate distant groups and forge new relations represents opportunities to improve transatlantic networking practices.

Overall, this book aspires to *contribute to the understanding of the "network factor"* as a more recent focal point of economic and political development. My particular interest is in the role of networks as generators and disseminators of knowledge that have the capacity to bridge global divides. While the concluding chapter elaborates on the book's contribution to the discipline, the distinctive techniques to examine virtual networking practices of transatlantic organizations is worth mentioning here. To my knowledge, *no other research to date has used social network analytical tools and visualization techniques to investigate transatlantic networks.*

The broader implication of this research resides in its ability to deliver insights and contribute to understanding whether and how *virtual networks,* understood as knowledge-based structures, have the ability to *act as "conduits of change"* and help resolve transnational policy problems in the environment of fast-paced change. Consequently, the findings of this research can breach important questions, such as: What roles do new modes of interaction, importantly online communication networks, play in the transformation of existing political and social structures transnationally? How might science and technology be an area of cooperation, which facilitates cooperation on other policy initiatives? As Thompson explains, networks emerged as explanatory devices in various fields and can be contrasted with other coordinating devices, such as hierarchies and markets.[20] Further elaborating on the issue, Wong argues, "[t]he importance of network analysis for international relations . . . is the implication of differences in network structure, including the notion of centrality and its implications [which ultimately] helps us understand the effects of interdependence and the implications of the variations in structure."[21]

THE PLAN OF THE BOOK

Methodology and Research Strategy

While the theoretical framework is described, in detail, in Chapter 2 and an in-depth review of the methodology is provided in Appendix A, a brief introduction of both is in order here.

This book draws on and synthesizes a broad range of theoretical and methodological approaches with the underlying idea that theories that reflect diverse approaches can capitalize on their complementarities. The overall theme of the book regards the opportunities and challenges of international communication and their implications to governance. An essential point the book conveys is that open communication transnationally fosters trust and understanding, and facilitates cooperative behavior. After addressing one of the key ideas, access to information and knowledge as a source of democratic politics and policies, the idea of transnational discursive democracy is discussed, which, as this study points out, constitutes the basis for consensus-making and cooperative behavior. The review then focuses on networks and network theory. A core idea that runs through the book is that, in addition to international institutions, the web of governmental and non-governmental transnational networks lay down the foundation for consensus-building, cooperation, and internationally negotiated agreed-upon law. This research clarifies how a flexible and innovation-prone brokering of connections among network-members, as well as disconnected network segments, creates opportunities that, in turn, have the ability to generate social capital. Next, the concept of epistemic-like communities, such as "knowledge networks," is explained. In line with Stone's contention, the book highlights the invaluable potential of policy-expertise grounded in scientific, "codified forms of knowledge," which is able to bridge knowledge gaps, facilitate "the delivery of (global) public goods," and provide a deliberative capacity for democratic governance.[22] As scholars of Internet governance began to investigate the diverse sources and competences of knowledge, they found that these can be understood, as well as depicted, as networked governance structures. This book incorporates these ideas into the theoretical framework. A closely related concept, science diplomacy, and its role in policy coordination and cooperation is also examined; then the review of the literature attends to the concepts of international order and governance, which are considered the ultimate goals as well as tools for transnational security and peaceful coexistence in the international system. Overall, these theories and concepts aim to serve both as a foundation of and a framework for the book.

As previously mentioned, this book looks at the "network factor" as it analyzes web-based connections of select transatlantic organizations via hyperlink analysis. Network analysis allows for their depiction as nodes connected by lines that represent relationships. The web-based connections these organizations create are called "hyperlinks," and they serve as references, as well as communicative channels. This book examines how virtual communication networks gather and disseminate policy-specific knowledge that might foster inter-organizational trust. A key assertion of this study is that these networks can be identified and verified empirically through their interactions on the Internet. This research hypothesizes that it is possible to locate, within a broader transatlantic network, a science and technology-specific sub-network that may contribute to policy change in regards to transatlantic scientific and technological cooperation.

The primary data gathered and analyzed in this study are network data, which were collected using Internet hyperlinks of organizations engaged in transatlantic relations. This involved network analysis and data-mining techniques. Institutions were selected in the following subcategories of knowledge networks: academic, research, and policy institutes; governmental organizations; inter-governmental organizations; think tanks; interest groups; and other building blocks of these information and knowledge systems. Social network data, data on networks of web pages or hyperlinks, and other data extracted from text documents are often called relational data. This is because it is the relationships that are considered central. The network perspective puts the emphasis on structural relations. As opposed to the more individualistic, variable-centered approaches, the argument is made that social context matters and, under certain circumstances, the structural setting within a network may drive behavior or action independent of attributes. Knoke and Yang argue, "social networks affect perceptions, beliefs, and actions through a variety of structural mechanisms that are socially constructed by relations among entities."[23]

In addition to the social network analyses, this research visually represents these networks by using "Pajek," a software program suitable for the analysis and visualization of large networks.[24] Performing various techniques of social network analysis, the study sought answers to the following network-specific questions: What are the key coalitions and backbone agencies in the network(s)?[25] How do they relate to the community structure of the network?[26] How do these structures relate to different types of KNET participants, such as policy research institutions, universities, public-interest NGOs, government agencies, and inter-governmental organizations (IGOs)? Does the transatlantic knowledge network system show similar characteristics to that of other forms of networked governance found in the literature?

Hypotheses

Several specific hypotheses are developed throughout the book. *First,* in line with liberal IR theory, non-state actors play a significant role in transatlantic relations constituting the communicative "linchpin" to catalyze virtual collaboration. *Second,* the more closely related a transatlantic network member's mission is to science and technology policy, the more likely it emerges as a key player in transatlantic cooperation. The basis for this assumption is that science and technology play an increasing role in finding policy solutions to increasingly complex foreign policy problems.[27,28] *Third,* potential knowledge network members, such as academic, research, and policy institutions, and also think tanks, provide a higher proportion of the membership in the virtual transatlantic science and technology (S&T) sub-network. This is grounded in Adler's finding that such entities play important roles in transnational cooperation in policy areas characterized by complexity and technical uncertainty. *Fourth*, if complexity in international relations stimulates new modes of interactions among new actors and transforms social structures, then the structure of the aforementioned transatlantic networks may conform to the forms commonly found in online social networks. *Fifth*, if there are opportunities to improve transatlantic virtual networking practices, then organizations that are in the position of brokering further connections will emerge from social network analysis. This might provide a basis for strategic policy recommendations pertaining to future improvement of the transatlantic partnership.[29]

Research Strategy: Embedded Case Study

This study includes an embedded case study. Yin suggests that the case study should be defined as a research strategy—an empirical inquiry that investigates a phenomenon within its real-life context. "The case study is preferred in examining contemporary events, when the relevant behaviors cannot be manipulated."[30] The embedded case study is especially suited for investigating an environment where the boundaries between the phenomenon under investigation and its context are not entirely obvious.[31] This research investigates transnational cooperative arrangements via hyperlink network analysis and uses transatlantic relations between the United States and the European Union as a case study. Nevertheless, it should be considered an embedded case study, because the sub-unit of analysis is transatlantic science and technology policy and the relevant cooperative agreement. There are advantages to conducting research using embedded case studies. First, the inclusion of sub-units allows for a more detailed level of inquiry. Second, as Yin explains, an embedded case study, similar to a case study, offers a means to integrate diverse methodology (quantitative and qualitative) into a single research, including the use of technology.[32] As Flyvbjerg argues, case studies lend themselves to both generating and testing hypotheses.[33]

It is important to address the issue of generalizability here. While individual case studies are unique, the findings and conclusions are generalizable.[34] As Gilgun explains, this kind of generalizability, sometimes termed "analytic generalizability," she suggests that these findings can be just as useful in different settings.[35] This research offers three aspects of generalizability. First, the findings can be applicable when researching other transnational networks. Second, the choice of science and technology policy is deliberate as it is crucial to the understanding of the actions and interactions of regional blocks, state or non-state actors in 21st-century international relations. As social, political, and economic impacts and determinants of intensified scientific and technological change become more salient to the general public, they motivate policy-makers to address issues, such as the generation of alternative energy resources, more aggressively. Science and technology, and its interaction with international politics, make foreign policy decision-making more complex than ever before. As the aforementioned interaction impacts social and political structures by providing a perpetually evolving context, new actors with new interests emerge while old actors' interests are continually being altered. Communication channels among scientists, policy-makers, and the public must adapt to these changes. Complexity and technical uncertainty impact all policy areas more extensively today than they did in the past, and, as a result science and technology are central to addressing all critical global issues and challenges. This trend, which is expected to continue in the coming decades, manifests in the active networking roles of organizations with S&T-related missions. This research supports these observations. Third, research on knowledge network participants, such as policy research institutions, universities, public-interest non-governmental organizations (NGOs), government agencies, and inter-governmental organizations (IGOs), can also be transferable to other transnational groups as these epistemic-like communities can act as catalysts of change in facilitating the development and implementation of international public policy.

Book Outline

Following the introductory chapter, **Chapter 2** is dedicated to reviewing the literature and explaining how, by bringing together seemingly different elements, multiple dimensions of knowledge can help us understand political processes that impact policies. The study draws on and synthesizes a broad range of theoretical and methodological approaches, as well as analytical concepts, such as networked governance, multi-stakeholder diplomacy, science diplomacy, epistemic communities, knowledge networks and network theory, as well as transnational communication. While this chapter focuses on reviewing the relevant theories and analytical concepts, it also seeks to highlight the idea of generating synergy among methodological, theoretical, or even empirical skills. As this research argues, this should contribute to the success of the researcher.

Chapter 3 begins with the question: Why should we care about transatlantic relations? After looking at the relevant literature, the chapter sets the stage for viewing transatlantic relations as an essential element of the international system. Considering that the inception of the institutionalization of transatlantic relations can be placed at the end of World War II, that is where this research begins. **Chapter 4** examines how and why science and technology policy is becoming increasingly critical to resolving global issues. On the one hand, the book's goal is to reinforce the idea that this policy area should be regarded as an integral element of the foreign policy process, while, on the other hand, the policy also serves as an example of the dynamics of cooperative arrangements within the transatlantic agenda. Science and technology induced changes result primarily from the interactions of new actors and their interest representation that modify not only social structures, but also the context in which policy issues arise and are debated on the transnational level.[36] This book builds on these insights.

Chapter 5 presents the empirical results and addresses the main approaches to answering key questions. The findings of the research demonstrate the existence of a structurally discernible network in cyberspace among transatlantic organizations. Additionally, results prove the existence of a science and technology-specific sub-network, where a range of network actors fulfilling various roles can be distinguished. Furthermore, findings indicate that *science and technology-related organizations,* or organizations whose mission is tied to science and technology promotion, emerge as rather *visible actors.* This confirms the idea that these types of organizations have an essential role in finding policy solutions to increasingly complex foreign policy problems in transatlantic relations and, potentially, in various other transnational relations.

This research is based on the assumption that if various organizations form a knowledge network (KNET), then it is feasible to represent them as such. In agreement with liberal IR theory, which emphasizes the role of non-state actors in cooperation and policy-coordination, this research finds that while state actors are not invisible, they are not predominant actors in these networks. Inter-governmental organizations; academic, research, and policy institutes; and think tanks all have a significant share. This chapter points out an evolving network of professionals and organizations in cyberspace which, if watched closely, can be a basis for improving strategic cooperation. Overall, the chapter aims to show how these new findings add to what is already known about transatlantic relations.

The **final chapter** elaborates on the research contribution, addresses theoretical implications, positions the research in the discipline, and considers policy implications, as well as future directions. The chapter summarizes what we can learn from the findings of the study and how the discovery of patterns could be applicable to other regions of IR. The interdisciplinary nature of network analysis and the benefits of such approach to social science research are discussed; the chapter then highlights two main arguments supported by the author. First, complex human behavior and sociopolitical complexities are better explained by the interdisciplinary approach. Second, problem solving in the 21st century increasingly necessitates the adoption of such approaches.

NOTES

1. Anthony Giddens, *Modernity and Self-Identity. Self and Society in the Late Modern Age*, 1st ed. (Cambridge, MA: Polity Press, 1991), 136.
2. Douglas P. Fry, *Beyond War: The Human Potential for Peace*, 1st ed. (Oxford University Press, 2007), xiv.
3. Ibid.
4. I use the EU and Europe in this research somewhat interchangeably, because even though the goal is to investigate US–EU relations and their partnership opportunities, some of the literature uses them rather interchangeably.
5. James N. Rosenau, *Turbulence in World Politics* (Princeton, NJ: Princeton University Press, 1990).; Margaret E. Keck and Kathryn Sikkink, *Activists Beyond Borders: Advocacy Networks in International Politics* (Ithaca, NY: Cornell University Press, 1998).; Albert L. Barabási, *Linked: How Everything Is Connected to Everything Else and What It Means for Business, Science, and Everyday Life* (Cambridge, MA: Perseus Publishing, 2002).
6. Mark Hanneman and Robert A. Riddle, *Introduction to Social Network Methods* (Riverside, CA: University of California, Riverside, publsihed in digital form, 2005), http://faculty.ucr.edu/~hanneman/.
7. Jeffrey Pfeffer and Gerald R. Salancik, *The External Control of Organizations: A Resource Dependence Perspective* (New York, NY: Harper and Row, 1978).
8. David Lazer, "Regulatory Capitalism as a Networked Order: The International System as an Informational Network," *The ANNALS of the American Academy of Political and Social Science* 598, no. 1 (March 1, 2005): 52–66.
9. AAAS, *2009–2010 Annual Review*, 2010, http://diplomacy.aaas.org/files/CSD_YIR_Year2_Web.pdf.
10. Vaughan C. Turekian, "Building a National Science Diplomacy System," *Science and Diplomacy* 1, no. 4 (2012), http://sciencediplomacy.org/files/building_a_national_science_diplomacy_system_science_diplomacy.pdf.
11. In brief, "epistemic communities" and "knowledge networks" refer to various forms of intellectual collaborations. These approaches that emphasize the role of policy-expertise grounded in systemized forms of knowledge are further explained later in this chapter.
12. Margaret Levi, "A State of Trust," in *Trust and Governance,* eds. V. Braithwaite and M. Levi (New York: Russel Sage Foundation, 1998), 77–101.; Diane Stone, "Think Tank Transnationalisation and Non-Profit Analysis, Advice and Advocacy," *Global Society* 14, no. 2 (April 2000): 153–172.; Peter M. Haas, "Introduction: Epistemic Communities and International Policy Coordination," *International Organization* 46, no. 01 (May 22, 1992); Diane Stone, "Knowledge Networks and Global Policy," in *Global Knowledge Networks and International Development,* ed. D. Stone and S. Maxwell, 1st ed. (New York: Routledge, 2005); Inderjeet Parmar, "American Foundations and the Development of International Knowledge Networks," *Global Networks* 1 (2002).
13. Diane Stone, "Knowledge Networks and Global Policy," in *Global Knowledge Networks and International Development*, ed. D. Stone and S. Maxwell, 1st ed. (New York, NY: Routledge, 2005).
14. A Hall and C.R. Taylor, "Political Science and the Three New Institutionalisms," *Political Studies* 44, no. 5 (1996): 936–957.

15. Levi, "A State of Trust."
16. Robert D. Putnam, *Bowling Alone: The Collapse and Revival of American Community*, 1st ed. (New York, NY: Simon & Schuster, 2000).
17. John Peterson, *Europe and America: The Prospects for Partnership*, 1st ed. (Cheltenham, UK: Edward Elgar Publishing Limited, 1993).; Thomas Risse-Kappen, *Cooperation Among Democracies: The Euroepan Influence on U.S. Foreign Policy* (Princeton, NJ: Princeton University Press, 1997).; Mark A. Pollack and Gregory C. Shaffer, *Transatlantic Governance in the Global Economy*, ed. Mark A. Pollack and Gregory C. Shaffer (Lanham, MD: Rowman and Littlefield Publishers, Inc., 2001).; Maria Green Cowles, James Caporaso, and Thomas Risse, eds., *Transforming Europe: Europeanization and Domestic Change*, 1st ed. (Ithaca, NY: Cornell University Press, n.d.).; Andrew Moravcsik, "Striking a New Transatlantic Bargain," *Foreign Affairs* 82, no. 4 (2003): 74–89.; JP Quinlan, *Drifting Apart Or Growing Together?: The Primacy of the Transatlantic Economy* (Washington, DC: Center for Transatlantic Relations, 2003), http://kms2.isn.ethz.ch/serviceengine/Files/RESSpecNet/46948/ipublicationdocument_singledocument/47F34B9C-04BA-4411–8738-D31867721737/en/2003_drifting+apart.pdf.; Sophie Meunier, *Trading Voices: The European Union in International Commercial Negotiations* (Princeton, NJ: Princeton University Press, 2005).; Rebecca Steffenson, *Managing EU-US Relations: Actors, Institutions and the New Transatlantic Agenda* (Manchester, UK: Manchester University Press, 2005).
18. Pollack and Shaffer, *Transatlantic Governance in the Global Economy*.; Pollack, "The New Transatlantic Agenda at Ten: Reflections on an Experiment in International Governance."
19. Hyperlinking serves as an approximation of social ties for organizations with online presence, which is a common practice in web-based research analysis.
20. Grahame F. Thompson, *Between Hierarchies and Markets: The Logic and Limits of Network Forms of Organization*, 1st ed. (Oxford, UK: Oxford University Press, 2003).
21. Wendy H. Wong, *Internal Affairs: How the Structure of NGOs Transforms Human Rights*, 1st ed. (Ithaca, NY: Cornell University Press, 2012), 55.
22. Peter M. Haas, "Introduction: Epistemic Communities and International Policy Coordination," *International Organization* 46, no. 1 (May 22, 1992).; Stone, "Knowledge Networks and Global Policy," 2005, 94, 102.
23. David Knoke and Song Yang, *Social Network Analysis, Quantitative Applications in the Social Sciences Series*, 2nd ed. (London, UK: Sage Publications, 2008), 5.
24. Vladimir Batagelj and Andrej Mrvar, "Networks/Pajek, Program for Large Network Analysis," 2005, http://vlado.fmf.uni-lj.si/pub /networks/pajek/.
25. The term *backbone* is often used to describe the main network connections; the main wire that connects nodes. It is a collection of links through which information is transmitted; essentially a central cable that connects other network components (Chakrabarti, 2003).
26. Communities are "subsets of actors among whom there are relatively strong, direct, intense, frequent or positive ties" (Wasserman and Faust, 1994, p. 249).
27. I hypothesize that a science and technology specific knowledge community can be uncovered within transatlantic relations due, in part, to the fact that an agreement in this policy area was reached and renewed twice between the transatlantic partners.

28. Eugene B. Skolnikoff, *The Elusive Transformation: Science, Technology, and the Evolution of International Politics* (Princeton, NJ: Princeton University Press, 1993).
29. Emanuel Adler, "The Emergence of Cooperation: National Epistemic Communities and the International Evolution of the Idea of Nuclear Arms Control," *International Organization* 46, no. 1 (1992): 101–145.
30. Robert K. Yin, *Case Study Research* (Thousand Oaks, CA: Sage Publications Ltd., 2003), 7.
31. Yin, *Case Study Research.*
32. Ibid.
33. B. Flyvbjerg, "Five Misunderstandings About Case-Study Research," *Qualitative Inquiry* 12, no. 2 (April 1, 2006): 219–245.
34. L.E.E.J. Cronbach, "Beyond the Two Disciplines of Scientific Psychology," *American Psychologist* 30, no. February (1975): 116–127.; Jane F. Gilgun, "Theory and Case Study Research," *Current Issues in Qualitative Research* 2, no. 1–6 (2011), http://scribd.com/doc/48231895/Theory-and-Case-Study-Research.
35. Ibid.
36. Skolnikoff, *The Elusive Transformation: Science, Technology, and the Evolution of International Politics.*

2 Synthesizing Theories
International Communication, Cooperation, Networks, and Governance

This is but a beginning [with] endless possibilities in both directions—a building of a human life with undreamt of wealth and dignity, or a sudden end in utmost misery . . . modern science has abolished time and distance as a factor in separating nations; on our shrunken globe today, there is room for one group only—the family of man.

—Albert Szent-Györgyi, 1970[1]

In order to put the issues this book investigates in context, it is necessary to first look at the most frequently used themes and establish the usage of concepts deemed most relevant to the research. As previously mentioned, the opportunities and challenges of international communication are an essential part of this research and, as such, they will be reviewed first in this chapter.

Networks are also considered to be vital elements, as well as a mode of organization, in today's information age.[2] Therefore, the book addresses how questions of global concern and the transforming of the transatlantic partnership are, and can be, related; and also, how the sharing of ideas and knowledge can, and should be, the "glue" for collective action.[3] As this research finds, the networking modes of operation of transatlantic think tanks, policy research institutions, academics, research analysts and other experts constitute a gap in the literature that demands attention.

INTERNATIONAL COMMUNICATION

In an increasingly globalized world, international communication is facilitated by rapid technological advances. As a consequence, global information networks and the ability to communicate effectively across cultures have become central to international relations. This raises several questions concerning information, misinformation, diffusion, and knowledge generation, as well as access to information and knowledge that is fundamental to the development of inclusive knowledge societies.

Information, Knowledge, and Access

While Sir Francis Bacon has enlightened us that "knowledge is power," it requires internalization, which, in turn, must be preceded by the ability to access information.[4] Access is an indispensable factor, especially when one considers the highly developed nature of contemporary transnational communications technology and its empowering capacity. In discussing synergy and complexity in today's world, Lucas shows that the prerequisite to novelty generation and innovation by communication is that we are able to access, and thus be aware of, such empowering capacities. In an environment where synergy is cultivated, new ideas may foster.[5,6]

An additional aspect, which is of primary significance in political science, is the way knowledge is created and distributed; its sources and truthfulness lay down the foundations of democratic societies and cooperative arrangements worldwide. The question then arises as to who or what has power over these processes and how? Discussing the role of international institutions in catalyzing democratic values, human rights, and the rule of law, Tetzlaff emphasizes that common threats increase the importance of global cooperation.[7] As he stresses however, the globalization of Western-based values, norms, and scientific knowledge has spurred anti-cosmopolitan sentiments in the developing world. Western democracies face a credibility problem as those who consider themselves the "losers" of globalization show a general lack of trust in the "winners" and their Western kind diplomacy: "[m]odern rational *knowledge* as the foundation of *'human capital'* really matters" and without that link no society stands a chance to flourish.[8] Tetzlaff points to an additional set of problems. First, in some of the developing areas, such as in Africa, "intellectuals . . . are becoming an endangered species . . . [due to] an unwholesome and disenabling intellectual and economic environment at home." Second, without rapid economic and social development within these countries, "the developed countries will be inundated by a human flood of third world immigrants far beyond their economic, social, and cultural capacity to absorb."[9] Tetzlaff concludes that a "minimal consensus on basic values and rules of the game" is needed for modern societies that face the challenges of globalization. An institutionalization of this also necessitates "the mutual acceptance of democratic principles, an active middle class, and . . . *committed democratic leaders*."[10]

In writing about the role and responsibility of well-known intellectuals who contributed to human development, Kucklick sees the issue as basically twofold. On the one hand, "men of knowledge" have a social role in collecting, disseminating knowledge, and educating the public that could easily be manipulated by populist ideologies.[11] On the other hand, as Dewey wrote nearly a century ago, such integrated, more discursive knowledge has enormous potential to provide the legitimacy of pragmatic social knowledge.[12] To Kucklick, "social science has to prove 'worthy of its mission' by demonstrating the connection between knowledge and democracy."[13] This connection to create "living knowledge" and a much more informed and educated public with a quality of life that, at a minimum, approximates the standards of living in human dignity is indeed what can get us closer to create order that is more cooperative and peaceful. *As the chapters that follow show, a core idea of this book is that it is networks, and the networked modes of operation, that are highly capable of facilitating and delivering a flow of reliable information and scientific knowledge, which can empower wider constituencies to improve the quality of their lives.*

Discourse and Legitimacy

The role of discourse in international communication is underscored by the idea that discourse and the presence of strong civil societies can be considered more receptive to ideas communicated by knowledge networks. They have a legitimating role, and they might be able to facilitate the work of cooperative transnational arrangements in their quest to address global issues.

Dryzek puts the social constructivist view of policy-making into practice when he explains that "discourse-related aspects of international affairs" are something to be seriously considered when facing global insecurities.[14,15] The discursive aspects in this book suggest that the particularities of exercising power should be taken into consideration in international relations. Also, the idea that free and open communication fosters trust, understanding, and facilitates cooperative behavior ought to be reflected upon. Consensus matters and, as such, it should be included into our investigations of the political world. When forming global public policies, a wider global civil societal dialogue can be crucial for legitimacy.[16] While acknowledging it as valuable, Dryzek critiques the cosmopolitan model and its attachment to constitutionalism and centrality of the rule of law, which he feels is inadequate in the post-9/11 era.[17] Instead, he suggests a "transnational discursive democracy [that] rests on the notion that discourses are consequential in producing international outcomes through their influence upon and constitution of actors."[18] As Risse discusses, "[t]he emphasis on communicative and discursive practices constitutes [an important] characteristic feature of social constructivist approaches."[19] This idea that human knowing and communicating, and the social and the political, are intimately intertwined and that "human agents do not exist independently from their social environment and its collectively shared systems of meanings" is at the heart of social constructivism.[20]

In Habermas' discursive or deliberative theory of democracy, the public sphere represents an activist aspect of politics and policy-making, which is based on the participation of civil society and a consensus between rational citizens.[21,22] Following in the footsteps of Habermas, Dryzek suggests that in a transnational discursive democracy the global public sphere is less constrained by the exercise of authority, than it certainly is in the constitutional exercise of authority and, as such, it represents a more informal and communicative realm.[23] Building on Káldor's work on civil society, Dryzek adds,

> transnational discursive democracy has not been so devastated by [the exercise of authority] as cosmopolitanism . . . [the impact of which] on the actions of states is impeded by polarization of the world by terror and counterterror, its discursive space is invaded by associated "war of ideas," and its normative commitments are attacked by unilateralists contemptuous of international public opinion.[24]

While these theorists aim to be critical of neoliberal institutionalist approaches to international relations, their models should not, in themselves, be considered incompatible with other theoretical approaches, such as Ikenberry's neoliberal "constitutional" world order or Slaughter's "new world order" that is based on internationally negotiated and agreed-upon law and a web of governmental and transnational networks.[25] Discourse and negotiation do not preclude subsequent law-making. The role of international institutions cannot be played down, but rather, what Dryzek's ideas add to the understanding of an evolving constitutional order is the depiction of a more discourse-oriented and participatory global democracy, in which NGOs and civil society manage to obtain a greater role in decision-making processes. They do so, as I point out in the next section, by capitalizing on the advantages of their networking potentials. Dryzek's claim, that deliberative and discursive aspects of democracy can also be applied to areas such as networked governance, affirms this idea.[26]

A related concept in the relevant literature is reflexivity. Berejikian and Dryzek explain that "[i]ntelligent international action is reflexive in that it attends to the world that actions help constitute, as well as take affect within."[27] This idea appeared in Beck's as well as in Giddens's writings, who affirm that in a "reflexively modern" society people ought to live their lives less as a fateful given, and more as a continuously conscious negotiation on the effects of a "risk society."[28] Beck's work, one of the most influential European social analyses, presents two interrelated ideas. One is reflexive modernization, which means that the negative effects of modernization can effectively be dealt with. Beck proposes that through reflexive modernization that is manifest in a broader set of societal responses and movements, science and progress can be "tamed" to be more in synch with societal and natural processes. The other key idea is that there are risks in today's societies, originating from the fact that scientific and technological development not only paves the way toward progress, but simultaneously represents risks to societies. Due to extreme levels of interconnectedness, these risks are neither contained in time or space.[29] As Beck puts it,

> structural change forces social actors to become progressively freer from structure. And for modernization successfully to advance, these

> agents must release themselves from structural constraint and actively shape the modernization process . . . [t]he axial principle of industrial society is the distribution of goods, while that of the risk society is the distribution of "bads" or dangers.[30]

A stronger claim that Beck makes is that "[r]eflexivity is excluded from the social and political interactions between experts and social groups over modern risks, because of the systematic assumption of realism in science."[31] In agreement with Giddens's idea that, in the post-traditional order, the reflexive nature of institutions represents not only risks, but also opportunities to change that can be facilitated by knowledge and expertise, this book suggests that the role of knowledge networks and their impact and interaction with transnational advocacy networks and other civil societal forces can enhance society's reflexive capacities.[32] Haas's notion, that while "epistemic communities are the transmission belts by which new knowledge is developed and transmitted to decision-makers . . . knowledge must also possess the substantive characteristics of usable knowledge: credibility, legitimacy, and salience," also underscores these ideas.[33]

As this book explains further in the section on science diplomacy, there is an evolutionary process in the information age where technology plays a more determining role in economic and political life: traditional "Mode 1" type knowledge production has been transformed to "Mode 2," and, recently, to "Mode 3" type.[34] In their quest to develop an understanding of knowledge creation and diffusion in the 21st century, Carayannis and Campbell formulate a new model and theoretical framework, called

> the "Quadruple Helix" model, through which government, academia, industry, and civil society are seen as key actors promoting a democratic approach to innovation through which strategy development and decision-making are exposed to feedback from key stakeholders, resulting in socially accountable policies and practices.[35]

NETWORKS AND NETWORK THEORY

Having established that knowledge and expertise "matter" in the global policy arena, the additional claim made here is that networks matter as bridges within and across societies. *Networks are also considered to be vital elements,* as well as a mode of organization, in today's information age.[36]

"Networks . . . facilitate collective action and cooperation, exercise influence, or serve as a means of international governance."[37] They also have the advantage of being less formal institutions, the boundaries of which are fluid. These characteristics provide networks with greater flexibility and adaptability that is much needed in a complex environment. According to Castells, an increasingly linked global society and the network-based logic of operation have the potential to modify traditional transnational modes of operation and codes of conduct and, subsequently, alter outcomes.[38] But where does network theory come from?

Origins of the Network Approach

This research uses social network analytical tools to unravel problems in political science. Social network analysis, a continuously and rapidly evolving field, has simultaneously evolved and drawn from various disciplines: psychology, anthropology, sociology, mathematics, and more recently, communication studies and political science. It is also a "branch of the broader study of networks and complex systems."[39] At its early stage, social network analysis could be associated with the "gestalt" tradition of the late 1920s and early 1930s based on the German psychologist Köhler's theory.[40] Followers of this tradition rejected to investigate the social world atomisticly, but rather, they stressed the organized patterns that structure thoughts and perceptions and emphasized how organized patterns were regarded as "wholes" with properties distinct from those of their parts.[41] Following that logic, individuals, or a group of individuals such as organizations, can be viewed as open systems in active interaction with their environment. Numerous scientists worked along this tradition; however, it was not until Moreno's introduction of sociometry in the mid-1930s when a major breakthrough occurred in social network analysis. Moreno's major contribution was that now scientists had the means to describe the interpersonal structures and concrete patterns of groups or social configurations. Moreno's sociogram was able to unravel leadership roles, asymmetry, and reciprocity, for example friendship, in social choices.[42]

Although graph theory emerged as a theory on its own right, there are various fields of inquiry, such as economics, strategic management, biology, chemistry, physics, and, recently, political science, that build on certain aspects of graph theory. Within political science, scholars of networked governance use it quite frequently as an important mathematical tool to assist their research. While some trace back the origins of graph theory as far as Euler's paper in 1736, it can be considered a relatively young science as it took root only during the last decade of the 19th century.[43] A frequently used branch called random graph theory was developed by two Hungarian mathematicians, Erdős and Rényi, as late as 1959.[44] Network theory is part of graph theory. Network analysis in general, and social network analysis particularly, makes use of the mathematical tools and concepts developed within graph theory. A network can model a communication group—organizational communication in our case. Also, there are several theories in various disciplines that are, in essence, network theories such as the theory of social capital, the strength of weak ties theory, or transaction cost economics.

The Network Approach in IR

Network analysis offers an alternative to conventional explanations in international relations. It does so through its ability to use network analytical tools and by interpreting power as inherently related to actors' structural properties and positions in the network.

> Network analysis complements existing structural approaches to international relation . . . [as] it emphasizes how material and social relationships create structures among actors through dynamic processes . . . provides methods for measuring these structures, allows for the operationalization of processes such as socialization and diffusion, and opens new avenues for reconsidering core concepts in international relations, such as power.[45]

The integration of network analytical tools to fundamental IR concerns has only begun with a "third wave of network applications, starting in the late 1990s."[46] Social network analysis that, in essence, is a study of relations of the actors in the network, empirically derives relationships among actors and characterizes a social network as a whole.[47] Network structure and relations among actors impact and shape information exchange and cooperation patterns; network actors either reproduce or change the structure of their organization.[48] *This book investigates how actors' network position can, potentially, influence the future of transatlantic relations.* The study concentrates on who the most important authorities and hubs are and what organizations appear to be the "structural holes" with brokering potential in the network. In that regard, this research is aiming to test as well as add to the existing body of network theory as it relates to international relations. As Lazer and Friedman point out, although there seems to be enough research done on the idea of social networks transferring information to individuals, research on systemic network structure and systemic-level success is, at best, scarce.[49]

As network properties influence the operational capacity of a network, this book explores important network theoretical concepts and their attributes as they relate to transatlantic connections.[50] Moreover, the quality of information that flows through these communication channels directly enhances their effectiveness and the prospects for successful policy outcomes. While this book constitutes an initial step in a *new research pathway to understanding transatlantic communication,* the peculiarities of transatlantic information flows through virtual networks, investigated in this study, require further research on the topic. One of the main assumptions of network analysis affirms that structural relations are viewed as dynamic processes; networks are not static, but rather they are changing due to the multitude of interactions constantly taking place.[51] These networks evolve over time and, consequently, a temporal analysis and a broad exploration of the lifecycle of these hyperlink networks and their implications for political, social, and cultural phenomena should be part of a broader research project. Although patterns of organizational networking practices change slowly, progressing in this way provides greater potential for unraveling long-term changes in online structures. Such investigations might further clarify in what particular ways do these networking patterns catalyze or constrain future cooperative action in transatlantic relations.

Bridges, Brokers, Structural Holes, and Social Capital

Granovetter's seminal 1973 paper, "The Strength of Weak Ties," is one of those studies that laid down the foundation for a growing body of network studies research in the past few decades. Granovetter argues that a distinction between strong ties (family members, close friends) and weak ties (acquaintances, distant friends) could be made insofar as the strength of the social relationship is concerned.[52] He explains that individuals relying exclusively, or mostly, on the former "will be deprived of information from distant parts of the social system . . . [which then] will not only insulate them from the latest ideas . . . but may put them in a disadvantaged position" elsewhere.[53] Relying on the latter, however, that is having numerous and diverse weak ties, might supply the individual with more innovative ideas and information overall. Therefore, these weak ties could not only be ties that bridge (ideas, ideologies, cultures, etc.), but also, they can be the sources of innovative information and knowledge. Understood in this way, the lack of global networking and a reduced capability to communicate impedes learning and human development. As Frederick observes, "accumulating evidence for world public opinion" and utilizing unbiased knowledge and expertise through various forms of communication channels seems essential to peace and security.[54]

This directly connects to the ideas of Sen and Nussbaum, who redefined the concept of development and formulated their so-called "capability approach."[55] This conceptual framework maintains that freedom should play a key role in social evaluation, and emphasizes that we should consider both: what it is that people are free to do and, also, what they do in actuality. Their approach accentuates functional capabilities and suggests, for example, that the abilities to participate in political activities or to live to an old age be understood as "substantial freedoms." Poverty then is defined as a capability-deprivation. Sen also illuminates that certain features of contemporary economic development are able to diminish the "capability deprivation" of poverty, which is then able to endow individuals with more freedom within the economic domain.[56] Investigating human values, beliefs, and behavior, Inglehart and Welzel contend that "socioeconomic modernization, rising liberty aspirations, and the quest for democratic institutions all reflect the common underlying process of human development, the theme of which is the broadening of human choice."[57] Building on these ideas, this book maintains that the ability to access accurate and unbiased information and knowledge about all areas of life, like the food that people eat, the air they breathe in, or the security threats they face, provides them with greater freedom to choose from among available alternatives more in synch with their needs and interests.

Another aspect of Granovetter's thesis is that in complex systems, such as the global system of societies, creating linkages and building bridges among actors and policies could be enhanced by the bridging ability of weak ties. Information-gaps, that may lead to miscommunication, misunderstanding, and have the potential to create hostilities towards the unknown, could be narrowed. Granovetter further explains, "one needs to show not only that ties bridging network segments are disproportionately weak but also that something flows through these bridges and that whatever it is that flows actually plays an important role in the social life of individuals, groups, and societies."[58] While the empirical challenges to the latter can be daunting, these have enormous implications for the value of social networks and the build-up of social capital. Unraveling the divergent performances of the Italian regional governments, Putnam finds that it is, what he calls, the building-up of "social capital" that had allowed people to cooperate in ways that made government and economy stronger.[59] Putnam's work on social capital illuminates the strong relationship between the intensity of associational life and the success of regional governments. Similarly, Fukuyama finds that "[s]ocial capital has benefits that go well beyond the economic sphere. It is critical for the creation of a healthy civil society . . . [which] is said to be critical to the success of democracy."[60] Burt, in his work on structural holes, also argues that "social capital is created by a network in which people can broker connections between otherwise disconnected segments."[61] Actors in the international system who are in a brokering position or act as bridges over structural holes then can transform that social capital into social power.[62]

In discussing the transfer of knowledge from one area of inquiry to another, Bourdieu and Wacquant define social capital as "the sum of the resources, actual or virtual, that accrue to an individual or a group by virtue of possessing a durable network of more or less institutionalized relationships of mutual acquaintance and recognition."[63] Coleman's opposing view asserts that social capital is created by network closure.[64] As Gudmundsson and Lechner illuminate, "[t]he opposing view argues that network closure would generate superior 'social capital' and thus superior 'economic rent' as we would have more trust, reputation and cooperation within a closed group with strong internal ties."[65] In their case study on multilateral airline alliances, they show that "a combination of opportunities to bridge 'structural holes' as well as a degree of cohesiveness are important in combination but not exclusive of each other."[66,67] This is in line with Burt's findings that "brokerage across structural holes is a source of value added, but closure can be critical to realizing the value buried in structural holes."[68] Burt sums up the merging of structural hole and social capital theories when he explains, "[c]ast in diverse styles of argument (e.g., Coleman, 1990; Bourdieu and Wacquant, 1992; Burt, 1992; Putnam, 1993), social capital is a metaphor about advantage."[69]

Another connection pointed out in the literature is the one that considers relations with their structural characteristics and outcomes. There seems to be a consensus in the network literature that structural and relational characteristics do influence outcomes. As Mergel and Langenberg illuminate, "studies found the network structure to be a good predictor of access and control over network partners."[70] Others like Hafner-Burton et al. argue that "[t]wo issues regarding network power are particularly important to international relations: whether actors can increase their power by enhancing and exploiting their network positions, and the fungibility of power—whether network power can be used to supplement or offset other forms of power."[71]

Combining network-efficiency and social capital related aspects of the literature allows us to recognize that communities are built on connections and better connections give rise to new opportunities.[72] While improved connectivity begins with mapping connections, followed by "weaving the network," it then follows that future network capacity increases.[73] Competing for connections in an increasingly interconnected world is crucial as "nodes always compete for connections because links represent survival."[74] Drawing on the analogy of the market, this kind of competition might lead to enhanced efficiency in the system. In reality, nodes or network actors that specialize and gain expertise and recognition will have a better chance to become more efficient parts of the network and contribute to the cross-pollination of policy learning within the community.

Linking network and social capital theories Lin explains, "[w]ith ever sharpening definitions and measurements, social network scholarship may have much to contribute to the sustained development of social capital as an intellectual enterprise."[75] In his earlier work Lin affirms that relationships can be considered as significant sources of material, informational, as well as emotional support.[76] These relationships, recognized as "embedded resources in social networks," are best characterized as a new form of social capital.[77] In regards to web-based connections and organizational hyperlinks, understood as communicative channels, this research considers those as cybernetworks or web-based social networks.

Knowledge Networks

As a world of scientific community is forming and science diplomacy becomes more internationally widespread, it is essential to look at the "policy-related roles of university researchers and other experts . . . who . . . enter and traverse the global agora."[78,79] International knowledge networks can be understood as "system[s] of coordinated research, disseminated and published results, study . . . intellectual exchange, and financing, across national boundaries."[80] Parmar adds that these networks may include a range of other actors, such as official policymakers or international agencies.[81] Stone explains that those who typically interact in such knowledge networks are "university researchers and other experts who may be based in consultancy firms, philanthropic foundations, independent research institutes and think tanks."[82] They contribute to knowledge production through "a complex interweaving of network interactions."[83] Being a "reputational intermediary," knowledge networks perform two broad functions. "First . . . acting as intermediaries within and between national and local (social) scientific/intellectual communities . . . [and by building] common infrastructure[s] for communication via websites . . . reports and other publications as well as through meetings and conferences." Second, they serve "as interlocutors with external audiences."[84] Additionally, "think tanks [and other potential epistemic-community-like entities] have the flexibility and autonomy to address policy problems as they arise rather than being dealt through a slower bureaucratic process."[85]

As knowledge network researcher Stone argues, networks can be useful in global governance, because they systemize knowledge from a wide variety of sources. They can also be considered "part of the global civil society."[86] As Stone explains, there are three systematic approaches to understanding the so-called knowledge networks. First is the epistemic communities approach, popularized by Haas, which insists that, based on an intellectual commitment to expert knowledge, an epistemic community is independent from governmental or other vested interests although members of the community typically seek access to policy makers based on their unique policy-expertise grounded in scientific, codified forms of knowledge.[87] Nevertheless, as Stone adds, even these "disinterested" pursuers of knowledge compete for attention and funding that leaves some room for criticism if one puts less emphasis on power as an explanatory variable.[88]

The second approach to investigating knowledge networks is the "discourse coalitions and communities" approach.[89] This framework stresses the role of discourse, as well as the transnational characteristics of professionals. It emphasizes that the work of these networks/communities transcends narrower national identities and interests; hence power and knowledge may "operate through discursively informed social and institutional practices such as [these] networks."[90] In this second case, professionals create a distinct transnational community. While power is not taken into consideration in the first approach and it serves as a basis for the approach taken in the third one, this second framework is somewhere in between those two approaches. In this second case, power is "tamed" by discourse within a wider range of narratives (participants and their representative views) and, based on the Foucauldian thought, it places the discourse community between power and knowledge.[91] As Foucault argues, "power is situated among the cacophony of social practices and situations."[92] Understood in this way, Stone adds, the aforementioned networks constitute "discursively informed social and institutional practices."[93]

The third approach stands for the neo-Gramscian (dis)embedded knowledge networks approach. This approach "treats knowledge, discourses or ideas as a tool of power used by dominant interests in maintaining the capitalist order."[94] Here knowledge networks are viewed as parts of the "'micro-politics of contemporary hegemony' . . . [or a] component of the 'globalizing elite.'"[95]

In addressing how a "knowledge network" can be differentiated from other forms of intellectual collaboration and discourse, Stone asserts,

> "knowledge network" is an umbrella category for a number of frameworks like epistemic community, or subaltern network, or "discourse coalitions" or neo-Gramscian "embedded knowledge networks" each of which comes from quite different foundations, and provide varying interpretations of the power of knowledge/ideas/expertise. "Epistemic community" is not the only concept available to comprehend knowledge networks. In short, epistemic community is only one kind of knowledge network concept.[96]

The idea of a (global) knowledge network grew out of trying to differentiate these kinds of networks from (global) public policy networks (GPPN) that are more of a common interest-based type, whereas the activities of knowledge networks are more research- and science-oriented. In sum, various network forms could be better understood by visualization along a differentiation spectrum. Here the more government-based transnational executive networks (TENs) are towards one end and the more neo-corporatist global public policy networks (GPPNs) are somewhere in the middle, whereas KNETs and transnational advocacy networks (TANs) that are more civil society-based, but frequently policy oriented, are situated closer to the other end of the spectrum.[97]

Regardless of the approach taken, however, Stone explains that these *"knowledge networks are able to bridge knowledge gaps, facilitate the delivery of global public goods, and have tremendous potential to provide a deliberative capacity for democratic governance."*[98] Even though KNETs may be resource-dependent, their interaction with and impact upon other civil societal actors can legitimate their actions further. One of the most significant studies written on the impacts of knowledge networks based on empirical evidence is that of Parmar.[99] His research examines and demonstrates how three American foundations, Rockefeller, Carnegie, and Ford, influenced US domestic and foreign policies, facilitated the spread of the idea of "liberal internationalism," and, ultimately, "constructed a key basis of America's rise to globalism."[100]

In writing about think tanks that are likely candidates for knowledge network hubs, Abelson suggests that even though we still "need a more nuanced understanding of what constitutes influence [of such entities] and how it is measured," the use of several indicators (direct and indirect) at the various points in the policy cycle, issue articulation, policy formulation, and policy implementation can be beneficial.[101] Hayes finds that suggested indicators of such entities may include, but do not exhaust, the following.[102] On the supply side are "funding and staffing level," and "*networks of key players*"; on the demand side are media exposure, briefings, and testimony; and, finally, considering *mission indicators,* these can be "recommendations considered or adopted by policy-makers," *listserv or website dominance,* and "publications in or citation of publications in academic journals."[103] This book builds on Hayes's suggestions.

A successful example of a knowledge community acting as a catalyst of change is described in Barth's study of a transnational coalition of American and Soviet scientists. These scientists ultimately succeeded in shaping Soviet foreign policy and, at the same time, altered the nuclear test ban debate in the United States during the 1980s.[104] A classic in this area is Haas' case study of the Mediterranean Action Plan, which relates to regional environmental cooperation, as well as it represents the role of scientific communities in the development and implementation of international public policy.[105] Last, but not least, attention needs to be drawn to Esterling's work on the role of policy research and expertise and the overall connection between information and efficiency as he demonstrates that ideas, evidence, experiences, and an efficient use of these for innovative policy practices matters.[106] While Esterling researches the importance and the building of expertise within American politics, his findings could provide further talking points for international relations scholars as well.

Networked Governance

Networks as systems in IR theorizing lead to the next concept investigated in this research: networked governance. Mueller et al. argue that IR scholars need to research and theorize global governance further if they want to have a deeper understanding of Internet governance and define the term "networked governance" more succinctly.[107] While these authors state that the conversation on networked governance is still ongoing, they suggest that it can be described as "a semipermanent, voluntary negotiation system that allows interdependent actors to opt for collaboration or unilateral action in the absence of an overarching authority."[108]

Networked governance scholar Lazer defines networked governance somewhat differently as "a system populated by autonomous, interdependent agents, where the interconnectedness of those agents affects systemic outcomes [where] those agents may be organizations or people; government or nongovernment."[109] Diverse sources and competences of knowledge, represented by networked governance structures, have the potential to create synergy as they benefit from the vitality and the legitimacy of civil societal forces and the financial strength of corporate interest groups, as well as "the enforcement and the rule-making power and coordination and capacity-building skills of states and international organizations."[110] Mueller et al. agree when they assert, "the idea of network governance has proved especially useful in studying transnational orders."[111]

After the millennium, scholars of Internet governance began to explore "non-hierarchical, bottom up arrangements for networking and the pooling of resources between traditional diplomatic and non-state actors."[112] The diffusion of Internet technologies, and the fact that an increasing number of national diplomatic systems rely on the expertise and policy advice of non-state actors, facilitate the creation of multi-stakeholder partnerships and various forms of networked diplomacy. "Multistakeholder partnerships between governments, civil society, and the private sector" develop, in which their "relationship [is] based on trust and the recognition of mutual interests."[113,114]

Cogburn, who investigates computer-mediated communication (CMC) practices of transnational civil society organizations, and Levinson, who explores knowledge transfer processes in regards to the Internet Governance Forum (IGF), combine global Internet governance with inter-organizational learning, collaboration, knowledge-transfer, and the roles of epistemic community-like entities as they explore new types of multilevel or multi-stakeholder governance.[115] These tie well with the *reciprocal relationship between communication technology and society and, in a broader sense, science, technology, and society, which is an important aspect of this book.* As Cogburn observes, "the failure of traditional state-centered governance solutions to complex problems with international dimensions" resulted in the emergence of a less state-centric and more multi-stakeholder approach to both public policy-making and diplomacy.[116] Cogburn further explains, "the principle of stake-holding [as the idea that] all those affected by, or with a stake in, the decisions of public authorities have the right to a voice in the governance of those matters."[117] He then further explains that this "principle of stakeholderism" is "central to the deliberative argument" in that scholars of deliberative democracy emphasize the discursive sources of existing governance systems at all levels.[118] They are also "concerned with the principles and necessary conditions for the creation of a genuine transnational public sphere of democratic deliberation."[119] These points reinforce the need to include discursive aspects of international relations into the theoretical framework. In sum, whether we discuss networked governance or multi-stakeholder governance and multi-stakeholder diplomacy (MSD), we certainly are considering newly emerged innovative ways of facilitating a more inclusive and democratic way of global public policy-making and governance. These approaches advocated by scholars of Internet governance, "bring about a synergy between state and non-state actors in their efforts to seek co-operative solutions to the most pressing problems of global" significance.[120,121]

SCIENCE DIPLOMACY

As this research considers science diplomacy to be an essential part of networked governance processes, it could be reviewed within multiple sections depending on the interpretation of the researcher. This book, however, takes the approach of discussing this topic under a separate sub-heading within the chapter as the subject matter is relatively new; further research on this matter is much needed, which can lead to a more refined understanding of its potential to support US foreign policy goals.[122]

What is science diplomacy? There are many definitions to approximate what the term stands for; one of these is Nina Fedoroff's, Science and Technology Adviser to US Secretary of State, suggestion that "science diplomacy is the use of scientific interactions among nations to address the common problems facing humanity and to build constructive, knowledge based international partnerships."[123] The same report suggests that, as the concept "science diplomacy" evolves, *three central dimensions* can be recognized as it relates to science, technology, and innovation policy: "informing foreign policy objectives with scientific advice (*science in diplomacy*); facilitating international science cooperation (*diplomacy for science*); [and] using science cooperation to improve international relations between countries (*science for diplomacy*)."[124] A brief assessment of these three dimensions is essential.

Science in Diplomacy

There are at least two aspects to consider in regards to the first dimension, *science in diplomacy*. First, sustainable development requires that foreign policy goals be formulated based on sound scientific evidence and advice. Second, potential politicization of scientific inquiry, that is rendering scientific evidence-based approaches secondary to particularistic political interests and goals may hurt policy outcomes.[125]

Considering the first aspect, the need for sound scientific evidence and advice to achieve foreign policy goals and keep up with sustainable development, it is important to underscore the role of epistemic community-like entities, or knowledge networks (KNETs). As the Royal Society's 2010 report, New Frontiers in Science Diplomacy, states, "[n]ational academies and learned societies are . . . an important source of independent scientific advice to international policymakers."[126]

As far as the second aspect, the potential politicization of scientific inquiry, is concerned, Jotterand explains that there is a difference between "traditional [and current] understanding of how to pursue scientific and technological knowledge."[127] A Kuhnian paradigm shift seems to have taken place in our societies as we entered a stage where technology plays a more determining role in economic and political life.[128] In this context, the meaning of science is no longer just this ideal of finding truth ("Mode 1" knowledge production), but rather, it seems to be in a symbiotic relationship with technological aspects and applications that have more immense implications for the acquisition of economic, as well as political, power in the 21st century. Using Ziman's approach, Jotterand discusses the era of "post-academic science," in which "culture and the epistemic structure of scientific research and development" has been transformed.[129] Not only is scientific inquiry more interdisciplinary, but it also is trans-disciplinary, by which he means an integration of all "knowledges" scientific or non-scientific. Lastly, Jotterand points out that, in this new era, *scientific knowledge production* is so much more *intertwined with technological development and IT-based production* than before that it is virtually impossible to separate it from *essential resource-dependencies.*[130] This combined with another dimension, the so-called "norm of utility" or the "usefulness of scientific projects . . . is also a moral concept determined by human ends, goals and values within the social context."[131] The problem, however, remains that these factors then contribute to creating an environment in which scientific inquiry becomes more politicized. An important question to ask then is what constitutes a balanced mode of knowledge production that aims to preserve the integrity of codified scientific knowledge, yet emphasizes and contributes to tacit and consensual, hence more legitimate, ways of conducting this so-called "Mode 2" knowledge production in knowledge networks. In trying to answer such questions, Carayannis and Campbell develop their "Quadruple Helix" model, in which the triple helix representing "university-industry-government relations" is joined by a fourth helix, which they call the "media-based and culture-based public, and civil society." This model goes another step further and establishes the idea of a

> multilayered, multimodal, and multilateral system, encompassing mutually complementary and reinforcing innovation networks and knowledge clusters [called] "Mode 3" [which] ensures a tighter and more robust coupling of vision with reality and helps reify the socio-economic and socio-political being and becoming by achieving between aspirations and limitations.[132]

Carayannis and Campbell argue that such dynamics are already developing; what is needed is a much more coherent strategy to reap full benefits of such systems. These authors also discuss the role of "knowledge clusters" and innovation networks and how these together "resemble a matrix, indicating the interactive complexity of knowledge and innovation."[133,134]

In conclusion, the politicization of scientific inquiry, understood as politics interfering with scientific inquiry and "cherry-picking" sides in scientific disputes depending on one's special interests, can become problematic. Nevertheless, as Pielke suggests, "rather than eliminating considerations of politics in the composition of science advisory [we should] focus our attention on developing transparent, accountable, and effective processes to manage politics in science—not to pretend that it doesn't exist."[135]

Diplomacy for Science

The second dimension of science diplomacy that foreign policy decision-makers should acknowledge is that resource-dependencies create a greater need for cooperation in the area of science, technology, and innovation policies. As Dehglan and Colglazier assert, "[c]ooperation on science, technology, and engineering around development challenges provides U.S. diplomats with a significant opportunity to leverage science as a tool of smart power."[136]

Science for Diplomacy

As for the third dimension of science diplomacy, using science cooperation to improve international relations between countries, not only is transatlantic cooperation significant on its own, but it also interacts with and has the potential to facilitate all cooperative relationships with other geographical regions. Science is a source of "soft power"; as the scientific community habitually works beyond national borders on issues of global interests, a vast network of governmental and non-governmental organizations has been building-up and is being facilitated by the information technology revolution of the 21st century. "If aligned with wider foreign policy goals, these channels of scientific exchange can contribute to coalition building and conflict resolution."[137] The National Intelligence Council's 2012 report, *Global Trends 2030,* identifies so-called "mega-trends" that will shape the world, such as a greater demand for scarce resources (food, water, energy), while the report points out that technological innovation will be a "game changer" that will ultimately shape the future.[138] In our increasingly complex and interconnected world, innovation is becoming the principal driving force to collectively resolve policy-issues of global significance.

The European Commission's 2009 report, on what drives international collaboration in research, finds that there is a growing trend for "policy attention for international research collaboration . . . due to external triggers." The same report also finds that there is a "diverse set of drivers interacting with each other." A major challenge, however, is that "envisaged outcomes and impacts are not well defined."[139]

While all facets of science diplomacy "played an important, if underappreciated, role in the U.S. foreign policy over the past 50 years," the question arises "[w]ho should lead a renewed effort toward science diplomacy . . . [but] unfortunately, there is currently no ideal U.S. government agency to lead such sustained effort." Lord and Turekian further explain,

> It is time for the scientific community to increase its role in diplomacy—and maybe even take the lead. Nongovernmental scientific organizations

are more credible, more nimble, and—as honest brokers—in many cases more respected than the U.S. government overseas.[140]

ORDER, GOVERNANCE, AND COOPERATION

An overarching theme of the book is global *governance and the reconfiguration of authority.* Scholars of transnational relations, like Nye and Keohane, took issue with the "classic state-centric paradigm" as early as 1971, and projected that the fast-paced change that characterizes world politics would demand a new model that better fits the realities of the international system. Furthermore, Nye and Keohane specifically address the role of transnational networks as they relate to intergovernmental cooperation and the notion of legitimacy, as well as the idea that "most if not all governments will find it very difficult to cope alone with many aspects of transnational relations."[141] In addressing new forms of governance, scholars of international relations today engage in exploring the various levels of institutionalization of the policy decision-making process. The role of public and private networking modes of operation is at the core of these scholarly endeavors, which try to re-conceptualize the idea of governance.

These new forms of governance are also intimately connected to the notion of order in the international system; therefore, it is necessary to first look at the diverse set of explanations to the question: What are the sources of international order? Depending on the various schools of thought, and the underlying assumptions, international order has been defined in various ways. For realists, order is borne out of the balancing and adjusting of power by the various states in the anarchic system.[142] Power politics, as described by Morgenthau, is the only phenomenon able to adequately describe international relations and stabilize the international system.[143] Balance-of-power explanations suggest that stabilization occurs not necessarily by peaceful means, but rather, through the balancing actions of states that may include militarized force. Part of the problem with these realist and neorealist theories is that power is explained in material terms only. Non-material terms and institutions are ignored. Therefore, a more thorough and comprehensive understanding requires the introduction of less coercive modes of order-creation, which might be better suited to explaining the kinds of, more institutionalized, orders that have emerged after World War II and in the post-Cold War era.

In his book, *After Victory: Institutions, Strategic Restraint, and the Rebuilding of Order After Major Wars,* Ikenberry defines political order as "the 'governing' arrangements among a group of states, including its fundamental rules, principles, and institutions."[144] This renders order to be seen as a settled arrangement among states. Others, like the constructivist Finnemore, suggest that order in the international system is "simply the *regularized patterns of behavior among states,* what some might call the structure of the system and others the rules of the system."[145] Finnemore describes international order as an evolving concept that is socially constructed, which is a reflection of the constructivist idea that socialization processes are important determinants of state behavior in international politics. Her conception of order then is one that is continuously influenced by societal forces and, also, by non-material sources of power within a particular historical context; "[n]ormative context is important because it shapes conceptions of interest."[146] As Finnemore sums up, whereas 19th-century "multilateralism was driven by shared fears and perceived threats," contemporary multilateralism is driven "by shared norms and principles."[147] This, however, does not preclude constructivist theorists from considering other factors in international processes; as Gourevitch et al. recognize the scholarly achievements of Peter Katzenstein, they state that "[e]conomic and political structures; history, norms, and culture; interests and power: all of these components are part of Katzenstein's rich conception of world politics."[148]

While liberal institutionalists and social constructivists may advocate the same policy options, their focus is different. In addressing change in the system, the neoliberal institutionalist approach relies heavily on the cooperative potential of international institutions and international law and, while acknowledging that there are non-state actors in the system, considers states to be the most important actors that may cooperate for mutual advantage.[149] International institutions are there to reduce uncertainty in the system and facilitate state cooperation in order to advance state interests, but changes in the system as they relate to changes in interests and identities for states or non-state actors are not fully addressed. Constructivists, on the other hand, put the emphasis on normative shifts caused by global knowledge dissemination and/or shared norms and principles. Yet, Keohane's assertion in his recent works reflects a certain evolutionary change in neoliberal institutionalist thinking, as he argues that 20th-century multilateral legitimacy should be upgraded to be more in line with 21st-century demands and challenges that multilateral organizations face today.[150] Since "governance implies the possibility of coercion, which requires justification," Keohane suggests that three criteria should be taken into account when considering "the normative legitimacy of multilateral institutions: *decisiveness, inclusiveness,* and *epistemic reliability.*"[151] By decisiveness, he refers to the idea that even if the strongest member of the international organization disagrees, the organization will still be able to take action. By inclusiveness he means that "all valid interests . . . must be represented effectively," and epistemic reliability implies sufficient transparency and openness to criticism in the decision-making process.[152] Higgott, addressing global governance from a similar point of view, also stresses that the "triad" of democratic, inclusive, and accountable should describe structures of governance regardless of the approach taken.[153]

As Wendt argues, states are not predisposed to either conflict or cooperation but, rather, interactions are critical as they continuously influence "intersubjective meanings" and the nature of relationships. Intersubjectivity here refers to interpretations or understandings among international actors, and it is derived from reflecting on exchanges and interactions. Constructivists also suggest that shared knowledge results from the exchange of ideas and emphasize how agency and interaction produce and reproduce structures of shared knowledge over time.[154] Additionally, transnational non-state activism is a major tool for spreading norms and ideas. "Advocates of deliberative democracy on a global scale tend to emphasize argument and persuasion as mechanisms by which cosmopolitan values can be furthered in an age of globalization."[155]

If *international social structure matters and the distribution of knowledge is in an interactive relationship* with the social, and political fabric, it is then easy to see how investigating international communicative networks, the main focus of this book, must be a fruitful endeavor.[156] Network dynamics impact conflict and cooperation in international relations; as an example, "social network studies of degree centrality and conflict find that more central nodes tend to be more aggressive . . . Network analysis [also] offers a method for measuring the sources of socialization and the diffusion of norms based on the strength of ties between states, collective state identities such as security communities, and the importance of individual states."[157]

Until the last decade of the 20th century, the Cold War and its ideological division provided the world with a certain kind of understanding of an international world order, but in the post-Cold War era and, especially, following the tragic events of 9/11, new divisions and conflicts have surfaced. The problem became that a so-called "new world order" is evolving, which should be channeled towards more peaceful, tolerant, and universally applicable norms and behavior through international law and enlightened and inclusive foreign policy discourses, the purpose of which is to overcome old, as well as newly surfaced, insecurities and resulting violence.

If we are to accept Ikenberry's theory of a constitutional international order, then we need to give more emphasis to his arguments that, not only the mechanisms of states have changed by putting restraint on power through institutions, but also, the character of order as well as conceptions of legitimacy have changed. The legitimacy of a constitutional order presumes a qualitatively different kind of legitimacy from the type we have witnessed in earlier periods in history. It requires a truly broad-based support of states and non-state actors. It also means overcoming fears and building trust and a much more predictable and cooperative kind of system than the current one. As Ikenberry explains, "the more complex, adaptable, and autonomous the institution, the more durable it will be and the more it can play a role in lowering the returns to power."[158] This responsiveness to change is becoming a critical element in the survival of today's international environment and can be pivotal in successful order-creation and maintenance in the future.

In a similar vein, Slaughter's ideas reflect such a constitutional type of order, which she says is increasingly becoming network-based, backed by international law, and, "describes a system of global governance that institutionalizes cooperation and sufficiently contains conflict such that all nations and their peoples may achieve greater peace and prosperity, improve their stewardship on the earth, and reach minimum standards of human dignity."[159] Measuring the success of these potential knowledge networks can be based on their contribution to establishing a common framework of ideas, values, norms, rules, and practices to resolve global issues. As Strange argues, the structural strengths of states within the international system refer to their ability to establish norms and rules that can facilitate governance.[160] To Volgy and Bailin, relational strength alone may not suffice to exert necessary influence in an exceedingly complex system.[161] Hence restructuring the dominant (and currently rather unstable) order requires that those who wish to facilitate the emergence of a more peaceful and new kind of post-Cold War world order are able to exert necessary influence by possessing the necessary structural strength to do so.[162]

This is not to say that this type of order would lack the necessary characteristics of Ikenberry's constitutional type of international order. On the contrary: to ensure legitimacy, here too, the constitutional "bargain" must be acceptable to all participants. However, on the analogy of the order that emerged after World War II, transatlantic partners, acting together as a political and ideological entity, would attempt to create and maintain order in which cooperation works at a higher level and where *learning and knowledge facilitates the emergence of norms, rules, and identities that are more congenial to a "culture of peace."* Exerting such "soft power" and using knowledge creation that focuses on progress and transformation to transcend narrow perspectives may let us benefit the most from changes spurred by globalization and transnationalization.[163]

Writing on the distinct challenges of twenty-first century global governance, Bradford explains that a key issue is that there is a considerable mismatch between current global institutions and global challenges. His policy recommendations involve higher levels of knowledge-integration and the creation of linkages among various sectors. Bradford notes that "[w]hile the 20th century relied on specialists, the 21st century may come to rely more on people who are *integrationists,* capable within their expertise but excelling in their grasp of the relationship between their area of expertise and those adjacent to it." As he illuminates, "[t]he linkages among challenges and between disciplines and approaches are major drivers of institutional inadequacy and mismatch." Progressing in this way, we will be able to "*generate* [better] *strategic guidance on the new inter-institutional relations,*" Bradford summarizes.[164]

In discussing issues of legitimacy, Bradford maintains that global governance does not mean that nation-states will be superseded by another set of international institutions, but rather, they will constitute the foundation for political legitimacy for those global institutional reforms necessary for effective and efficient 21st-century governance. Additionally, there are two other key elements to successful global governance that Bradford emphasizes. First, an important characteristic of this 21st-century governance ought to be that it is more inclusive, meaning that countries of the Middle East and other, less represented, developing regions should participate actively in summit mechanisms. This idea of an inclusive world order resonates well with what numerous scholars concluded before, for example it is exactly what Slaughter has put an emphasis on as well. Second, monitoring and evaluation systems are also necessary to ensure accountability and transparency. Finally, Bradford calls for an overall summit reform of global leadership.[165] Snyder, Hermann, and Lasswell had already suggested the establishment of a global monitoring system (GMS) 30 years ago, which, as they explained, "would use standardized indicators to monitor governmental actions and their impacts on professed official goals and on the attainment and distribution of basic human values." Preferred outcomes would also need to be "compared to avowed goals and the fundamental values associated with human dignity."[166]

Corning asserts that there seems to be a growing interest in the concept of a "political evolution," which might include reordering and reconfigurations in the international system. He draws attention to the ubiquitous nature of synergistic processes, not only in the natural sciences, but virtually in all systems. He explains, "[p]olitical scientists observe synergistic effects in voting processes, interest group activity, coalition behavior, and a host of organizational phenomena, among other things." Synergistic effects acted as sources of creativity in evolution and in the emergence of more complex social systems.[167] This ties into Modelski and Thompson's evolutionary approach, which is based on the idea that "global political structures undergo change that can be characterized as evolutionary," and that "an evolutionary perspective is applicable . . . because global politics involves social evolution at the level of the macro-organization of the human species," which enables strategic innovation and provides a wider range of opportunities such as "creating new patterns of association and cooperation." In their broader context, called "the co-evolutionary context," a range of other phenomena evolves simultaneously, such as the global information/ knowledge-based economy, which, in turn, gives rise to a more informed public that becomes progressively more involved in defining and resolving global problems. Barriers to information and knowledge break down, and new networks of solidarity appear transforming the characteristics of the "global community" into a more inclusive one, these authors add rather optimistically. Overall, Modelski and Thompson suggest that all these co-evolutionary processes have the ability to enhance the overall human evolutionary potential; consequently, emerging new norms and value-sets and social and political learning can facilitate alternative global policies.[168]

As mentioned earlier, transatlantic knowledge networks can be viewed as building blocks of cooperation and order-creation. In an era in which we are experiencing the proliferation of global challenges that are being addressed through a multitude of international organizations that face serious policy dilemmas, these networks can be regarded as essential mechanisms of global governance. In *After Hegemony: Cooperation and Discord in the World Political Economy,* Keohane argues that treating states as non-unitary actors, accounting for the variations in domestic politics, and the role of non-governmental organizations (NGOs) and transnational networks call for a different approach to unraveling patterns of cooperation in the 21st century.[169] In *Power and Interdependence,* Keohane and Nye show that, in an era of complex interdependence, multiple channels of interactions and cooperative patterns prevail, there is an absence of hierarchy among issues of global significance due to the fact that a great number of issues overlap, and there is a greater need to rely on forces that project power by other means.[170,171]

Greater interdependence in our global political, economic, and cultural systems may lessen the significance of local, traditional, and more personalized kinds of influences that have long driven the way our social and political systems dealt with all facets of human interaction. Problems or risks were created and addressed more on the lower-level setting, where the individual was able to find moral support when dealing with challenges. When systems reach higher levels of complexity in which the intrusion of system-level problems, or risks, into the daily lives of individuals requires that other forms and facets of "moral rewards" be available, then the seeking out of these mechanisms becomes inevitable.[172] These new mechanisms need to build trust at the system-level and, hence, become the facets of coordination, cooperation, and order-creation. This research investigates those institutional aspects of order-formation that involve professional collaborations and their transformative power in transnational politics. Whether knowledge networks, in general, and transatlantic connections, in particular, can help construct such building-blocks is investigated in this project. A core insight of this book is that *viewing transatlantic communication networks as new spaces where political order is being formed* allows us to assess the character of this new political order by identifying key actors or organizations and the unique structure of their interactions in cyberspace.

NOTES

1. Albert Szent-Györgyi, *The Crazy Ape*, 1st ed. (New York: Philosophical Library, 1970), 29.
2. Jan van Dijk, *The Network Society: Social Aspect of New Media* (London, Thousand Oaks, New Delhi: Sage Publications Ltd., 1999).; Manuel Castells, *The Information Age, Volumes 1–3: Economy, Society and Culture (Information Age Series)* (Chichester, West Sussex: Wiley-Blackwell, 1999).
3. Diane Stone, "Knowledge Networks and Global Policy," in *Global Knowledge Networks and International Development*, ed. Diane Stone and Simon Maxwell (New York, NY: Routledge, 2004).

4. Francis Bacon, "Religious Meditations, of Heresies, 1597," in *The Essays of Sir Francis Bacon*, Limited Sl (New York, NY: The Heritage Press, 1944).
5. Synergy is the idea that wholes have properties that are different from those of the parts. Considered as such, synergy lies at the heart of human inquiry.
6. Chris Lucas, "Synergy and Complexity Science," *Complexity & Artificial Life Research Concept for Self-Organizing Systems, Educational Website by CALResCo*, 2006.
7. Rainer Tetzlaff, "International Organizations (World Bank, IMF, EU) as Catalyst of Democratic Values, Rule of Law and Human Rights—Successes and Limits" (Denver, CO, 2006), http://partners.civiced.org/paw/tools/people_download.php?%0Agroup=event&id=193.
8. Ibid.,19, emphasis in original.
9. Omonyi Adewoye, "Leadership and the Dynamics of Reform in Africa," in *Reflections on Leadership in Africa. Forty Years after Independence*, ed. Haroub Othman (Brussels, Belgium: VUB University Press, 2000), 46–47. Quoted in Tetzlaff, "International Organizations (World Bank, IMF, EU) as Catalyst of Democratic Values, Rule of Law and Human Rights—Successes and Limits," 14.
10. Ibid., 20, emphasis in original.
11. Bruce Kuklick, *Blind Oracles: Intellectuals and War from Kennan to Kissinger* (Princeton, NJ: Princeton University Press, 2007).
12. John Dewey, *The Public and Its Problems* (New York, NY: Holt, 1927).
13. Kuklick, *Blind Oracles: Intellectuals and War from Kennan to Kissinger*, 11.
14. Schmidt (2011, p. 60) argues that "change (but also continuity) [is better explained] through ideas and discursive interaction."
15. John S. Dryzek, *Discursive Democracy: Politics, Policy, and Political Science* (New York, NY: Cambridge University Press, 1990).; John S. Dryzek, "Transnational Democracy in an Insecure World," *International Political Science Review/ Revue Internationale de Science Politique* 27, no. 2 (April 1, 2006): 104.
16. Dryzek, "Transnational Democracy in an Insecure World."
17. Ibid.
18. Ibid., 104.
19. Thomas Risse, "Social Constructivism and European Integration," in *European Integration Theory*, ed. Antje Wiener and Thomas Diez (Oxford, UK: Oxford University Press, 2004), 7.
20. Ibid., 5.
21. Although Habermas' work was translated between 1984 and 1987, the original work was published in 1981.
22. Jürgen Habermas, *The Theory of Communicative Action* (Cambridge, MA: Polity Press, 1981).
23. Dryzek, "Transnational Democracy in an Insecure World."
24. Mary Káldor, *Global Civil Society: An Answer to War* (Cambridge, MA: Polity Press, 2003).; Dryzek, "Transnational Democracy in an Insecure World," 103.
25. John G. Ikenberry, *After Victory: Institutions, Strategic Restraint, and the Rebuilding of Order after Major Wars* (Princeton, NJ: Princeton University Press, 2001).; Anne-Marie Slaughter, *A New World Order* (Princeton, NJ: Princeton University Press, 2004).
26. John S. Dryzek, *Foundations and Frontiers of Deliberative Governance* (Oxford, UK: Oxford University Press, 2012).
27. Jeffrey Berejikian and J. S. Dryzek, "Reflexive Action in International Politics," *British Journal of Political Science* 30, no. 2 (2000): 193.

28. Ulrich Beck, *Reflexive Modernization: Politics, Tradition and Aesthetics in the Modern Social Order* (Stanford, CA: Stanford University Press, 1995).; Anthony Giddens, *Modernity and Self-Identity. Self and Society in the Late Modern Age* (Cambridge, MA: Polity Press, 1991).
29. Beck, *Reflexive Modernization: Politics, Tradition and Aesthetics in the Modern Social Order.*
30. Ulrich Beck, *Risk Society: Towards a New Modernity* (London, UK: Sage Publications Ltd., 1992), 2–3.
31. Beck, *Risk Society: Towards a New Modernity*, 4.
32. Anthony Giddens, *The Constitution of Society: Outline of the Theory of Structuration* (Cambridge, MA: Polity Press, 1984).
33. Peter Haas, "When Does Power Listen to Truth? A Constructivist Approach to the Policy Process," *Journal of European Public Policy* 11, no. 4 (January 2004): 587.
34. "'Mode 1' of knowledge production refers primarily to basic university research (basic research performed by the higher education sector) that is being organized in a disciplinary structure." Elias G. Carayannis and David F. J. Campbell, *Mode 3 Knowledge Production in Quadruple Helix Innovation Systems* (New York, NY: Springer New York, 2012), 3.
35. Ibid., 1.
36. van Dijk, *The Network Society: Social Aspect of New Media.*; Castells, *The Information Age, Volumes 1–3: Economy, Society and Culture (Information Age Series).*
37. Emilie M. Hafner-Burton, Miles Kahler, and Alexander H. Montgomery, "Network Analysis for International Relations," *International Organization* 63, no. 03 (July 15, 2009): 559.
38. Castells, *The Information Age, Volumes 1–3: Economy, Society and Culture (Information Age Series).*
39. Hanneman, Robert A. Riddle, *Introduction to Social Network Methods*, 1.
40. Gestalt is a German term, which translates to "essence or shape of an entity's complete form" (Wikipedia.org).
41. John Scott, *Social Network Analysis: A Handbook*, 1st ed. (Newberry Park, CA: Sage Publications Ltd., 1991).
42. Jacob L. Moreno, *Who Shall Survive?: Foundations of Sociometry, Group Psychotherapy, and Sociodrama* (Washington, DC: Nervous and Mental Disease Publishing Company, 1934).
43. Richard J. Trudeau, *Introduction to Graph Theory* (Mineola, NY: Dover Publications, 1994).
44. Paul Erdős and Alfréd Rényi, "On Random Graphs I," *Publ. Math.* 6 (1959): 290–297.
45. Hafner-Burton, Kahler, and Montgomery, "Network Analysis for International Relations," 559.
46. Ibid., 562.
47. Caroline Haythornthwaite, "Social Network Analysis: An Approach and Technique for the Study of Information Exchange," *Library and Information Science Research* 342 (1996): 323–342.
48. Ronald S. Burt, *Structural Holes: The Social Structure of Competition*, Cambridge, (Harvard University Press, 1992).
49. David Lazer and Allan Friedman, "The Dark Side of the Small World: How Efficient Information Diffusion Drives Out Diversity and Lowers Collective Problem Solving Ability." *Harvard Program on Networked Governance Working Paper* No. 06–001, 2006. www.hks.harvard.edu/netgov/files/png_workingpaper_series/PNG06-001_WorkingPaper_LazerFriedman.pdf.

50. Albert L. Barabási, *Linked: How Everything Is Connected to Everything Else and What It Means for Business, Science, and Everyday Life* (Cambridge, MA: Perseus Publishing, 2002).
51. David Knoke and Song Yang, *Social Network Analysis, Quantitative Applications in the Social Sciences Series* (2nd ed. London, UK: Sage Publications, 2008).
52. Mark S. Granovetter, "The Strength of Weak Ties," *American Journal of Sociology* 78, no. 6 (1973): 1360–1380.
53. Ibid., 202.
54. Howard Frederick, "Computer Networks and the Emergence of Global Civil Society," in *Global Networks: Computers and International Communication*, ed. Linda M. Harasim (Cambridge, MA: MIT Press, 1993), 8.
55. Martha Nussbaum and Amartya Sen, *The Quality of Life (Studies in Development Economics)*, ed. Martha Nussbaum and Amartya Sen (New York, NY: Oxford University Press, 1993).
56. Ibid.
57. Ronald Inglehart and Christian Welzel, *Modernization, Cultural Change, and Democracy: The Human Development Sequence* (Cambridge, MA: Cambridge University Press, 2005), ix.
58. Granovetter, "The Strength of Weak Ties," 228–229.
59. Robert D. Putnam, *Making Democracy Work: Civic Traditions in Modern Italy* (Princeton, NJ: Princeton University Press, 1993).
60. Francis Fukuyama, "Social Capital," in *Culture Matters: How Values Shape Human Progress*, ed. L.E. Harrison and S.P. Huntington (New York, NY: Basic Books, 2000), 99.
61. Ronald S. Burt, "The Network Structure of Social Capital," *Research in Organizational Behavior* 22 (2000): 345–423.
62. Hafner-Burton, Kahler, and Montgomery, "Network Analysis for International Relations."
63. Pierre Bourdieu and Loïc J.D. Wacquant, *An Invitation to Reflexive Sociology* (Chicago, IL: University of Chicago Press, 1992), 119.
64. J.S. Coleman, "Social Capital in the Creation of Human Capital," *American Journal of Sociology* 94 (1988): S95–S120; James S. Coleman, *Foundations of Social Theory* (Cambridge, MA: Harvard University Press, 1990).
65. Sveinn Vidar Gudmundsson and Christian Lechner, "Multilateral Airline Alliances: Balancing Strategic Constraints and Opportunities," *Journal of Air Transport Management* 12, no. 3 (May 2006): 153.
66. "Structural holes" is a term used mainly in social network analysis to designate connections of nonredundant ties, which can be regarded as latent opportunities.
67. Ibid., 154.
68. Burt, *The Network Structure of Social Capital*, 1.
69. Ibid., 1.
70. Ines Mergel and T. Langenberg, "What Makes Online Ties Sustainable? A Research Design Proposal to Analyze Online Social Networks," *Harvard Program on Networked Governance* (2006): 6, http://hks.harvard.edu/netgov/files/png_workingpaper_series/PNG06-002_WorkingPaper_MergelLangenberg.pdf.
71. Hafner-Burton, Kahler, and Montgomery, "Network Analysis for International Relations," 573.
72. N. S. Contractor and P. R. Monge, "Managing Knowledge Networks," *Management Communication Quarterly* 16, no. 2 (November 01, 2002): 249–258.
73. Valdis E. Krebs and June Holley, "Building Sustainable Communities Through Network Building," 2002, http://orgnet.com/BuildingNetworks.pdf.

74. Barabási, *Linked: How Everything Is Connected to Everything Else and What It Means for Business, Science, and Everyday Life*, 106.
75. Nan Lin, "Building a Network Theory of Social Capital," *Connections* 22, no. 1 (1999): 48.
76. Lin, "Building a Network Theory of Social Capital."
77. Ibid., 31.
78. "The dictionary definition of this Greek word differ to mean 'market-place' or 'place of assembly' or a 'public space'. In its contemporary meaning, the term is borrowed from Nowotny et al., who refer to a social or public space in which science interacts and is constituted" (Stone 2005, p. 89).
79. Diane Stone and Andrew Denham, *Think Tank Traditions, Policy Research and the Politics of Idea* (Manchester, UK: Manchester University Press, 2004), 89.
80. Inderjeet Parmar, "American Foundations and the Development of International Knowledge Networks," *Global Networks* 1 (2002): 13.
81. Parmar, "American Foundations and the Development of International Knowledge Networks."
82. Stone, "Knowledge Networks and Global Policy," 89.
83. Diane Stone, "Knowledge in the Global Agora: Production, Dissemination and Consumption," in *Reshaping Globalization: Multilateral Dialogues and New Policy Initiatives*, ed. Andrea Krizsán (Budapest, Hungary: Central European University Press, 2003), 55. Also available at www2.warwick.ac.uk/fac/soc/ pais/staff/stone/publications/kga.pdf.
84. Stone, "Knowledge Networks and Global Policy," 93.
85. Stone, "Think Tank Transnationalisation and Non-Profit Analysis, Advice and Advocacy," 161.
86. Stone, "Knowledge Networks and Global Policy," 102.
87. Peter M. Haas, "Introduction: Epistemic Communities and International Policy Coordination," *International Organization* 46, no. 01 (May 22, 1992): 1.
88. Stone, "Knowledge Networks and Global Policy," 94.
89. Ibid.
90. Ibid., 95.
91. Ibid., 95.
92. Michel Foucault, *Power/Knowledge: Selected Interviews and Other Writings, 1972–1977* (New York, NY: Pantheon Books, 1980), 133.
93. Stone, "Knowledge Networks and Global Policy," 95.
94. Ibid., 96.
95. Stephen Gill, "Structural Change and Global Political Economy: Globalizing Elites and the Emerging World Order," in *Global Transformation: Challenges to the State System*, ed. Yoshikazu Sakamoto (Tokyo: United Nations University Press, 1994). Quoted in Stone, "Knowledge Networks and Global Policy."
96. Personal communication with Diane Stone on August 9, 2007.
97. Slaughter, *A New World Order*.; Wolfgang H. Reinicke et al., *Critical Choices. The United Nations, Networks, and the Future of Global Governance*, ed. Wolfgang H. Reinicke et al. (Ottawa, Canada: International Development Research Center Books, 2000).; Keck and Sikkink, *Activists Beyond Borders: Advocacy Networks in International Politics*. While TENs are accurately described in Slaughter's (2004) writings, GPPNs can be best understood from Reinecke's (2000) research, and TANs are examined by Keck & Sikkink (1998). Personal communication with Diane Stone on August 9, 2007.
98. Stone, "Knowledge Networks and Global Policy."
99. Parmar, "American Foundations and the Development of International Knowledge Networks."

100. Ibid., 13.
101. Donald E. Abelson, *Do Think Tanks Matter? Assessing the Impact of Public Policy Institutes* (Montreal, CA: McGill-Queens University Press, 2002), quoted in Peter Hayes, "The Role of Think Tanks in Defining Security Issues and Agendas," 2004, http://nautilus.org/collaborative/essay/2004/1021_Hayes.pdf.
102. Peter Hayes, "The Role of Think Tanks in Defining Security Issues and Agendas."
103. Ibid., 4.
104. Kai-Henrik Barth, "Catalysts of Change: Scientists as Transnational Arms Control Advocates in the 1980s," in *Global Power Knowledge. Science and Technology in International Affairs*, ed. John Krige and Kai-Henrik Barth (Chicago, IL: University of Chicago Press, 2006).
105. P.M. Haas, "Do Regimes Matter? Epistemic Communities and Mediterranean Pollution Control," *International Organization* 43, no. 3 (Summer 1989): 377–403.
106. Kevin M. Esterling, *The Political Economy of Expertise: Information and Efficiency in American National Politics* (Ann Arbor, MI: University of Michigan Press, 2004).
107. Milton Mueller, Andreas Schmidt, and Brenden Kuerbis, "Internet Security and Networked Governance in International Relations," *International Studies Review* 15, no. 1 (March 10, 2013): 86–104.
108. Ibid., 86.
109. David Lazer, "The Challenges of Networked Governance," 2005, 13.
110. Reinicke et al., *Critical Choices. The United Nations, Networks, and the Future of Global Governance*, 29.
111. Mueller, Schmidt, and Kuerbis, "Internet Security and Networked Governance in International Relations," 89–90.
112. J. Kurbalija and V. Katrandjiev, "Multistakeholder Diplomacy: Challenges and Opportunities," 2006, viii, http://scholar.google.com/scholar?hl=en&btnG=Search&q=intitle:Multistakeholder+Diplomacy:+Chanllenges+and+Opportunities#1.
113. The EU structure can be regarded as a success of multi-stakeholder governance.
114. Ibid.
115. D.L. Cogburn, "Diversity Matters, Even at a Distance: Evaluating the Impact of Computer-Mediated Communication on Civil Society Participation in the World Summit on the Information Society," *Information Technologies & International Development* 1, no. 3 (2004): 15–40; Nanette S. Levinson, "Unexpected Allies in Global Governance Arenas? Cross-cultural Collaborative Knowledge Processes & the Internet Governance Forum. Paper Presented at the Annual Meeting of The International Studies Association's Annual Convention," in *"Theory Vs. Policy? Connecting Scholars and Practitioners"* (New Orleans: International Studies Association, 2010), http://allacademic.com/meta/p413163_index.html.
116. Derrick L. Cogburn, "In Whose Name?: A Multimodal Exploration of Transnational Deliberative Democratic Practices in Multistakeholder Global Information Policy Formulation Processes" (San Diego, CA: International Studies Association, 2006), 8, http://allacademic.com/meta/p100585_index.html.
117. Ibid., 8.
118. Ibid.
119. Dryzek, *Discursive Democracy: Politics, Policy, and Political Science.*; Philip Pettit, *Republicanism: A Theory of Freedom and Government* (Oxford, UK: Oxford University Press, 1997).; Michael Saward, *The Terms*

of Democracy (Cambridge, MA: Polity Press, 1998), 64–65. quoted in Anthony McGrew, "Transnational Democracy: Theories and Prospects," in *Democratic Theory Today: Challenges for the 21st Century*, ed. Geoffrey Stokes and April Carter (Cambridge, UK: Polity Press, 2002), 269–294.

120. The World Summit on the Information Society (WSIS) is probably the most important platform that brings these scholars of Internet governance together.
121. Kurbalija and Katrandjiev, "Multistakeholder Diplomacy: Challenges and Opportunities," vii.
122. Kristin M. Lord and Vaughan C. Turekian, "Time for a New Era of Science Diplomacy," *Science and Society Policy Forum*, n.d., http://sciencemag.org/content/315/5813/769.full.pdf.
123. The Royal Society & AAAS, *New Frontiers in Science Diplomacy*, 2010. www.aaas.org/sites/default/files/New_Frontiers.pdf.
124. Ibid.
125. Ibid.
126. American Association for the Advancement of Science, Center for Science, Technology and Security Policy, *Science Policy Is Crucial for U.S. Foreign Policy*, 5.
127. Fabrice Jotterand, "The Politicization of Science and Technology: Its Implications for Nanotechnology," *The Journal of Law, Medicine & Ethics: a Journal of the American Society of Law, Medicine & Ethics* 34, no. 4 (January 2006): 658.
128. M. W. Wartofsky, "Technology, Power, and Truth: Political and Epistemological Reflections on the Fourth Revolution," in *Democracy in the Technological Society*, ed. L. Winner (Dordrecht: Kluwer, 1992), quoted in Jotterand, "The Politicization of Science and Technology: Its Implications for Nanotechnology."
129. Ibid.
130. Ibid.
131. John Ziman, *Real Science: What It Is, and What It Means* (New York, NY: Cambridge University Press, 2002), 74, quoted in Jotterand, "The Politicization of Science and Technology: Its Implications for Nanotechnology," 659.
132. Carayannis and Campbell, *Mode 3 Knowledge Production in Quadruple Helix Innovation Systems*, 14.
133. "Here, a cluster represents a specific configuration of knowledge, and possibly also of knowledge types" (Carayannis and Campbell, 2012, p. 14).
134. Ibid., 14.
135. Roger A. Pielke, "Accepting Politics In Science," *Washington Post*, January 10, 2005, 17, http://washingtonpost.com/wp-dyn/articles/A61928-2005Jan9.html.
136. Alex Dehgan and E. Colglazier, William, "Development Science and Science Diplomacy," *Science and Diplomacy*, 2012, http://sciencediplomacy.org/print/100.; Joseph S. Nye, *Soft Power: The Means to Success in World Politics*, 1st ed. (New York: Public Affairs, 2004).; Massimo Calabresi, "Hillary Clinton and the Rise of Smart Power," *Time Magazine*, November 7, 2011, http://content.time.com/time/magazine/article/0,9171,2097973,00.html.
137. American Association for the Advancement of Science, Center for Science, Technology and Security Policy, *Science Policy Is Crucial for U.S. Foreign Policy*, 6.
138. National Intelligence Council, *Global Trends 2030: Alternative Worlds*, 2012, http://globaltrends2030.files.wordpress.com/2012/11/global-trends-2030-november2012.pdf.

139. P. Boekholt et al., "Drivers of International Collaboration in Research," *Final Report* (2009): 40, http://eurosfaire.prd.fr/7pc/doc/1266832886_drivers_of_international_cooperation_in_research.pdf.
140. Lord and Turekian, "Time for a New Era of Science Diplomacy."
141. Joseph S. Nye and Robert O. Keohane, "Transnational Relations and World Politics: A Conclusion," *International Organization* 25, no. 03 (May 22, 1971): 721.
142. Kenneth N. Waltz, *Man, the State, and War: A Theoretical Analysis* (New York, NY: Columbia University Press, 1979).
143. Hans J. Morgenthau, *In Defense of the National Interest: A Critical Examination of American Foreign Policy* (New York, NY: Alfred A. Knopf, 1951).
144. John G. Ikenberry, *After Victory: Institutions, Strategic Restraint, and the Rebuilding of Order after Major Wars* (Princeton, NJ: Princeton University Press, 2001), 23.
145. Martha Finnemore, *The Purpose of Intervention: Changing Beliefs About the Use of Force* (New York, NY: Cornell University Press, 2003), 83. (Emphasis in original.)
146. Martha Finnemore, "Constructing Norms of Humanitarian Intervention," in *The Culture of National Security: Norms, Identity, and World Politics*, ed. Peter J. Katzenstein (New York, NY: Columbia University Press, 1996), 1.
147. Finnemore, *The Purpose of Intervention: Changing Beliefs About the Use of Force*, 81.
148. Peter A. Gourevitch et al., "The Political Science of Peter J. Katzenstein," *APSA* (2008): 894.
149. Robert O. Keohane, *After Hegemony: Cooperation and Discord in the World Political Economy* (Princeton, NJ: Princeton University Press, 1984).
150. Robert O. Keohane, "The Contingent Legitimacy of UN-Based Multilateralism," in *Legitimacy and Power in the Post-9/11 World* (University of Southern California, Stanford Center for Advanced Study in Behavioral Sciences, 2006).
151. Ibid., 2, 13, emphasis in original.
152. Ibid., 21.
153. Richard Higgott, "The Theory and Practice of Global and Regional Governance: Accommodating American Exceptionalism and European Pluralism," *GARNET Working Paper*, no. 01 (2005): 1–32. www2.warwick.ac.uk/fac/soc/garnet/workingpapers/0105.pdf.
154. Alexander Wendt, "Anarchy Is What States Make of It: The Social Construction of Power Politics" 46, no. 2 (1992): 391–425.
155. Thomas Risse, "Social Constructivism Meets Globalization," in *Globalization Theory: Approaches and Controversies*, ed. Anthony McGrew and David Held (Cambridge, UK: Polity Press, 2007), 131.
156. Peter J. Katzenstein, Martha Finnemore, and Alexander Wendt, *The Culture of National Security: Norms and Identity in World Politics*, ed. Peter J Katzenstein (New York, NY: Columbia University Press, 1996).
157. Hafner-Burton, Kahler, and Montgomery, "Network Analysis for International Relations," 569.
158. Ikenberry, *After Victory: Institutions, Strategic Restraint, and the Rebuilding of Order after Major Wars*, 2001, 269.
159. Slaughter, *A New World Order*, 15.
160. Susan Strange, "Toward a Theory of Transnational Empire," in *Global Changes and Theoretical Challenges: Approaches to World Politics for the 1990's*, ed. Ernst-Otto Czempiel and James N. Rosenau (Lexington, MA: Lexington Books, 1989).

161. Thomas J. Volgy and Alison Bailin., *International Politcs and State Strength* (Boulder, CO: Lynne Rienner Publishers Inc., 2003).
162. For now, this study assumes that those who make public written statements on trying to achieve such goals wish to follow their statement with actions that are consistent with those statements.
163. William H. Mott, *Globalization: People, Perspectives, and Progress* (Westport, CT: Praeger Publishers, 2004).
164. Colin I. Bradford, "Global Governance Reform for the 21st Century," (2005): 1–29, http://brookings.edu/~/media/research/files/papers/2005/10/24globaleconomics bradford/20051024bradford.pdf.
165. Bradford, "Global Governance Reform for the 21st Century."
166. R.C. Snyder, C.F. Hermann, and H.D. Lasswell, "A Global Monitoring System: Appraising the Effects of Government on Human Dignity," *International Studies Quarterly* 20, no. 2 (1976): 221.
167. P.A. Corning, "Synergy, Cybernetics and the Evolution of Politics," *International Political Science Review* 17, no. 1 (1996): 96.
168. George Modelski and W.R. Thompson, "The Long and the Short of Global Politics in the Twenty-first Century: An Evolutionary Approach," *International Studies Review* 1, no. 2 (1999): 120–121.
169. Keohane, Robert, *After Hegemony: Cooperation and Discord in the World Political Economy*.
170. Power by other means refers to using various forms of "soft power," to replace "hard power."
171. Robert O. Keohane and Joseph S. Nye, *Power and Interdependence* (New York, NY: Longman, 2001).
172. Giddens, *Modernity and Self-Identity. Self and Society in the Late Modern Age*, 1991.

3 All Is Well in Transatlantic Relations?

An investment in knowledge pays the best interest.

—Benjamin Franklin, 1758[1]

This chapter begins with a rationale for the case selection. After establishing why transatlantic relations matter, I discuss the earliest stages of cooperative arrangements between the transatlantic partners. The next section offers a brief account of early Atlanticism, followed by a description of the stages of transatlantic cooperative arrangements and the further institutionalization of relations leading to the New Transatlantic Agenda (NTA) of 1995. Finally, the chapter highlights some of the key points of the ongoing scholarly debate about transatlantic relations, which then leads to the process of institutionalization of various cooperative initiatives starting with the Marshall Plan and leading to the 1995 framework program, the New Transatlantic Agenda.

WHY CARE ABOUT TRANSATLANTIC RELATIONS?

This book argues that, despite having policy differences between the EU and the US in the early post-Cold War era and the difficulties of adopting to changes in the global environment, transatlantic relations and connections still matter in transnational politics. Based on the review of the literature, it becomes evident that a 21st-century world order is fundamentally influenced by the actions of the economically and democratically most developed segments of the world—the United States and the European Union. As the Streit Council for a Union of Democracies states, "[t]he transatlantic community represents the foundation of the world's wealth and security. The very size of the transatlantic economy (nearly 50% of global GDP and 40% of world trade) grants the US and the EU a privileged position to design and implement measures leading to economic growth . . . Yet great opportunities also entail great responsibilities."[2] From a security point of view, Meunier suggests, "while transatlantic security relations may not matter as much as to the traditional security allies . . . their impact on those traditionally outside of the European alliance remains profound."[3] Due to the unique security threats of the 21st century, the Atlantic Council puts an emphasis on collaboration on "research and development of technologies that will aid in preventing terrorism or alleviating its effects."[4] The significance of the transatlantic connection is also manifest in the transatlantic economy's role in the global economy; reaffirmed by negotiations, already underway, for a new agreement establishing a unified transatlantic market. This Trans-Atlantic Trade and Investment Partnership (TTIP) would drive transatlantic relations towards an entirely new direction "liberaliz[ing] one-third of global trade and generate millions of new jobs." "Divergent or duplicative regulatory policies" are among the greatest obstacles to concluding this new agreement, but policy-makers on both sides of the Atlantic should realize that this is an opportunity not to be missed to provide a template that can be emulated globally.[5]

As this book argues, the various aspects of cooperative relations are fundamentally intertwined due to the complexities of global politics and policies. Only a consensus-based, development-friendly, and well-articulated strategy, communicated through various transatlantic networks, has the potential to bring about change that reinforces, as well as goes beyond, transatlantic cooperation to address global challenges. The overall importance of the transatlantic partnership makes it one of the most representative and richest cases to be studied in the context of international cooperation and communication. While it is not a goal of this book to engage in a detailed examination of past century historical processes, in order to be able to understand the present and predict the future of the transatlantic partnership, it is essential to briefly look at the past.

EARLY ATLANTICISM

In order to unravel the earliest stages of transatlantic relations, we can go back more than a century or two to find exploratory cooperative connections between the two worlds, "old" and "new." Rennella and Walton describe the journeys of 19th- and 20th-century transatlantic voyagers as "planned serendipity." It was not until the late 19th century, when "transatlantic voyage became cheaper, safer, and shorter," that a visible increase in Americans' traveling to Europe could be registered.[6] These authors claim that this newly found opportunity had broadened travelers' horizon and imagination, and gave rise to some sense of internationalism. Improvements in shipbuilding technology not only boosted the number of travelers, but also facilitated competition between trading companies over the sea. Especially after the Civil War, more and more transatlantic shipping occurred as competition between transatlantic shipping companies became more pronounced.[7] Prominent voyagers, such as Henry and William James, used these opportunities as an "access to networks of accomplished foreign colleagues—networks that, in many ways, anticipated the vibrant intellectual circles that would be emerging a few decades later with the institutional support of the modern American university." Crossing the Atlantic "allowed people to think and act in ways that they might not allow themselves to do otherwise," which, in turn, resulted in their developing an admiration of the cultural values of others parallel to their own; perhaps an unusual endeavor at the time.[8] These serendipitous experiences expanded the professional horizon of travelers, as well as facilitated their intellectual development. As the authors put it, they provided travelers with "the opportunity to engage in a constructive questioning and self-examination of previously unquestioned beliefs and habits."[9]

Writing on the British Atlantic World, which excludes other parts of Europe during the past centuries, an international team of historians describes how that world had been created by the movements and early networking of people, goods, ideas, cultural values, and practices that ultimately shaped development.[10] This could be an important point of departure for it "takes us beyond institutional and political histories, drawing us towards studies of connection, identity, and solidarity in their broadest senses."[11] However, as Armitage and Braddick explain, Atlantic history has been traditionally understudied until recently and "[t]he particular strain of international engagement that would give birth to Atlantic history had its roots in World War I but flourished most vigorously during and after World War II."[12] They draw attention to the various forms of Atlanticism that had characterized Atlantic history and identify transatlantic history to be "the history of the Atlantic world through comparisons."[13] While these authors presume the existence, as well as significance, of nation-states and other economic formations during this historical period, Norman Angell's perspective at the beginning of the 20th century reflects a visionary view of transatlantic relations.

Angell, a political figure and author who has been understudied in the discipline, has certainly impacted both transatlantic relations as well as international relations in general with his work. In his book, *The Great Illusion,* Angell proves to be one of the predecessors of liberal internationalism as he argues for a new model in the international system. Considering the historical context in which he wrote *The Great Illusion,* one should not be surprised that the horrors of World War I made him question the efficiency of war, as well as concerned about the connection between nations' military might and the acquisition of wealth. Angell's philosophy, just like his predecessor Kant's, as well as his contemporary Schumpeter's, followed the logic that international commerce and development does not fare well with the destructive nature of war. In fact, it should be considered futile due to growing economic interdependence. Angell, worrying about the future of his beloved Europe, and reflecting on the interconnection between social and political change and its implications for change in international relations, already projected the type of development-oriented system that is based on the rule of law that would resemble the future European community.[14]

As an early form of institutionalized transatlantic relations, the US Postal Agreement with Great Britain on October 1, 1908, when the rate of postage to Great Britain was regulated to become the same as the rate within the territory of the Unites States should be mentioned here. When comparing this regulatory step to great inventions like steam, electricity, telegraph, and various other ways of facilitating commercial and industrial relationships, the drafters of the law claim that this move accelerated communication and a freer flow of ideas, ultimately bringing people together in the international arena.[15]

COMPLEMENTING RATHER THAN COMPETING VISIONS

There is a broad range of literature, especially since the inception of the New Transatlantic Agenda in 1995, which addresses the present, as well as the future, of the relationship between the United States and the European Union. Most scholars seem to agree that the transatlantic relationship does not live up to its full potential. Also, shifting domestic social and political structures influence policy approaches at the international level, and the way in which the literature evaluates the transatlantic partnership mirrors these shifts.[16] This phenomenon is clearly demonstrated by the body of literature that has been generated during the Bush administration vis-à-vis the Obama administration. Considering the European side, however, it seems more difficult to disentangle what drives policy change at the EU level. The subtleties of the supranational bodies, the diversity of various national leaders' style, charisma, and power-position within the union, combined with the ups and downs of the economy, make it rather complex to unravel the sources of policy change in the European Union at any point in time.

Part of the literature refers to existing value-gaps as an underlying issue that jeopardizes the success of the transatlantic partnership. Others insist that these partners share the same goals and values, but the source of recent disagreement lies, rather, in the preferred tools to achieve those goals. Only a few scholars suggested that the partnership might be beyond repair. The source of such pessimism seems to have resulted from the policies of the recent Bush era, when there was a special strain on transatlantic relations resulting from divergent policy prescriptions to 21st-century challenges. In fact, Daalder writing during this era suggests, "the gratuitous unilateralism that has marked the Bush administration's first two years in office . . . has had a profoundly negative impact on European elite and public opinion." He then continues,

> [e]ither their long marriage comes to an end, or it will be renewed. Which one of these futures comes true will depend especially on the United States, which, as the senior partner, has the greatest power to put the alliance back on track or to push it off the road completely.[17]

On the European side, a UK governmental website presents a similar perspective on the issue, "Atlanticism in Europe seems to be strongly correlated with political leadership, and the same is true for the US."[18] While Daalder puts the emphasis on the US's role in recovering transatlantic relations, both statements clearly show the insufficiency of only one level of analysis in international relations. In order to understand patterns of policy on the transnational level, one needs to understand not only the global, but also the domestic political structure and context.[19]

Risse also sees the major crisis in the transatlantic relationship to stem from domestic developments on both sides, as well as from different perceptions of security threats and approaches to address those. Risse suggests that the post-9/11 period provided a "window of opportunity" for policymakers and experts with divergent ideological backgrounds. This "window of opportunity" refers to pursuing a strategic dialogue on how to create successful transnational and transgovernmental coalitions across the Atlantic, which proved to be rather successful in the past. Risse's prescription to repair the transatlantic relationship calls for an overall institutional renewal for the transatlantic community.[20] He stresses that the United States needs to understand that the European partner has the potential to "deliver the international legitimacy required to make U.S. foreign policy effective" and successfully fulfill a "new transatlantic bargain."[21] Keohane brings up another key concern: the issue of sovereignty. He argues that the "concept of sovereignty can help us understand contemporary disagreement between Europe and the United States." While Europe has moved away from the classical conception of sovereignty and "converted to a conception of limited and pooled sovereignty," the United States and, especially, the "Bush administration has very effectively deployed the symbols of sovereignty," and became its strong defender.[22] "To Europeans . . . Bush seems unwilling to engage in reasonable persuasion, which models of pooled sovereignty recommend and even glorify."[23] Keohane warns, however, "a divorce between America and Europe is likely to be disastrous for order in world politics."[24]

Another scholar, Ash, advocates that a stronger value-and-interest consensus between these two main economic blocs is much needed, and America could really use Europe's soft power expertise to address common global challenges. Even a crisis situation, such as the threat of global terrorism, might hold unprecedented opportunities. On the analogy of the collapse of the Soviet empire in 1989 Ash suggests that there are similar opportunities to achieve change in the international system by means of soft power. Calling for greater citizen involvement, he emphasizes that ideas and actions of individuals and NGOs might accelerate change, similar to what happened during the Cold War. Ash conveys the message that through the networking of people and a myriad of "granovetterian" weak ties, new ideas are able to spread.[25] These, in turn, would have the power to impede ideologies and policies that represent obstacles to what Inglehart and Norris define as people "pursuing their liberty aspirations."[26] Finally, as Ash succinctly put it in an interview, "Blair . . . having refused to choose [between Europe and the United States] . . . ended up choosing—against Europe, and . . . against much of European public opinion, and much of British opinion [which] destroyed his credibility in continental Europe."[27] This indicates that even if public opinion, trust, and perceptions of legitimacy do not seem to matter as much in the short run, political leaders in democratic societies do not have the luxury to be ignorant of those in the longer run.

In preparing President Bush's trip to Europe in 2005, a subtle change in direction became visible when, American and European foreign policy and national security experts from both sides of the Atlantic signed a "Compact between the United States and Europe." This document stated that differences between the United States and Europe neither resulted from miscommunication, nor were they inherent, but rather "arose because each side has taken actions the other strongly opposes, or declined to join in actions the other strongly favors."[28] As a demonstration to their commitment in the same fundamental values and interests, such as promoting peace and the acknowledgement that transatlantic consensus fosters legitimacy, the Compact laid out a comprehensive strategy to address challenges to global stability.[29] Irrespective of whether one subscribes to these policy-makers' interpretation of the root-causes of the differences between the US and the EU, what is significant here is the recognition that there are common values and interests, and the acknowledgement that acting together strengthens legitimacy—a vital issue in contemporary world politics.

In an interview to BBC, Moravcsik explains that the disagreement, or misunderstanding, between America and Europe is in their conceptions and the instruments of power. Moravcsik further clarifies these diverse conceptions and argues that one is essentially coercive and "underestimates the importance of civilian power," while the other seeks to persuade or "entice countries to accept a form of international order" and, perhaps, "undervalues the importance of military force."[30] Moravcsik adds that the misconception between the United States and Europe is embedded in their institutions. As an example, he brings up the necessity of European bureaucracy to support integration that is, perhaps, beyond the comprehension of people in Washington—just like Eurocrats, he adds, do not get the imperatives of the American security strategy. He then concludes that as long as this bureaucratic misfit persists, without a new transatlantic bargain, problems may remain.[31]

Drezner explains the transatlantic divide over the role and effectiveness of international organizations as more of a clash on process, not outcome.

He then further clarifies, "[f]or Americans, multilateralism is strictly a means to an end; for Europeans, multilateralism remains an end in itself."[32] Banchoff represents a different point of view when he argues that there is a deeper underlying value-conflict between these partners, the US and the EU. According to Banchoff, the post-Cold War era and globalization processes have contributed to and made value-conflicts more visible. As he expounds, after 9/11 "Bush emphasized the value of freedom, a cornerstone of American civil religion . . . [and his] narrative conflated the interests and security of the United States with that of the entire world . . . Bush's choice of vocabulary ruled out the idea that in acting alone the U.S. would be acting for itself and acting against others."[33] Nevertheless, he was only able to do that because it resonated with prevailing American culture. As scholars like Almond and Verba, Elazar, Inglehart and others point out, the underlying values and the way ideas are communicated or conveyed matters; political culture shapes politics and policies.[34] Banchoff concludes that even though both American and European positions are rooted in their distinct institutional and historical contexts, values can change and develop. He suggests that the partners should find ways and uncover mechanisms, such as deliberation and persuasion, in which value-conflicts could be resolved and consensus could be attained to achieve common goals.[35]

In sum, these ideas reinforce the notion that it is *complementarity, rather than competition,* between the United States and the European Union that should *serve as the foundation for the transatlantic partnership.* While public opinion on both sides of the Atlantic remains relatively stable, the actions of political leaders reflect a renewed interest in further strengthening US–EU cooperation at all levels. As the German Marshall Fund's 2012 public opinion survey indicates, more than half of EU citizens assert that it is "desirable that the United States exert strong leadership in world affairs" and two third of Americans believe that the EU should do the same, while there are also signs that policy decision-makers have been actively broadening the range of cooperative relationships.[36]

In *Cooperation among Democracies: the European Influence on U.S. Foreign Policy,* Risse-Kappen argues that, historically, Europe had a great influence on US foreign policy and used the US open system to strike alliances.[37] This is a policy that Europe could still capitalize on in the future. Similarly, Quinlan asserts that the deepness and the broadness of the relationship between the United States and Europe is without precedent and still progressing despite occasional political differences. He affirms that the networks of interdependence between these two are becoming so dense that their quality is on another level when contrasted with networks that either one of them have with any other continent:

> If globalization is going to proceed as its promoters suggest, the U.S. and Europe will have to show that they can deal with the challenges generated by the deep integration of their economies. If the U.S. cannot

> resolve such differences with Europe, it is unlikely to resolve them with economies much less like its own. The possibilities—and potential limits—of globalization are likely to be defined first and foremost by the successes or failures of the transatlantic relationship.[38]

Modelski and Thompson suggest that it is the US–EU partnership that has the potential to constitute "the premier foundation for the twenty-first century world order."[39] Therefore, stronger collaborative efforts between the United States and Europe can be a step towards overcoming global challenges. After all, the enlargement process of the EU and the European neighborhood policy resulted in an historical leap towards a peaceful integration process that is without precedence. European integration, as we know it, would have been unthinkable even just a few decades ago.

In discussing US–EU partnership strategies Hamilton and Burwell recommend building "on the acquis Atlantique and the exceptional density of transatlantic interconnections." Their recent study suggests the acceptance of 10 initiatives due to the fact that

> a "multistakeholder" system now exists across the Atlantic, based on a thick web of networks that are now so dense, in fact, that they have attained a quality far different than those either continent has with any other . . . The sheer breadth and depth of the relationship means that no single framework will suffice.[40]

These initiatives include security issues, creating a barrier-free Transatlantic Marketplace, and addressing problems of global economic governance.[41]

STAGES OF COOPERATIVE ARRANGEMENTS: INSTITUTIONALIZATION

In *Managing EU-US Relations: Actors, Institutions and the New Transatlantic Agenda,* Steffenson examines three transatlantic agreements: the Transatlantic Declaration (1990), the New Transatlantic Agenda (1995), and the Transatlantic Economic Partnership (1998).[42] She tests the hypothesis that these agreements played a decisive role in the institutionalization of EU–US relations during the 1990s. Although the institutionalization process of EU–US relations, outside the confines of NATO, is not entirely evident and well-defined in the literature, Steffenson's argument that these agreements were most probably significant "building blocks" in this process seems to hold. When discussing the institutionalization of ideas, beliefs, and practices, it is essential to establish how institutionalization is understood. Steffenson uses Peters' as well as Ruggie's definition, which both assume that the general characterization of institutionalization includes

> formal and informal structures, including networks and shared norms; patterned and sustainable interaction between actors; constraints on the behavior of its members; and some sense of shared values. Thus, institutionalization is a process whereby a coordination and pattern of behavior between actors is established and developed.[43]

When Peters sets the criteria for the institutional approach in political science, he emphasizes structure (formal or informal), stability of some sort, and, also, putting constraint on human behavior (individual or organizational).[44] However, considering Huntington's definition of institutionalization as "a process by which organizations and procedures acquire value and stability," a somewhat different image emerges. Huntington shows that "the level of institutionalization . . . can be defined by the adaptability, complexity, autonomy, and coherence of its organizations and procedures."[45] Even though the context of Huntington's definition is that of the political system and order, it can be argued that his definition is applicable to the institutionalization of the transatlantic networks, considered as political systems. It then follows that the characteristics of networks, transatlantic or otherwise, put these on the adaptability-rigidity scale towards the adaptable, flexible end, while on the complexity-simplicity scale they emerge as complex by their nature. Considering Huntington's argument that "the more adaptable . . . the more highly institutionalized . . . the more complicated . . . the more highly institutionalized," these first two measures of institutionalization can put the networking modes of operations in a favorable light.[46] As far as the other two measures are concerned, autonomy versus subordination, as well as coherence versus disunity, the level of institutionalization for these measures becomes less clear. For the purposes of this study, the important question is whether transatlantic institutions matter and to what extent.

The institutionalization of the relationship between the United States and Europe began to shape during the postwar period in the late 1940s, and there is consensus in the literature on the significance of the Marshall Plan within this process. Peterson follows the evolution of US–EU relations and divides it into three major epochs: US–EC postwar relations, fundamental changes in the relationship due to a paradigm shift in international relations after the 1989 collapse of the bipolar world order, and the era following the birth of the Transatlantic Declaration.[47] As the German Marshall Fund of the United States' website describes, a most significant step towards building bridges between Europe and the United States is marked by US Secretary of State George C. Marshall's speech, delivered at Harvard University on June 5, 1947. This initiative led to the creation of the Marshall Plan that ultimately contributed, to a large extent, to the full recovery of Western Europe.[48] It was only 25 years later that a permanent memorial to that plan had been created through the establishment of the German Marshall Fund "dedicated to the promotion of greater understanding and common action between Europe and the United States."[49]

The transatlantic relationship has gone through a progression of stages. In the early stages, the United States, emerging as the strongest economy in the postwar world, was an avid supporter of European unity driven less by altruistic reasons than by strategic concerns and economic interests.[50] The creation of the Western European Union (1948), the North Atlantic Treaty Organization (1949), the European Coal and Steel Community (1952), the European Atomic Energy Community (1957), and the European Economic Community (1957) are all manifestations of that. It was Kennedy's "Grand Design" that brought up the idea of "a partnership of equals," as well as that the design envisioned a "'declaration of inter-dependence' between the United States and a united Europe."[51] However, there were factors that hindered the success of such optimistic initiatives, the most significant of which were the following. First, the institutional design of the US foreign policy-making system made it difficult to achieve consensus between decision-makers and pursue efficient foreign policies. Second, European unity was not present, either, to facilitate speaking with one voice. Third, French President De Gaulle's openly expressed anti-Americanism also weakened potential cooperation. Although later, during the Nixon years, there were attempts to redirect the relationship through the launch of the "New Atlantic Charter," it had actually gotten to be more of a rivalry than a partnership of equals due to rather divergent foreign policy preferences. During the Carter era, US-European relations took a backseat, while Reagan's attitude to European foreign policy directions was "overtly hostile," Peterson explains.[52]

It was not until the 1990s that considerable changes occurred in the nature of transatlantic relations. A number of critical factors played a role in this process, although most of these can be attributed to the pivotal changes and the transformation of the international system following the collapse of the bipolar order. The fundamental question arose: Now that the common security threat was over, what is it that could hold the alliance together? Is it common values and ideas, economic interests, and if so, is there enough commonality to make it work or even to bring transatlantic cooperation to a higher level? As later developments of the US–EU partnership make it clear, American dominance becomes much less obvious as Europe emerges as a more capable actor, slowly moving towards speaking with one voice through its extensive institution building and the broadening of supranational initiatives.

The New Transatlantic Agenda of 1995

Relations between the United States and the European Union reached a new level when the framework agreement, representing a "novel experiment in international governance," the New Transatlantic Agenda was called into being on December 3, 1995.[53] The New Transatlantic Agenda (NTA) represents a milestone as it signifies a commitment to a systematic cooperation between the US and the EU in four major areas: promoting peace, stability, "development, and democracy around the world"; responding to global challenges; contributing to the expansion of world trade and closer economic relations; and "building bridges across the Atlantic," which refers to closer people-to-people communications.[54] As Pollack sums up the NTA's 10-year performance, some of the aspects of the cooperative agreement, such as the Transatlantic Business Dialogue, were more successful, while others like the civil society dialogue were less so.[55] Nevertheless Pollack explains, "[t]he significance of the NTA lies not in its unblemished record of success," but rather in "seeking deep integration through shallow institutions."[56] Steffenson writes that "the structure of governance created by the NTA . . . facilitated policy-coordination . . . [and] produced policy outcomes that would be unimaginable" otherwise. In addition, she observes that the NTA contributed to the decentralization of decision-making.[57]

Yet another aspect of looking at transatlantic relations is through the level of institutionalization and the way it impacts the ability to exercise governance. While Peterson and Steffenson emphasize the continued significance of the alliance, they claim that there are "limitations of networked governance in transatlantic relations" and that these partners should be mindful of "trying to manufacture partnership using imperfect institutions."[58] Appraising the process toward institutionalization of transatlantic relations, Peterson and Steffenson point out that there are multiple channels through which transatlantic relations are manifest. Though they claim that "the US and EU remain far from an institutionalized partnership," they praise this new wave of institutionalism that began with the NTA of 1995 as they maintain that it "changed the nature of the transatlantic relationship . . . [and] the NTA system is an integral part of a wider dialogue that keeps both sides focused on a pragmatic agenda of policy co-operation."[59] The Obama administration's multilateralist stance is an added benefit that will, hopefully, foster this institutionalization process further.

As discussed earlier, a significant point this book examines is the pivotal leadership role that the United States and Europe can undertake in shaping global trends and overcome challenges. This research investigates this role in global governance through the transatlantic partners' networking practices. Steffenson's argument that "transatlantic institutions, no matter how loose, matter because they form the basis of a transatlantic governance structure" underscores this objective.[60]

NOTES

1. Benjamin Franklin, "The Way to Wealth," in *The Works of Benjamin Franklin Vol. 2.*, ed. Jared Sparks (Boston, 1758), 292–103.
2. The Streit Council for the Union of Democracies, "Transatlantic Cooperation," 2009, http://streitcouncil.org/index.php?page=transatlantic-cooperation.

3. S. Meunier, "Do Transatlantic Relations Still Matter?" *Perspectives on Europe (Council for European Studies)* 40, no. 1 (2010): 16.
4. David L. Aaron et al., "The Post-9/11 Partnership: Transatlantic Cooperation Against Terrorism," 2004, x, http://scholar.google.com/scholar?hl=en&btnG=Search&q=intitle:The+Post+9+/+11+Partnership+:+Transatlantic+Coopera tion+against+Terrorism#2.
5. Thomas J. Bollyky and Anu Bradford, "Getting to Yes on Transatlantic Trade," *Foreign Affairs* (July 10, 2013), http://foreignaffairs.com/articles/139569/thomas-j-bollyky-and-anu-bradford/getting-to-yes-on-transatlantic-trade?page=show.
6. Whitney Walton and Mark Rennella, "Planned Serendipity: American Travelers and the Transatlantic Voyage in the Nineteenth and Twentieth Centuries," *Journal of Social History* 2 (2004): 368.
7. Walton and Rennella, "Planned Serendipity: American Travelers and the Transatlantic Voyage in the Nineteenth and Twentieth Centuries."
8. Ibid., 368.
9. Ibid., 366.
10. David Armitage and Michael J. Braddick, *The British Atlantic World, 1500–1800* (New York, NY: Palgrave Macmillan, 2002).
11. Ibid., 1.
12. Ibid., 13.
13. Ibid., 18.
14. Norman Angell, *The Great Illusion*, (Cosimo Classics, 2007).
15. American Society of International Law, "Postal Agreement with Great Britain," *The American Journal of International Law* 2, no. 4 (1908): 849–853.
16. Robert D. Putnam, "Diplomacy and Domestic Politics: the Logic of Two-Level Games," *International Organization* 42, no. 3 (1988): 427–460.
17. I. H. Daalder, "The End of Atlanticism," *Survival* 45, no. 2 (June 2003): 148, 162.
18. Government Office for Science, "Europe Looks West: A Resurgence of Pro-Atlanticism Within the EU?" *Department for Business, Innovation, and Skill at GOV.UK*, 2012, http://sigmascan.org/Live/Issue/ViewIssue/35.
19. Robert D. Putnam, "Diplomacy and Domestic Politics: The Logic of Two-Level Games," *International Organization* 42, no. 03 (May 22, 2009): 427; Peter J. Katzenstein, Martha Finnemore, and Alexander Wendt, *The Culture of National Security: Norms and Identity in World Politics*, ed. Peter J. Katzenstein. (New York, NY: Columbia University Press, 1996).
20. Thomas Risse, "The Crisis of the Transatlantic Security Community," in *Multilateralism and Security Institutions in an Era of Globalization*, eds. Dimitris Bourantonis, Ifantis Kostas, and Tsakonas Panayotis (New York, NY: Routledge, 2007), 78–100.
21. Ibid., 25.
22. R. O. Keohane, "Ironies of Sovereignty: The European Union and the United States," *JCMS: Journal of Common Market Studies* 40, no. 4 (November 2002): 743.
23. Ibid., 760.
24. Ibid., 762.
25. Timothy G. Ash, *Free World: America, Europe, and the Surprising Future of the West* (New York, NY: Random House, 2004).
26. Ronald Inglehart and Pippa Norris, *Sacred and Secular: Religion and Politics Worldwide* (Cambridge, MA: Cambridge University Press, 2004).
27. Ash, *Free World: America, Europe, and the Surprising Future of the West*, 3.
28. Brookings Institute, "A Compact Between the United States and Europe" (Brookings Institute, 2005), 1, http://brookings.edu/fp/cuse/analysis/USEU Compact.pdf.

29. Brookings Institute, "A Compact Between the United States and Europe."
30. James Cox, "Transcript of Interview with Andrew Moravcsik 'The World This Weekend'" (UK: BBC, 2002), 3, http://princeton.edu/~amoravcs/library/bbc.pdf.
31. Cox, "Transcript of Interview with Andrew Moravcsik 'The World This Weekend.'"; Andrew Moravcsik, "Striking a New Transatlantic Bargain," *Foreign Affairs* (August 2003), http://jstor.org/stable/10.2307/20033650.
32. Daniel Drezner, "Lost in Translation: The Transatlantic Divide Over Diplomacy," in *Growing Apart: America and Europe in the 21st Century*, ed. Jeffrey Kopstein and Sven Steinmo (Cambridge, MA: Cambridge University Press, 2007), 194.
33. Thomas Banchoff, "Value Conflict and US-EU Relations: The Case of Unilateralism," *ACES Working Paper Series* (June 2004): 16.
34. Gabriel A. Almond and Sidney Verba, *The Civic Culture: Political Attitudes and Democracy in Five Nations* (Princeton, NJ: Princeton University Press, 1963).; Daniel J. Elazar, *American Federalism: A View from the States* (New York, NY: Crowell, 1966).; Inglehart and Norris, *Sacred and Secular: Religion and Politics Worldwide.*
35. Banchoff, "Value Conflict and US-EU Relations: The Case of Unilateralism."
36. The German Marshall Foundation, "Transatlantic Trends 2012 Partners; Key Findings" (2013): 3, http://trends.gmfus.org/files/2012/09/TT-2012-Key-Findings-Report.pdf.
37. Thomas Risse-Kappen, *Cooperation Among Democracies: The European Influence on U.S. Foreign Policy* (Princeton, NJ: Princeton University Press, 1997).
38. J. P. Quinlan, *Drifting Apart Or Growing Together?: The Primacy of the Transatlantic Economy* (Washington, D.C.: Center for Transatlantic Relations, 2003), vi.
39. George Modelski and W. R. Thompson, "The Long and the Short of Global Politics in the Twenty-first Century: An Evolutionary Approach," *International Studies Review* 1, no. 2 (1999): 131. http://onlinelibrary.wiley.com/doi/10.1111/1521-9488.00157/full.
40. Daniel S. Hamilton et al., *Shoulder to Shoulder: Forging a Strategic U.S.–EU Partnership* (2009), 83, http://transatlantic.sais-jhu.edu/publications/books/us-eu_report_final.pdf.
41. Ibid., 13.
42. Rebecca Steffenson, *Managing EU–US Relations: Actors, Institutions and the New Transatlantic Agenda* (Manchester, UK: Manchester University Press, 2005).
43. Ibid., 5.
44. B. Guy Peters, *Institutional Theory in Political Science. The "New Institutionalism"* (London, UK: Pinter, 1999).
45. Samuel P. Huntington, *Political Order in Changing Societies* (New Haven, CT: Yale University Press, 1968), 12.
46. Ibid., 13.
47. John Peterson, *Europe and America: The Prospects for Partnership* (Cheltenham, UK: Edward Elgar Publishing Limited, 1993).
48. Even though the economic aid through the Marshall Plan was initially offered to the rest of Europe as well, the Soviet Union refused such help from the an ideological enemy, the United States, and commanded the Eastern block to do the same.
49. GMF, "The German Marshall Fund," 2006, http://gmfus.org/template/index.cfm.

50. Peterson, *Europe and America: The Prospects for Partnership*.; Steffenson, *Managing EU-US Relations: Actors, Institutions and the New Transatlantic Agenda*.
51. Ibid., 28.
52. Peterson, *Europe and America: The Prospects for Partnership*.
53. Mark A. Pollack, "The New Transatlantic Agenda at Ten: Reflections on an Experiment in International Governance," *JCMS: Journal of Common Market Studies* 43, no. 5 (December 2005): 899.
54. "Fact Sheet: The New Transatlantic Agenda," *U.S. Department of State Dispatch, 10517693*. 6, no. 49 (1995), http://web.ebscohost.com/ehost/detail?vid=7&hid=113&sid=0abe2326-b562-4cf9-abdd-f37a3f057b18%40sessionmgr107.
55. Pollack, "The New Transatlantic Agenda at Ten: Reflections on an Experiment in International Governance."
56. Ibid., 916.
57. Steffenson, *Managing EU-US Relations: Actors, Institutions and the New Transatlantic Agenda*, 5.
58. John Peterson and Rebecca Steffenson, "Transatlantic Institutions: Can Partnership Be Engineered?" *The British Journal of Politics and International Relations* 11 (2009): 25.
59. Ibid., 40–41.
60. Ibid., 3.

4 Why Science and Technology Policy?

> *"Whether it's improving our health, or harnessing clean energy, protecting our security or succeeding in the global economy, our future depends on reaffirming America's role as the world's engine of scientific discovery or technological innovation"*
>
> —President Barack Obama, 2010[1]

This chapter begins with laying down the foundations for demonstrating the significance of EU–US cooperation on science and technology as it recounts the main developments in science and technology (S&T) policy in the United States, as well as in the European Union. Two important milestones, the "scientification" of national economies and the development of research support systems are examined. As the institutional developments provide the framework in which policy decision-makers operate, investigating the historical foundations of science and technology policy in both the United States and Europe is important. The sections that follow outline the major turning points of the evolution of legislative action on science and technology policy, from the 1950s to the current era. As this study highlights, both in the United States and in Europe, the legislative process facilitated institutionalization.

The chapter then focuses on the significance of EU–US cooperation on science and technology and identifies some of the pivotal projects that culminated in the *EU-US Agreement for Scientific and Technological Cooperation.* This agreement was signed in 1998, first renewed in 2004, and expanded in July 2009 to include security and space research as well.[2] Lastly, the chapter hones in on the book's focus on policy areas in which the *EU-US Agreement for Scientific and Technological Cooperation* is active. This dynamic cooperative action is also confirmed by the agreement, which indicates that, along with a few other areas, it is policies that concern biotechnology, alternative energy resources, and nanotechnology, where the most active cooperation takes place. Energy-related policy issues in general, and looking for alternative energy resources specifically, are at the top of the US's foreign policy agenda and will remain so in the foreseeable future.[3]

Additionally, as the EU–US Science and Technology Portal indicates, alongside environmental issues, these areas are the most influential in shaping the quality of life of future citizens.[4]

FOUNDATIONS AND SIGNIFICANCE OF SCIENCE AND TECHNOLOGY POLICY

To get a deeper understanding of cooperative arrangements in science and technology policy among transatlantic partners, it is important to look at how this policy has been perceived and has evolved on both sides of the Atlantic. An overview of the historical foundations of scientific and technology policy in both the United States and Europe is essential, because it can be argued that the institutional developments provide a framework in which policy decision-makers could operate. Both in the United States and in Europe, the legislative process facilitated institutionalization.

United States

According to the first report of the National Science Foundation in 1952, "[t]he history of the Science Foundation legislation begins on November 17, 1944 when President Roosevelt wrote a letter to Dr. Vannevar Bush, Director of the wartime Office of Scientific Research and Development, asking him to prepare for him a report on a postwar science program."[5] However, one needs to be careful when assessing such a "quantum leap" concerning scientific discoveries, or any kind of political or historical progression for that matter. The reason is because, more often than not, these are a result of a series of events and efforts of groups of individuals that culminate in such major shifts. The major point is that the *application of science*, formerly an endeavor supported by private initiatives, *gained recognition and support at the federal level.*[6]

Taking a brief look at the evolution of this process, the National Science Foundation document reports that there were several important steps preceding mid-20th-century developments in the history of state-level recognition of science and its advancement.[7] Over a century before the creation of the National Science Foundation, the Smithsonian Foundation was established in 1846 by Congressional legislation—to quote Smithson, for the "increase and diffusion of knowledge among men."[8] In 1863, President Lincoln signed into law the Congressional act establishing the National Academy of Sciences. During World War I, President Wilson initiated the establishment of the National Research Council, the primary task of which was to *organize scientific resources*. As the advancement and the impacts of scientific research were becoming more of a *public concern*, during the Depression's recovery program in 1933, President Roosevelt appointed a Science Advisory Board to the National Research Council.[9] It is interesting to observe that the same historical NSF record notes that during the *early 1940s,* as the conservation and the development of research resources became a priority, *research was declared to be one of the most important national resources* of the United States. The US's involvement in World War II had led to the mobilization of scientific resources and the creation of the National Defense Research Committee, headed by Vannevar Bush. In 1941 this organization was transformed, by Executive Order, into the Office of Scientific Research and Development. As the National Science Foundation records indicate, "out of its activities grew the United States radar program, the proximity fuse, and the atomic bomb," just to name a few.[10]

It might seem perplexing why the same executive, President Truman, had first vetoed the National Science Foundation Act of 1947, but signed it into law approximately three years later on May 10, 1950.[11] However, the political context of science policy provides an answer to the enigma. A remarkable breakthrough occurred when, on September 13, 1948, President Truman addressed the American Association for the Advancement of Science Centennial Meeting in Washington and proposed a national science policy, an element of which was to establish a National Science Foundation. According to The American Association for the Advancement of Science's Science and Technology Yearbook,

> Congress, it seems, did not take NSF seriously until it decided that university basic research might contribute to the Cold War, or at least bolster the U.S. position in its rivalry with the Soviet Union. On the other hand, *Science: the Endless Frontier* and *Science and Public Policy*[12] had both envisioned an NSF that would function in a peacetime context.[13]

Vannevar Bush's famous 1945 report, *Science: the Endless Frontier,* perhaps, had made a naïve mistake and put the emphasis on "policy-for-science" rather than the other way around, "science-for-policy." Also, as the AAAS's document remarks, "the President could not delegate his constitutional authority to oversee the disbursement of public funds to a part-time board of private citizens." Even though Bush's report was to advance governmental authority and responsibility in supporting basic research and recommended that a separate agency, the National Science Foundation, be established for that purpose, it is interesting to note that it was never to be a master plan of an overarching future science policy.[14]

In the United States, it was the introduction of the National Science and Technology Policy, Organization, and Priorities Act of 1976 (Public Law 94–282) and the subsequent creation of the Office of Science and Technology Policy, which could be considered a milestone in advancing science and technology-related issues. It is the OSTP's mission to advise the President and the Federal Government on the effects of science and technology on domestic and international affairs. It is also its mission to get involved with other policy actors such as the private sector and state and local governments and the science and higher education communities, as well as international actors for the purposes of developing sound science and technology policies and budgets.[15] As the Congressional Research Service's Report of 2009 evaluates overall science and technology performance in the United States, it emphasizes that S&T-related development and funding is still designed to be democratic and decentralized. Figure 4.1 demonstrates how the policy decision-making process involves numerous actors.[16]

In debating whether it is enough what the United States invests in R&D to return to or sustain its leadership position in S&T, the Rand Corporation's 2008 report points out that the slowing rate of growth in federal funding has weakened, while that of the industry-funded research has grown at a much faster pace. Another interesting phenomenon that this report clarifies is that looking at the federal obligations of research funding, almost half of the resources are allocated to the Department of Defense.[17] An overall summary of the development of federal funding of science and technology in the United States is shown in Table 4.1.[18]

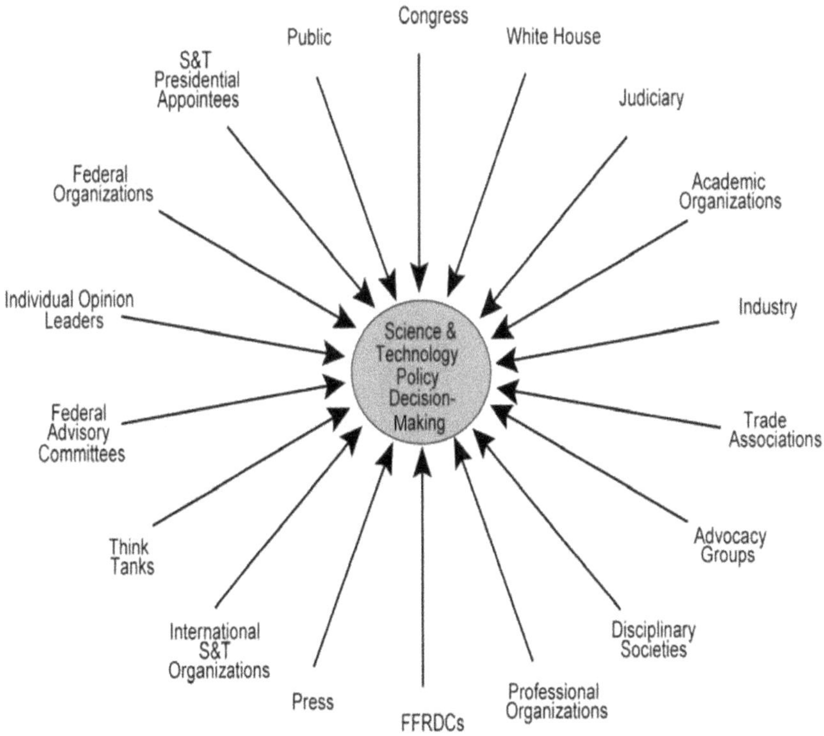

Figure 4.1 Organizations and Individuals Who Influence Science and Technology Policy Decision-Making in the United States

Source: CRS Report for Congress, *Science and Technology Policymaking: A Primer,* by Stine, Deborah D., 2009, p. 27., http://fas.org/sgp/crs/misc/RL34454.pdf.

Table 4.1 Significant Dates and Events in Federal Funding of Science and Technology in the United States

Pre-1940s	1940–1949	1950–1975	1976–Present
Research on commercial applications of knowledge by federal industrial laboratories.	1940: National Defense Research Council established.	1950: National Science Foundation (NSF) established.	1976: NSF funds research on effects of S&T on local, state, national, and international economies.
Funding from endowments, private fundraising, industry, and state funds.	1941: Federal Office of Scientific Research and Development established, which contracted for R&D.	1957–present: Launch of Sputnik catalyzes greater funding of university research.	1978: NSF begins to support state S&T councils.
	1941–1945: Federal laboratories supported war effort for WW II. 1945: Publication of *Science—The Endless Frontier.*	1957: President's Science Advisory Council and position of presidential advisor for science began. Both were abolished in 1973.	1979: NSF establishes Experimental Program to Stimulate Competitive Research for states with low levels of research support.
	1946–1950: Many federal agencies began funding large amounts of research in university	1973: NSF's Industry/University Cooperative Research Program established.	1980: Bayh-Dole Act assigns intellectual property rights for university research to university
		1974: OSTP established in the Executive Office of the President; Director of OSTP named as president's science advisor.	

Source: National Academy of Sciences, National Academy of Engineering Institute of Medicine. *State Science and Technology Policy Advice: Issues, Opportunities, and Challenges: Summary of a National Convocation*. Ed. by Steve Olson & Jay B. Labov. National Academies Press, 2008, p. 6.

European Union

In the EU, legislative action on science and technology policy should be looked at separately: policies preceding EU common directives and policies afterwards. The European Commission describes the stages of development in science and technology policy, and states that the overall European effort had started with the European Coal and Steel Community's first projects in March 1955. This was followed by the EURATOM treaty and the establishment of the Joint Nuclear Research Centre which, to a significant extent, had been induced by the Suez war-initiated energy crisis of 1957. However, it was not until the 1980s that the EU switched its focus from solely nuclear energy, considered a key area for economic and military security, to a broader framework of research and technological development (RTD). A major shift occurred with the set-up of the "ESPRIT Programme" in 1983, because prior to this program it was the privilege as well as the responsibility of national governments to promote IT-related industries in Europe. This program signals that science and technology policy cooperation was set in motion on another level. A key motivation for this change was to remain competitive with other regions in the world.[19] Table 4.2 summarizes subsequent development, while the related budget growth is depicted in Figure 4.2.[20]

Table 4.2 Stages of Development in Science and Technology Policy in the European Union

Year	Name of the Program	New Directions of the Program
1983	ESPRIT Programme	IT-technology promotion becomes an intergovernmental endeavor; contributes to the development of internationally accepted standards
1984	First Framework Programme	Joint funding
1987	European Single Act	Science becomes a community responsibility
	Second Framework	Joint projects
1990	Third Framework Programme	Joint projects; economic objectives
1993	Treaty of the European Union	Role of RTD in the EU enlarged
1994	Fourth Framework Programme	Valorization, benefit for society
1998	Fifth Framework Programme	Specified themes and objectives

(*Continued*)

Table 4.2 (*Continued*)

Year	Name of the Program	New Directions of the Program
2000	European Research Area	Development of a European research policy; creation of an "internal market" in research; better coordination within EU
2002	Sixth Framework Programme	Support for strategic research
2007	Seventh Framework	Lisbon pressure

Source: EURESEARCH, 2009.

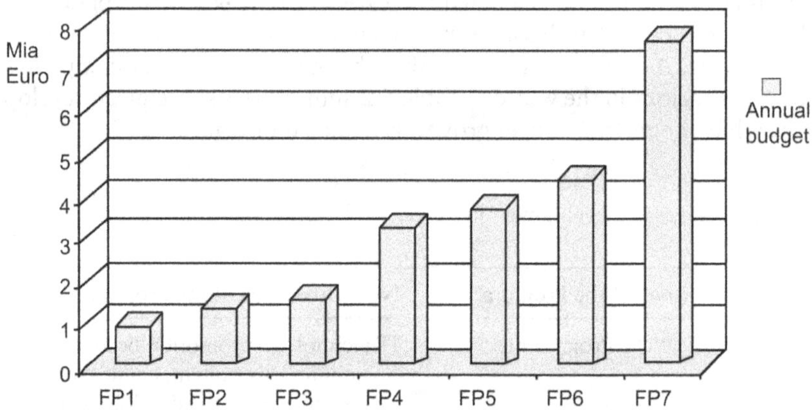

Figure 4.2 Budget Growths of Framework Programs
Source: EURESEARCH 2009

This reorientation signified that the EU has put research and development (R&D) at the center of policy and began to develop a programmatic approach towards long-term collaborative projects. Additionally, the need for the policy process to be more inclusive resulted in collaborating patterns that not only incorporated academic and research institutes, but companies as well. This established the industrial aspect of R&D policies, the policy aspect that continues to be a distinct feature of current EU policy-initiatives. Another major change in EU research planning is a shift in the ratio of national to EU funding through the Framework Programs. Figure 4.3 shows how the Framework Program boosted EU contribution to national R&D development.[21]

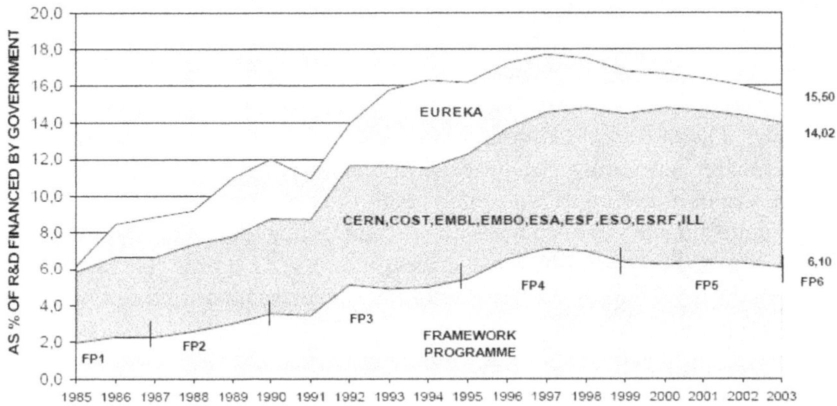

Figure 4.3 European Research: Increasing Budgets
Source: European Commission, Research DG, 2005

During the last decade of the 20th century when the Treaty on European Union (TEU) and the single market became a reality, the EU found that the overall results of Research and Technological Development (RTD) policies were still not successful enough to compete in a fast-paced increasingly global economy. In regards to the current institutional design of EU innovation policy-making, two main problem areas have stood out: "(a) the *lack of horizontal, inter-systemic cooperation and coordination* and (b) *the institutional fragmentation.*"[22] In fact, as the European Commission website describes the current state of affairs in innovation policy, they "are facing a situation of 'innovation emergency' [and] Europe is spending 0.8% of GDP less than the US and 1.5% less than Japan every year on Research & Development (R&D)."[23] Consequently, a new strategic direction became the focus of European policy-makers. Ideas to jumpstart EU economies and the emergence of innovation policies characterized the second part of the 1990s.[24] As Borrás observes, "The notion that innovation was partly the solution to the economic problems of the EU indicated the extent to which the new cognitive parameters . . . had penetrated the EU's political strategic thinking."[25] This broader policy vision of EU plans to create an institutional environment that is propitious to innovation at all levels of policy-making.

A New Era in research development and innovation diffusion (RDI) began with the Lisbon Strategy, when the problem of poorly translating knowledge into public policies was addressed. The Treaty of Lisbon, entered into force on December 1, 2009, underscores the diverse challenges facing Europe in the 21st century and the paramount role that science, technology, knowledge, and innovation plays in resolving those. As highlighted in the Lisbon Strategy, in the long-term, the evolving knowledge economies of the Union can only be strengthened through increased investment in R&D and innovation, and "Europe must renew the basis of its competitiveness, increase its growth potential and its productivity . . . placing the main emphasis on knowledge, innovation, and optimisation of human capital.[26] The 2009 EU Commission report found that member states were given greater autonomy, the bureaucratic framework had been eased, and the variety of aids rose as well. As a result of these changes, modernization of the state aid rules proved to be an efficient policy tool. The Commission's review states that one of the most successful tools in EU practice was proved to be that "the Commission has facilitated the dissemination of good practice via a network of national experts."[27]

The Lisbon Treaty has certainly put innovation policy, along with research and education, at the center of EU policy. The most recent development in EU policy is the "Innovation Union" project, which is one of the seven flagship initiatives of the "Europe 2020 strategy," the EU's growth strategy for the next decade. The overall goal of the strategy can be summarized as the realization of a "smart, sustainable and inclusive economy," and making sure that successful research materializes in better products and services.[28] The essence of the new "Innovation Union" plan is that the EU would make greater use of private funds to better address growth-related issues and create jobs through patent reform and by expanding the financing sources of RDI. EU policy-makers also hope that this will translate into enhancing the overall quality of life of EU citizens, and, at a minimum, preserving the level of European competitiveness worldwide.[29]

An important aspect that Kuhlman brings up is that public research, technology, and innovation policies are no longer exclusively governed by national governments in Europe. Rather, we are experiencing a change in the governance of the European innovation policy. This means that the European Union has already laid down the foundations for a "postnational" European innovation policy governance, characterized by "horizontally and vertically interwoven multi-level innovation policymaking arenas."[30]

EU–US AGREEMENT FOR SCIENTIFIC AND TECHNOLOGICAL COOPERATION

The aforementioned agreement was signed in 1998, first renewed in 2004, renewed again, expanded in July 2009 to include security and space research as well, and finally extended until October 2013.[31] The significance of the cooperative agreement and its subsequent renewals is, in no small part, due to the increased role of science and technology policy in foreign policy decision-making. The initial agreement, signed before the millennium, indicates the importance of science and technology for economic and social development, as well as recognizes that the partners pursue R&D activities in countless areas of common interest on a basis of reciprocity, which provides mutual benefits.[32] This formal statement and subsequent renewals of the agreement signify a stronger commitment to cooperate in this policy area within institutional confines. Beginning with the Obama Administration, the role of this policy area, with special regards to energy policy, is even more pronounced on this side of the Atlantic. As the American Association for the Advancement of Science's (AAAS) new science diplomacy center states, science and scientific cooperation promotes international understanding and prosperity,

> [m]any of our most pressing foreign policy challenges—energy, climate change, disease, desperate poverty and underdevelopment, and WMD proliferation—demand both technological and policy solutions. In these and other areas, U.S. national security depends on our willingness to share the costs and benefits of scientific progress with other nations.[33]

A comprehensive study on transatlantic science and technology cooperation, based on several interviews and surveys with EU and US experts, was published in 2013 by Herlitschka, which suggests that scientists and scientific organizations are the perceived drivers of S&T cooperation. The study also finds that 81% of those targeted "key stakeholders" believe that "there is a need for coordinated transatlantic European-U.S. science diplomacy approaches" and 56% of those surveyed indicated that US–European S&T cooperation needs considerable improvement.[34]

Among the initiatives to advance transatlantic relations is the "BILAT-USA 2.0" project, which is a series of meetings between the project's representatives as well as EU and US authorities. Under this initiative, the partners' goal has been to institute a platform for all relevant stakeholders to launch a sustainable transatlantic dialogue between 2009 and 2012. The project put a heavy emphasis on S&T-related areas. Its priorities were established as follows: "energy; material science and nanotechnology; environment, including climate change; metrology; information technology; space and security; food, agriculture & fisheries, and biotechnology (FAB); and health."[35]

The most recent development in transatlantic relations, the Transatlantic Trade and Investment Partnership (TTIP), was launched in February 2013, signifying a major step towards integrating the two largest markets. As a recent post on the European Commission's website states, "[o]n 14 June, Member States gave the European Commission the green light to start trade and investment talks with the United States." "The EU and the US economies account together for about half the entire world GDP and for nearly a third of world trade flows" and can already be considered the "most integrated economic relationship in the world."[36] Yet the European Commission's March 2013 Impact Assessment Report on the future of EU–US trade relations underscores the need "to harness the full benefits of trade and foreign investment . . . [i]n times where any budget-neutral source of economic growth is precious."[37] Not only could a successful conclusion of the TTIP bring considerable economic gains for both partners, but transatlantic trade liberalization also has the potential to positively impact the world economy "increasing global income by almost €100 billion." The economic assessment of the Center for Economic Policy Research reports several key findings in terms of the anticipated benefits of the TTIP. Among these are income gains due to trade growth, but the vast majority of potential gains would originate from significantly reducing bureaucracy and regulations, "as well as from liberalizing trade in services and public procurement."[38]

While the TTIP's main goal is trade liberalization, especially the reduction of non-tariff barriers (NTBs) to trade, it is important to note that there is a synergy between the trade and investment partnership and scientific cooperation, in that liberalized trade regimes necessitate dynamic and flexible systems to meet the demands of fast-paced change in the global economy. As a recognition of science-based principles for the harmonization of policies, on July 17, 2013, the "European Commission's Joint Research Centre (JRC) and the US National Institute of Standards and Technology (NIST) . . . agreed to expand their current scientific co-operation to 10 different areas." *These developments have implications on the research agenda, which forms the basis for this book,* for at least two reasons. First, the JRC-NIST Implementing Agreement has been concluded *"under the auspices of the Agreement for Scientific and Technological Cooperation* between the EU and US signed in 1997 . . . [with the] purpose [of] form[ing] an overarching arrangement, including and expanding on the previous co-operation." Second, the *agreement prioritizes energy, security, nanotechnology, and information and communication technologies (ICT)* on the partners' collaborative research agenda, all of which are at the *core of the author's overall research project.*[39]

Despite all these developments, Fisher asserts that a main challenge to systematic transatlantic cooperation remains that "[t]ransatlantic S&T collaboration and transatlantic policy cooperation thrive in parallel, but separate, worlds."[40] While she maintains that transatlantic scientific collaboration is typically a bottom-up process, propelled by the quest for new knowledge and progress, she also points out that there are numerous top-down official initiatives and dialogues within, and between, the two sides of the Atlantic. The idea that *science diplomacy has the potential to strategically integrate* and lay the foundation for sustainable development, which would address the complex tasks we face in the global commons, is one of the key arguments of this author's research.[41]

CONCLUSION

Writing about science, technology, and their interaction with international politics, Skolnikoff argues, "[t]here is no doubt that international politics is quite different, in almost all dimensions, than it has been . . . evolving under the influence of technological advance . . . making foreign policy more complex."[42] Science and technology-induced changes result, primarily, from the interactions of new actors and their interest representation that modify not only social structures, but also the context in which policy issues arise and are being debated on the transnational level.[43]

NOTES

1. Barack Obama, "Remarks by the President on the 'Educate to Innovate' Campaign and Science Teaching and Mentoring Awards" (The White House, 2010), http://whitehouse.gov/the-press-office/remarks-president-educate-innovate-campaign-and-science-teaching-and-mentoring-awar.
2. European Commission, "23–24 May 2013—The Atlantic: A Shared Resource" (European Commission, 2013), http://ec.europa.eu/research/iscp/index.cfm?lg=en&pg=usa.; EU-US, *COUNCIL DECISION of 30 March 2009 Concerning the Extension and Amendment of the Agreement for Scientific and Technological Cooperation Between the European Community and the Government of the United States of America*, vol. 2009, 2009, http://ec.europa.eu/world/agreements/downloadFile.do?fullText=yes&treatyTransId=13421.
3. Paula J. Dobriansky, "Science, Technology, and Foreign Policy: The Essential Triangle," 2003, http://state.gov/g/rls/rm/2003/20250.htm.
4. EU-U.S. Science and Technology Portal, "The Framework of EU-U.S. S&T Cooperation," *BILAT-USA and Link2US, EU-U.S. Agreements*, 2009, http://archive.euussciencetechnology.eu/home/st_agreement.html.
5. National Science Foundation, *Justification of Estimates on Appropriations, Fiscal Year 1952* (81st Congress, n.d.), Appendix II. p. 1, http://nsf.gov/pubs/1952/b_1952.pdf.
6. National Science Foundation, *Justification of Estimates on Appropriations, Fiscal Year 1952*.
7. Ibid.
8. Ibid., Appendix I, p. 1.
9. Ibid.
10. Ibid., Appendix I, p. 4.
11. Ibid.
12. *Science and Public Policy* is a report oftentimes referred to as the "Steelman Report" because it was prepared by Truman's newly appointed President's Scientific Research Board (PSRB) in 1946, by Executive Order, and chaired by economist John R. Steelman.
13. William A. Blanpied, "Science and Public Policy: The Steelman Report and the Politics of Post-World War II Science Policy," in *AAAS's Science and Technology Policy Yearbook of 1999* (American Association for the Advancement of Science [AAAS], 1999), http://aaas.org/spp/yearbook/chap29.htm.
14. Ibid.
15. OSTP, "The Office of Science and Technology Policy, Executive Office of the President," 2009, http://ostp.gov/cs/about_ostp/history.
16. Deborah D. Stine, "Science and Technology Policymaking: A Primer," Congressional Research Service Report, 2009. http://fas.org/sgp/crs/misc/RL34454.pdf.
17. Ronald L. Olson et al., *Setting Politics Aside*, 2008, http://rand.org/content/dam/rand/pubs/corporate_pubs/2010/RAND_CP1-2008.pdf.

18. National Academy of Engineering Institute of Medicine National Academy of Sciences, *State Science and Technology Policy Advice: Issues, Opportunities, and Challenges: Summary of a National Convocation*, eds. Steve Olson and Jay B. Labov (National Academies Press, 2008), http://books.google.com/books?hl=en&lr=&id=34YPVFqTW0MC&oi=fnd&pg=PR1&dq=State+Science+and+Technology+Policy+Advice:+Issues,+Opportunities,+and+Challenges:+Summary+of+a+National+Convocation&ots=A-MaygAvOX&sig=2MISrXCc6F6QKoVdFJAvPEdSEiw.
19. Euresearch, "Swiss Guide to European Research and Innovation," 2009, http://euresearch.ch/index.php?id=306.
20. Ibid.
21. European Commission, Research D.G. *Towards the Seventh Framework Programme 2007–1013, Building Europe Knowledge*, 2005, http://eurosfaire.prd.fr/bibliotheque/pdf/FP7_Complete_presentation_April_2005.pdf.
22. Dietmar Braun, "New Governance for Innovation—Keynote Presentation," in *Workshop Held at the Occasion of the 30th Anniversary of the Fraunhofer Institute for Systems and Innovation Research (ISI)* (Karlsruhe, Germany, 2002), 7. Quoted in Jakob Edler, Stefan Kuhlmann, and Ruud Smits, *Report on a Workshop Held at the Occasion of the 30th Anniversary of the Fraunhofer Institute for Systems and Innovation Research (ISI)* (Karlsruhe, Germany, 2003), http://academia.edu/2902629/New_Governance_for_Innovation._The_Need_for_Horizontal_and_Systemic_Policy_Coordination.
23. European Commission, "Innovation Union: A Europe 2020 Initiative," 2013, http://ec.europa.eu/research/innovation-union/index_en.cfm?pg=why.
24. Susanna Borrás, *The Innovation Policy of the European Union: From Government to Governance* (Cheltenham, UK: Edward Elgar Publishing, 2003).
25. Ibid., 15.
26. Council to the European Union, *EU Presidency Conclusion*, vol. 2005 (Brussels, 2005), 2, http://consilium.europa.eu/uedocs/cms_data/docs/pressdata/en/ec/84335.pdf.
27. EUEC, *Communication from the Commission to the European Parliament, the Council, the European Economic and Social Committee and the Committee of the Regions—Reviewing Community Innovation Policy in a Changing World*, 2009, http://eur-lex.europa.eu/smartapi/cgi/sga_doc?smartapi!celexplus!prod!DocNumber&lg=EN&type_doc=COMfinal&an_doc=2009&nu_doc=442.
28. European Commission, "Europe 2020," 2013, http://ec.europa.eu/europe2020/index_en.htm.
29. European Commission, "Innovation Union: A Europe 2020 Initiative," 2013, http://ec.europa.eu/ research/innovation-union/index_en.cfm.
30. Stefan Kuhlmann, "Future Governance of Innovation Policy in Europe—Three Scenarios," *Research Policy* 30, no. 6 (June 2001): 972.
31. European Commission, "Review of the Science and Technology Cooperation Between the European Community and the United States of America" (2008).; BILAT USA 2.0, "EU-US S&T Agreement," 2013, http://euusscience technology.eu/content/eu-us-st-agreement.; EU-US, *COUNCIL DECISION of 30 March 2009 Concerning the Extension and Amendment of the Agreement for Scientific and Technological Cooperation Between the European Community and the Government of the United States of America.*; EU External Action Service, "EU-US Co-Operation by Sector," 2013, http://eeas.europa.eu/us/sector_en.htm.
32. Commission of the European Communities, *Communication from The Commission to The Council, The European Parliament, The European Economic And Social Committee and The Committee Of The Regions: On the*

Progress Made Under the 7th European Framework Programme for Research (Brussels,2009),http://eur-lex.europa.eu/LexUriServ/LexUriServ.do?uri=SEC:2009:0589:FIN:EN:PDF.
33. AAAS, *2009–2010 Year in Review*, 2010, 13.
34. Sabine E. Herlitschka, *Transatlantic Science and Technology: Opportunities for Real Cooperation Between Europe and the United States* (New York, NY: Springer, 2013), 42.
35. EUEC, *Report on the Analysis of U. S. Participation in the 6th and 7th Framework Programmes—Second Update*, 2010, http://archive.euussciencetechnology.eu/uploads/docs/D2_1_US_FP_Participation_secondUpdate.pdf.pdf.; EUEC-US, "BILAT-USA 2.0," 2010, http://euussciencetechnology.eu.
36. EUEC, "EU-US Trade Policy," 2013, http://ec.europa.eu/trade/policy/countries-and-regions/countries/united-states/.
37. European Commission, "Impact Assessment Report on the Future of EU-US Trade Relations, Accompanying the Document Recommendation for a Council Decision Authorising the Opening of Negotiations on a Comprehensive Trade and Investment Agreement, Called the Transatlantic Trade and Investment Partnership, between the European Union and the United States of America," 2013, 14, http://trade.ec.europa.eu/doclib/docs/2013/march/tradoc_150759.pdf.
38. Joseph Francois et al., *Reducing Transatlantic Barriers to Trade and Investment: An Economic Assessment* (London, UK, 2013), 7, http://trade.ec.europa.eu/doclib/docs/2013/march/tradoc_150737.pdf.
39. EUEC, "EU–US Trade Policy."; EU External Action Service, "EU-US Co-Operation by Sector."
40. Cathleen Fisher, "The Invisible Pillar of Transatlantic Cooperation: Activating Untapped Science & Technology Assets," *Scienceandiplomacy.org* 2, no. 1 (2013): 2, http://scienceandiplomacy.org/files/the_invisible_pillar_of_transatlantic_cooperation_science_diplomacy_0.pdf.
41. Fisher, "The Invisible Pillar of Transatlantic Cooperation: Activating Untapped Science & Technology Assets."
42. Eugene B. Skolnikoff, *The Elusive Transformation: Science, Technology, and the Evolution of International Politics* (Princeton, NJ: Princeton University Press, 1993), 7.
43. Ibid., 10.

5 Who Are the Movers and Shakers in Transatlantic Relations?

New frontiers of the mind are before us, and if they are pioneered with the same vision, boldness, and drive with which we have waged this war we can create a fuller and more fruitful employment and a fuller and more fruitful life.

—Franklin D. Roosevelt, 1944[1]

This chapter presents the empirical results and addresses the main approaches to answering key questions. The chapter then describes the transatlantic network structure and key findings. Several network attributes are discussed, such as clustering, prominence or prestige. The networks' backbone connections are identified, along with the transatlantic science and technology policy sub-network, as well as the distribution of types of institutions in these transatlantic networks.

A visual representation of the findings of the social network analysis, generated by Pajek software, depicts the constellation of institutional actors engaged in transatlantic collaboration. Taken together, the *findings demonstrate that there exists an active and structurally discernible network in cyberspace among transatlantic organizations*. Also, as this research documents, *there exists a science and technology specific sub-network*. Additionally, as the chapter reveals, a *range of actors fulfilling various roles in this network can be distinguished*. By applying social network analysis to science and technology collaboration in Europe and North America, we gain greater understanding of the shape of knowledge networks (KNETs) in the emerging era of "virtual" collaboration. A key element of the chapter is a description of how the findings reinforce or challenge what is already known about cooperative arrangements and epistemic communities in transatlantic relations.

Additionally, the chapter sheds light on how network structure relates to the various types of KNET participants in these networks. As has been indicated in previous chapters, all organizations in this study were categorized into the following types: academic, research and policy institutes, government agencies, inter-governmental organizations, think tanks, and interest groups (see Appendices C and D for details).[2] There are two main reasons for this strategy. The first is to determine what types of network members fulfill various roles in the network. Second, as was pointed out earlier, while evaluating the transatlantic partnership, Pollack and Shaffer argued that it might be the network of experts and professionals based at various types of transatlantic organizations that constitute the "linchpin" to foster transatlantic relations.[3] As it will be explained further in the concluding chapter, these have important theoretical and policy implications.

FINDINGS FOR OVERALL NETWORK STRUCTURE AND CLUSTERING

Transatlantic Network—Backbone Connections

The presentation of the findings begins with introducing the results of the network analysis for the broader transatlantic network investigated in this book. First is shown, in Figure 5.1, a visual layout of the overall transatlantic network with the 87 core organizations.

These organizations are represented as nodes, while the connections or hyperlinks among them are drawn as directed links or arcs at two additional "depths" (see Figures 5.2 and 5.3).

To summarize the procedure briefly, each depth refers to a web page's shortest distance path length to any of those 87 core sites or URLs.[4] The path length is the number of hyperlinked pages that needs to be traversed to get from one page to another.[5] It might be interpreted as *the number of "clicks"* one needs to make to get to the destination page from the homepage.[6]

Looking at Figures 5.1 through 5.3, it becomes immediately apparent that there are a number of nodes that are clustering together close to the center, while others are situated in the periphery of the network. It is important to note that "loops," i.e., self-references, were deleted from the networks before final visualization and analysis, because self-references do not represent information exchange among organizations.[7] Still, after removing these loops, some of the organizations that were considered to be most active in their hyperlinking practices demonstrate more than 100,000 virtual connections to other network members, while others seem to have only a few. Additionally, the visualization of the network reveals that there are four organizations that are so-called "isolates," which are not part of the larger transatlantic network (labeled as "D1" network for the purposes of this study). These isolates are the National Science Foundation (NSF), the French Institute of International Relations (IFRI), the Center for Strategic and International Studies (CSIS), and Nature Publishing Group (NATJ). However, except for NSF, which remains an isolate even in the network through tertiary links ("D3" network), the other three

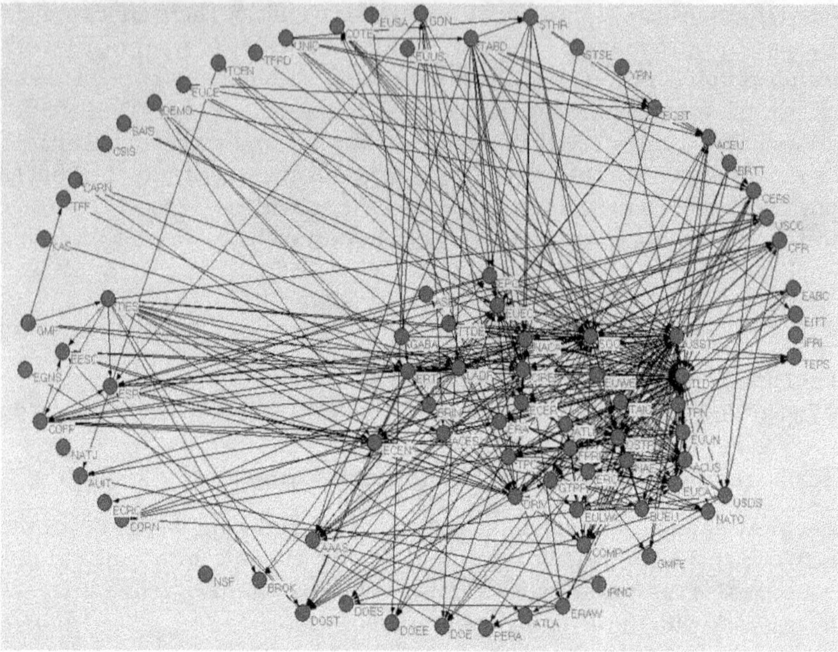

Figure 5.1 Visualization of the Transatlantic Network Connections through Direct Links[1]

Nodes represent the 87 core organizations' web pages, while the lines with arrows designate all established links (hyperlinks) among these network members. Names of organizations are shown with 3–4 letter acronyms.[2]

[1] *Loops, i.e., self-references, deleted form all networks.*

[2] *Acronyms of all organizations are listed, in detail, in Appendix B.*

essentially become part of the networks, both through secondary and tertiary links ("D2" and "D3" networks).[8] This suggests that IFRI, CSIS, and NATJ can be considered network members via secondary or tertiary links *only* (i.e., the number of "clicks" these pages are away from the starting page, which are the 87 core or root pages here). Because there are interesting changes in the network structure, this shows that it can be a valuable research endeavor to further investigate these "deeper" links in the future.

The most commonly linked-to pages, excluding the 87 core transatlantic organizations, found in this research project, are reported in Table 5.1. I report this to make boundary specification of the networks more refined.

These findings are organized by "depth," that is, the shortest-path distance from any of the core web pages. It is interesting that only a few additional organizational websites with a significant number of connections to network members emerged from the initial "depth1" web crawl.

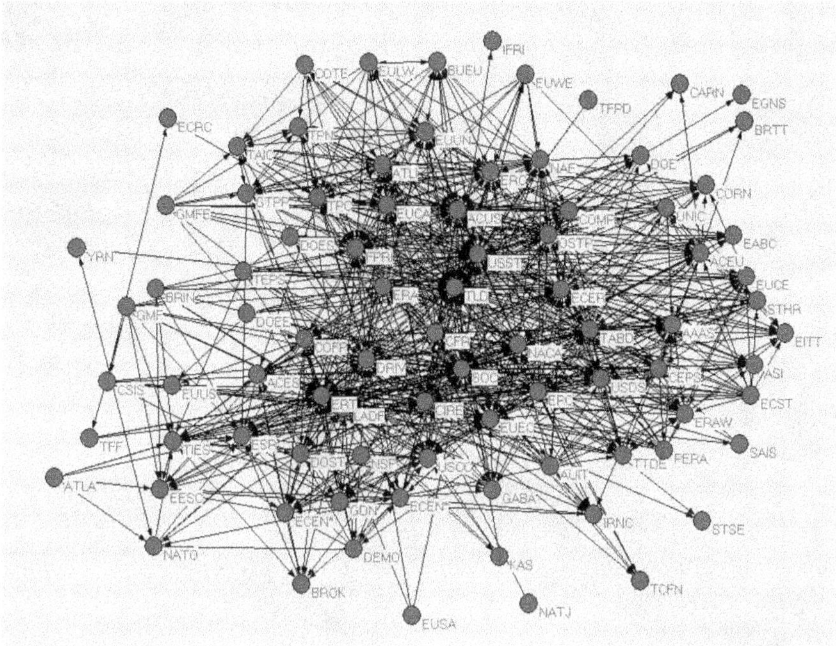

Figure 5.2 Visualization of the Transatlantic Network Connections through Secondary Links

Nodes represent the 87 core organizations' web pages, while the lines with arrows designate all established links (hyperlinks) among these network members. Names of organizations are shown with 3–4 letter acronyms.

Two corporate sites stand out: The Boeing Company's and Daimler AG's, each representing more than 18,000 links to the 87 core transatlantic organizations investigated in this study. Also, two US governmental websites, the Office of the Citizen Services and Communications information site and the US Department of State Freedom of Information Act (FOIA) were found to have more than 10,000 links within the network. An intriguing finding is, however, that the program has found over 15,000 links to "Add This social book marking and sharing" in this network. Considering the "depth2" and "depth3" findings, nodes with the most number of links found at these "depths" are either among the "core" organizations already, strongly associated with those, or they are some sort of Wikipedia or Wikimedia information pages.

Overall, at depths two and three, the number of links decreases significantly. Consequently, additional organizational websites do not appear to have a significant enough impact on the network—especially in comparison with the most important organizations, which can have as many as over 160,000 connections. Therefore, this study will not consider analyzing the emergence of these websites in detail.

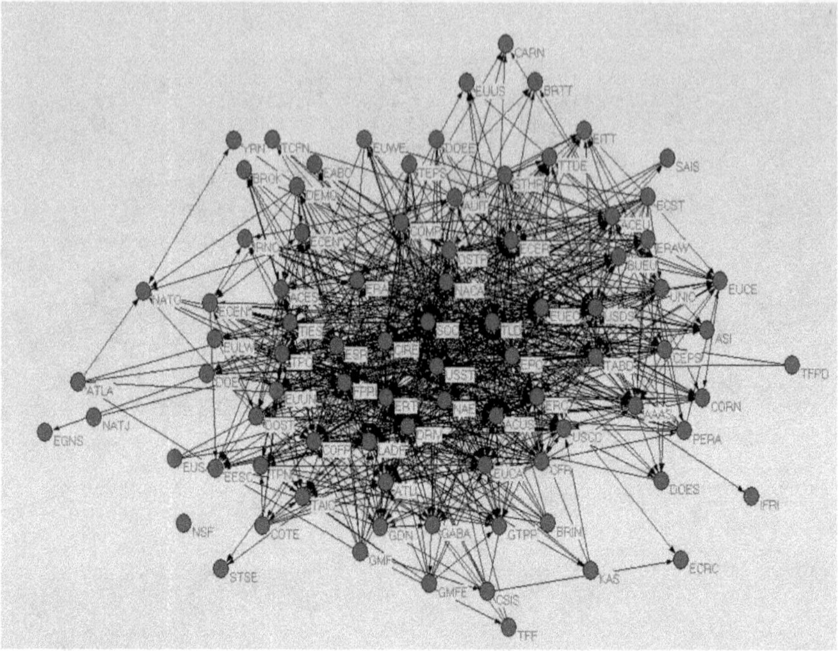

Figure 5.3 Visualization of the Transatlantic Network Connections through Tertiary Links

Nodes represent the 87 core organizations' web pages, while lines with arrows designate all established links (hyperlinks) among these network members. Names of organizations are shown with 3–4 letter acronyms.

Table 5.1 Most Commonly Linked-to Web Pages Excluding the Core Transatlantic Organizations

	count	URL	Organization
Top pages at "depth1"	18245	www.boeing.com	The Boeing Company
	18241	www.daimlerchrysler.com	Daimler Chrysler AG[1]
	15655	www.addthis.com/bookmark.php	Add This social bookmarking and sharing
	10423	www.usa.gov	US citizen information site
	10378	http://foia.state.gov	US Department of State Freedom of Information Act (FOIA)

(*Continued*)

Table 5.1 (*Continued*)

	count	URL	Organization
Top pages at "depth2"	2444	http://publications.europa.eu	Office for Official Publications of the European Communities
	2115	www.europarl.europa.eu/default.htm	European Parliament
	1811	http://eur-lex.europa.eu/Europa.do[2]	Gateway to the European Union
	723	www.ceps.eu/rss1.php	Center for European Policy Studies
	709	www.adobe.com	Adobe
Top pages at "depth3"	6848	http://publications.europa.eu	Office for Official Publications of the European Communities
	6118	www.mediawiki.org	EUROPA Publications Office
	6050	http://wikimediafoundation.org	MediaWiki[3]
	5422	http://en.wikipedia.org/wiki/Main_Page	Wikipedia the free encyclopedia
	4995	www.wikimediafoundation.org	Wikimedia Foundation, Inc.
	3904	http://eur-lex.europa.eu/Europa.do[2]	Gateway to the EU

[1] Due to a recent restructuring, this website stopped operating as Daimler AG recently sold Chrysler.

[2] Currently, this website can be found at europa.eu/index_en.htm, which is identical to one of the 87 core organizations on the main EU website.

[3] MediaWiki is a free software wiki package written in PHP, originally for use on Wikipedia.

Transatlantic Science and Technology Policy Sub-network

Next, the various forms of the science and technology-specific network are revealed, followed by a discussion of the various social network analytical measures and network characteristics. As specified in the research methodology appendix, a list of keywords and key terms was used to narrow down the search field and identify those transatlantic sub-networks that were involved in science and technology (S&T) cooperation by their hyperlinking practices. This sub-network, generated by a refined search, is visualized in Figure 5.4. This figure shows the resulting sub-network, which involves the direct links from one website to another (identified as "d1-kw" sub-network in the analysis).[9]

It is immediately apparent that, *after narrowing the search by incorporating S&T-specific keywords and key terms, the majority of the transatlantic network remains still intact.* Two major differences can be pointed out, however. First, it is visible that some of the network members of the larger network are not part of this newly generated policy-specific network. These organizations are listed in Table 5.2.

Nevertheless, further analysis of the S&T sub-network, at "depth" levels two and three, reveals that three more organizational websites essentially become part of the network through secondary and tertiary links.[10] These include the Brookings Institution's Hamilton Project (BROK) referencing the institute's science and diplomacy program, the Network of European Union Centers of Excellence (EUCE), and the European Research Area "ERAWATCH" (ERAW). Second, *the number of links of node pair connections, on average, decreases by a factor of five. This is about the same order*

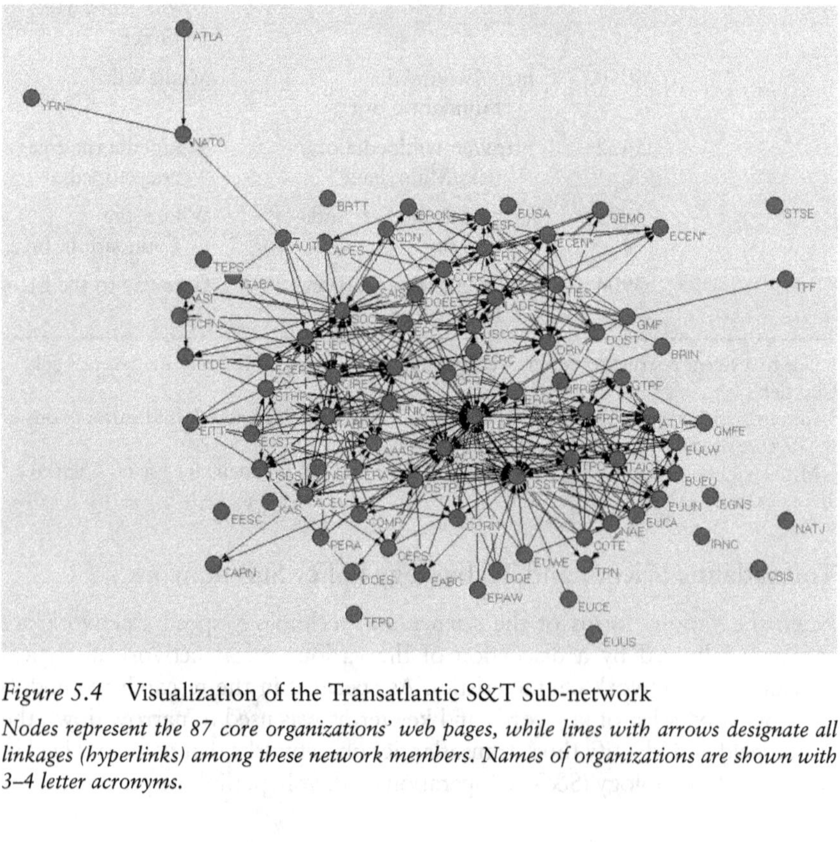

Figure 5.4 Visualization of the Transatlantic S&T Sub-network

Nodes represent the 87 core organizations' web pages, while lines with arrows designate all linkages (hyperlinks) among these network members. Names of organizations are shown with 3–4 letter acronyms.

Table 5.2 Organizational Websites That *Are Not* Members of the S&T Sub-network

1	Brookings Institution, The Hamilton Project (BROK)[2]
2	BRUEGEL, Brussels European and Global Economic Laboratory, (BRTT)
3	Center for Strategic and International Studies (CSIS)
4	Joint Research Centre (ECRC)
5	European Economic and Social Committee (EESC)
6	European Global Navigation Satellite System Supervisory Authority (EGNS)
7	The Network of European Union Centers of Excellence (EUCE)[2]
8	The European Union Studies Association (EUSA)
9	EU Delegation to the US, European Union Centers of Excellence in the United States (EUUS)
10	The European Research Area "ERAWATCH" (ERAW)[2]
11	French Institute of International Relations (IFRI)
12	NSF's International Research Network Connections (IRNC)
13	The Konrad-Adenauer-Stiftung (KAS)
14	Nature journal (NATJ)
15	National Science Foundation (NSF)[1]
16	SAIS Center for Transatlantic Relations, Johns Hopkins University (SAIS)
17	Science, Technology, and Innovation Subcommittee of the Unites States Senate Committee on Commerce, Science, and Transportation (STSE)
18	Trans European Policy Studies Association (TEPS)
19	Transatlantic Foreign Policy Discourse (TFPD)

[1] Based on the more extensive network analysis, NSF seems to be an isolate that cannot be considered a network member in any of these networks after all.
[2] BROK, EUCE, and ERAW essentially do become part of the S&T sub-network through secondary and tertiary links.

of magnitude reduction as the reduction of network members, which reflects a proportional decrease to network size.

It is somewhat curious to observe how certain organizations seem to be inactive in building their connections in this virtual transatlantic community, whereas their mission indicates a need to be involved in S&T research and policy-related cooperative arrangements. The *lack of web presence is especially puzzling in regards to the following organizations: the National Science Foundation; the Joint Research Centre; NSF's International Research Network Connections; and the Science, Technology, and Innovation Subcommittee of the Unites States Senate Committee on Commerce, Science, and Transportation* (see Figure 5.4 for these isolates). It is plausible that these institutions give priority to building their off-line connections. Also, this research reveals that there are several transatlantic organizations, within the network, that pursue projects with NSF-funded resources. It is plausible that the *NSF plays an indirect role in the promotion of transatlantic cooperation* and, as such, this agency can be regarded as a "behind-the-scenes" network actor. The same might be true for the European Research Council (ERC), which is the European equivalent of NSF, and was established in 2007. Although the ERC is part of the S&T network, it is neither extensively connected, nor does it emerge as a significant network member in any other way.

Network Clusters

Clustering, in general, is the task of classifying a collection of objects, such as documents, machines, or biological organisms, into natural categories.

Table 5.3 Transatlantic Network Clusters

	Clusters							
	1 1	22	33	44	55	66	77	88
Transatlantic Organizations	TPN	STSE	GMF	TCFN	DEMO	GABA	KAS	TFF
	FPRI	BRTT	BRIN	IRNC	LADF	STHR	CARN	CSIS
	TAIC	EABC	TIES	AUIT	USCC	TTDE	SAIS	EUCE
	ATLI	IFRI	ACES		SOC	ASI	EUUS	GDN
	TPC	NSF	ERT		ERA	ECST	YRN	EUSA
	TFPD	EGNS	DRIV		ECEN	EPC	ACEU	TEPS
	UNIC	EESC	DOST			USDS	EITT	NATO
	COTE		COFP			ECER	DOES	ATLA
	TABD		ESR			CIRE	BROK	PERA
	USST[1]					ERAW	NATJ	CORN
	EUWE					DOE		
	ACUS					DOEE		
	CEPS					AAAS		
	CFR					NACA		
	BUEU					EUEC		
	COMP							
	EULW							
	TLD							
	EUUN							
	EUCA							

(*Continued*)

Table 5.3 (*Continued*)

Clusters							
1	2	3	4	5	6	7	8
GMFE							
GTPP							
OSTP							
ERC							
NAE							

[1] Bold fonts specify highly connected network members.

Table 5.4 Transatlantic S&T Sub-network Clusters

Clusters								
1	2	3	4		5	6	7	8
GABA	TPN	LADF	GMF	EITT	UNIC	TIES	SOC	ECST
TTDE	FPRI	DRIV	KAS	IFRI	TABD	COFP	ERA	CFR
EPC	TAIC	ECEN	BRIN	TEPS	STHR	ESR		ECER
	ATLI		TFF	USDS	ACEU			CIRE
	TPC		CARN	NATO	CEPS			DOEE
	COTE		SAIS	GMFE				NACA
	USST[1]		CSIS	IRNC				EUEC
	EUWE		DEMO	ERAW				
	ACUS		EUCE	ATLA				
	BUEU		TCFN	PERA				
	COMP		TFPD	DOE				
	EULW		GDN	DOES				
	TLD		EUSA	DOST				
	EUUN		ACES	BROK				
	EUCA		EUUS	AAAS				
	GTPP		STSE	NSF				
	OSTP		ASI	CORN				
	ERC		YRN	ECRC				
	NAE		BRTT	AUIT				
			USCC	NATJ				
			ERT	EGNS				
			EABC	EESC				

[1] Bold fonts specify highly connected network members.

To analyze the various network clusters, spectral clustering has been used, as detailed in the methodological appendix. Nodes that belong to specific clusters are depicted using different shades of grey to represent these discrete clusters, depending on how many clusters the network was partitioned into. Membership of the transatlantic organizations in these clusters is analyzed next. The graphs shown in Figures 5.5 through 5.7 are images of a sample of the numerous clusters generated in this research at all three depths.

Figures 5.5 and 5.6 visualize the transatlantic core network, while Figure 5.7 is a representative sample of the S&T specific sub-network. Although clustering generated in this study ranges from a minimum of three to 15 clusters, with a given number of nodes, the division of eight clusters seems to be an optimal number of clusters for this investigation.

Cluster analysis reveals that the *structure* of the hyperlink-affiliation network, understood as a knowledge network, *is influenced by the intensity or the frequency of interaction of ties* between each pairs of actors. This is important because these transatlantic networks are regarded as valued or weighted directed graphs, in which *the lines have values indicating the*

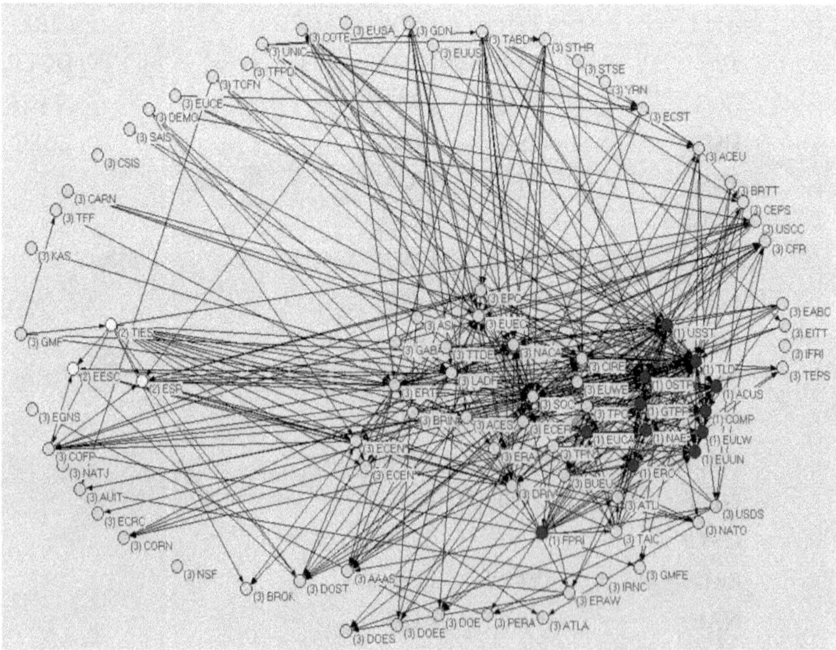

Figure 5.5 Visualization of the Clustering of the Transatlantic Network through Direct Links

Three clusters generated by spectral clustering.

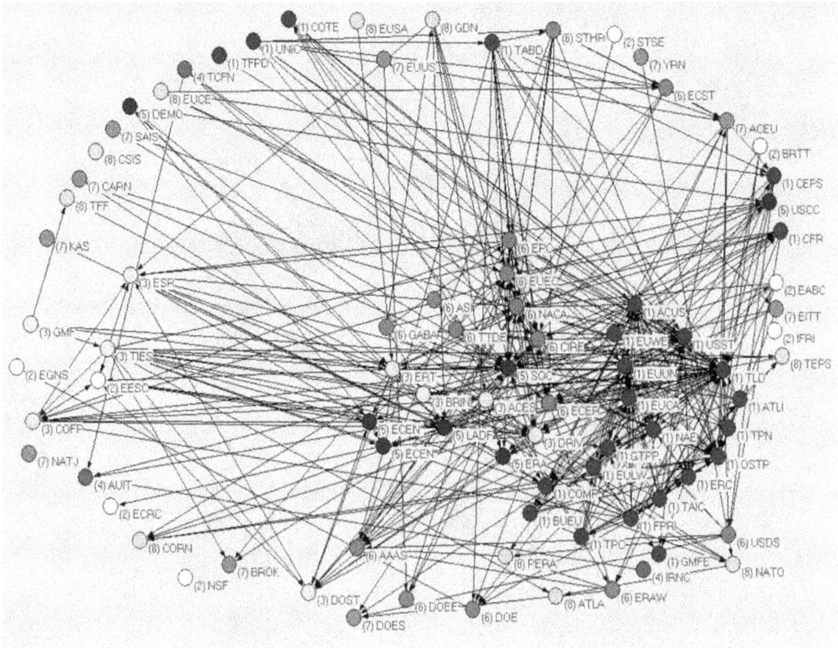

Figure 5.6 Visualization of the Clustering of the Transatlantic Network through Direct Links

Eight clusters generated by spectral clustering.[1]

[1] *We can observe that the rather cohesive cluster #1 is situated towards the bottom right side of the network image.*

strength of the relationship between pairs of directly connected nodes in the network.[11] Intuitively, higher numbers indicate more frequent, intense, or important interactions. As this chapter points out later, this has implications for further analysis of the network, especially in terms of evaluating network attributes such as cohesion.

Cluster analysis helped to identify groups of web pages that are representative of their hyperlinked relations. A group of network members is found that cluster in a similar fashion in all networks—in the larger network as well as in the policy-specific sub-network. As indicated in Tables 5.3 and 5.4, this group seems cohesive and includes *four highly connected network members: the Department of State, US–EU Cooperation in Science and Technology (USST); the Transatlantic Legislators' Dialogue (TLD); the Delegation of the European Commission to Canada (EUCA); and the National Academies of Engineering (NAE).* Because of the implications of these results to network attributes, a detailed evaluation follows in the section that discusses cohesion.

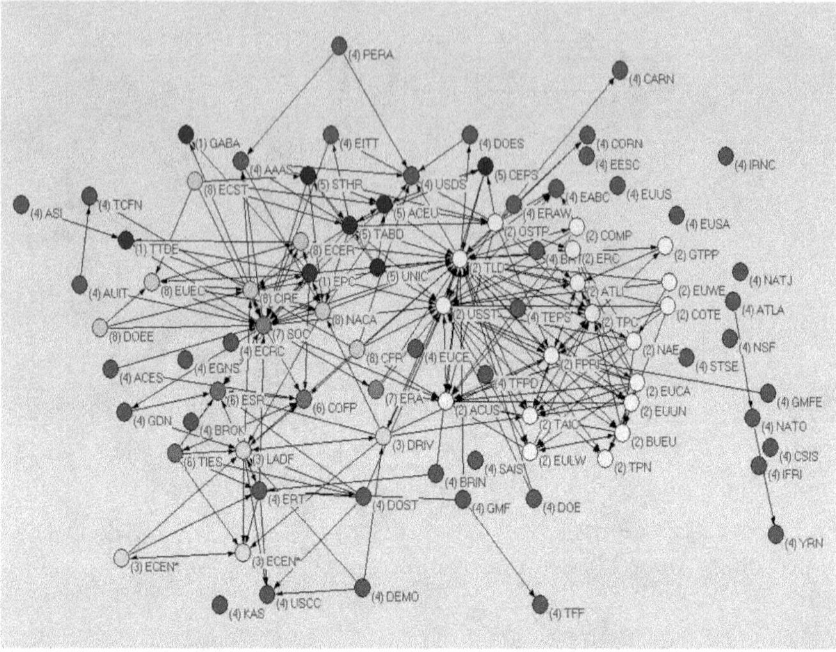

Figure 5.7 Visualization of the Clustering of the S&T Sub-network through Direct Links

Eight clusters generated by spectral clustering.[1]

[1] *We can observe that the rather cohesive cluster #2 is situated towards the right side of the network image.*

Transatlantic Network Structure

As hypothesized earlier, the structure of the transatlantic knowledge networks conforms to the forms commonly found in web-based social networks, such as power-law distribution. To find out whether this hypothesis holds the observed degree distribution, or the probability distribution of the degrees over the entire network, was charted and fit by the power-law equation.[12] This special kind of mathematical relationship, described by $P(k) \sim k^{-\gamma} + C$, illustrates that there is no typical size of the nodes, so there is no maximum of the distribution. Rather, most of the connections, about 80%, belong to 20% of the nodes, a pattern similar to the Pareto rule that describes the distribution of wealth in economics. Power laws govern a wide variety of natural and man-made phenomena, such as solar or lunar activities, earthquakes, genetics, popularity of people or ideas, and citations, just to name a few. Countless empirically observed networks, commonly called scale-free networks, appear to follow a power-law distribution in which the number or frequency of an object or event varies as a power of some attribute of that object.[13]

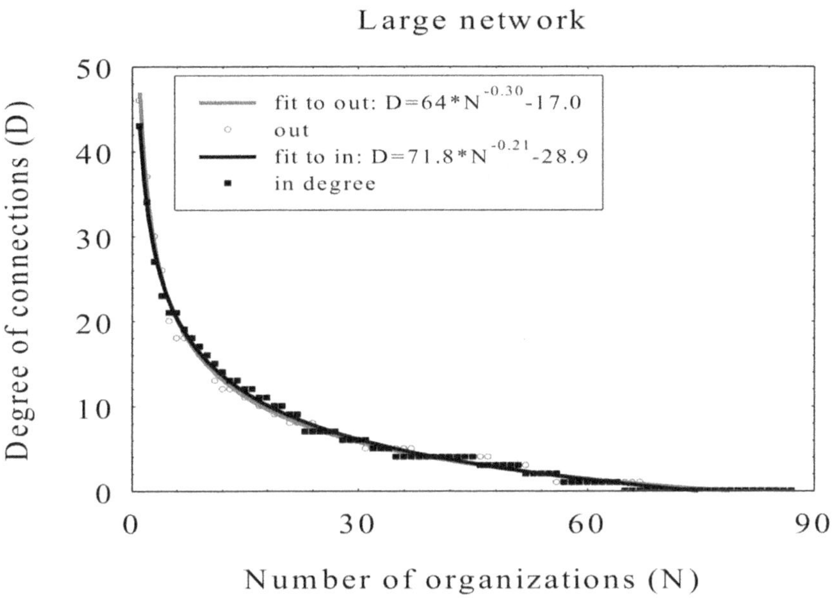

Figure 5.8 Transatlantic Network: Degree of Connections

Number of connections versus number of organizations and their fit with power law functions of the entire group.

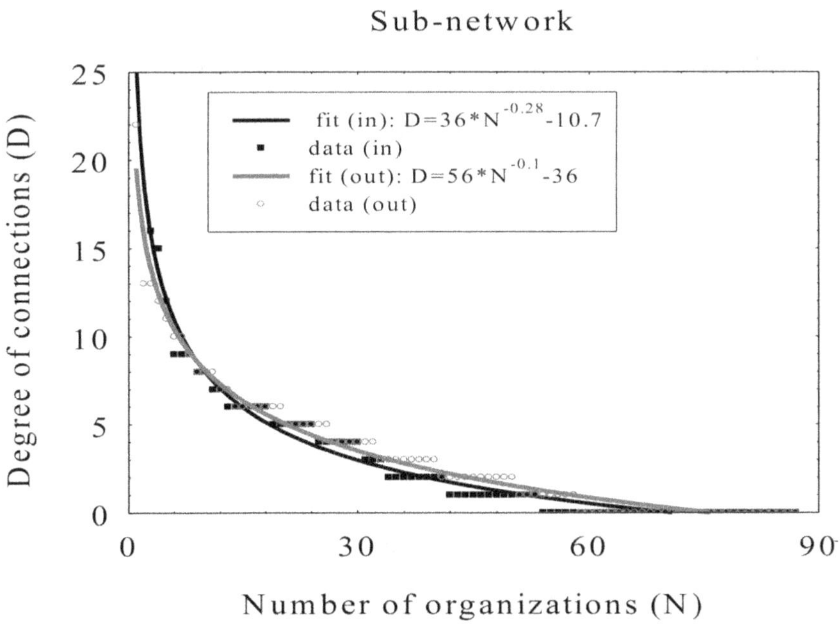

Figure 5.9 Science and Technology Specific Transatlantic Sub-network: Degree of Connections

Number of connections versus number of organizations and their fit with power law functions of the entire group.

Figures 5.8 and 5.9 represent network structures for both the larger transatlantic network (D1) as well as the science and technology sub-network (d1-kw).

While the first two figures mirror in- and out-degree distribution induced fitting, Figure 5.10 is a comparison of both networks for all degrees, in and out. Lastly, Figure 5.11 represents the strength of connections as the function of the number of organizations.

As I state in the figure caption, interestingly, this describes *exponential decrease, which shows even stronger centralization than the power law that describes the behavior of the degree of connections. This is because the weight of more popular nodes is even higher, i.e., fewer network members share more of the power in the network.*

The first impression we get from looking at these graphs is that the fit is rather perfect. These fitted power-law distribution figures are, typically, of

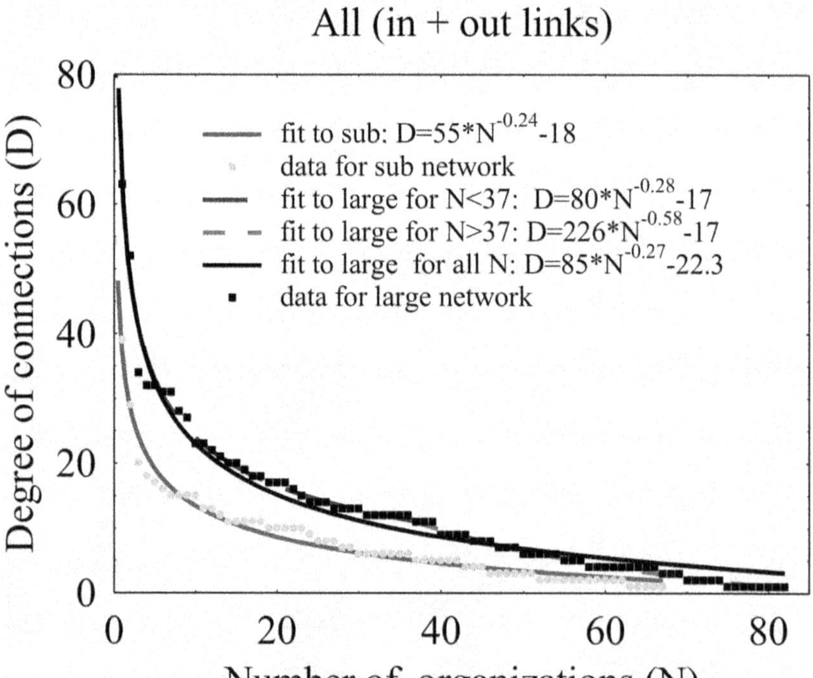

Figure 5.10 Comparison of Both Transatlantic Networks: Degree of Connections

Number of all (in + out) connections versus number of organizations and their fit with power law functions of the large and sub-group. Note the behavior of the large group: It splits into the top 37 organizations that have most connections and to the others that have less. The subgroup behavior does not split.

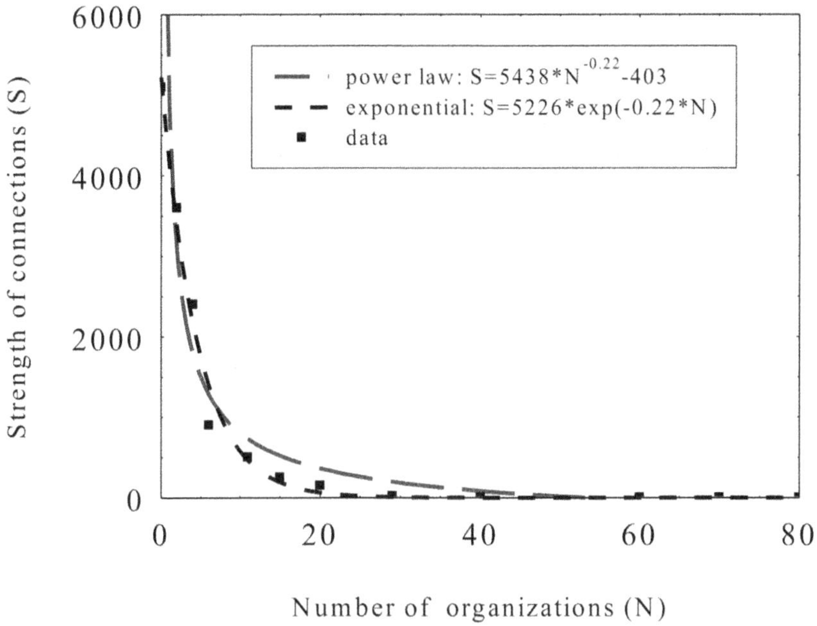

Figure 5.11 Science and Technology Specific Transatlantic Sub-network: Strength of Connections

Sample of the strength of connections as the function of number of organizations. Interestingly this describes exponential decrease that shows even stronger centralization than the power law that describes the behavior of the degree of connections. According to my best knowledge, this has not ever been found in the literature that usually describes only the degree of connections.

great scientific interest, mainly because they have significant consequences for our understanding of the natural world as well as man-made phenomena. The *preferential attachment process that they demonstrate, in everyday parlance "the rich gets richer" phenomenon,* is when some quantity is distributed among a number of individuals or objects, according to how much they already have. As Chakrabarti explains, "preferential attachment, which dictates that a new node is linked to existing nodes not uniformly at random, but with higher probability to existing nodes that already have large degree, [is] a 'winner take all' scenario."[14] *This is exactly what this research has found in these transatlantic networks.* Connectivity is concentrated to a number of actors who seem to collaborate among themselves and only slowly reach out to less active network-members.

This study also finds that, in the S&T sub-network depicted in Figure 5.11, the *strength of connections as the function of the number of organizations describes an exponential decrease. This demonstrates an even stronger centralization than the power law, which describes the behavior of the degree of connections. This means that the weight of the most popular nodes is even higher than that of the less popular ones.* Therefore, instead of having a pattern in which about 80% of connections belong to 20% of the nodes, as described by the power-law, the pattern can be explained rather as almost 90% of connections belonging to 10% of the nodes. *According to my best knowledge, this has not ever been found in the literature that usually describes only the degree of connections and does not account for their strength.*

KEY FINDINGS BASED ON NETWORK ATTRIBUTES

Network attributes measure different characteristics of a social network; a summary of these and their measurement, used in this study, can be found in Table 5.5.

While this section provides a brief introduction to the social network theoretical concepts and network analytical tools, these are elaborated on in greater detail in the methodological appendix, Appendix A. This section shows how various network attributes help unravel the structure of the network system and, consequently, guide us in *discovering not only the current "movers and shakers" of the network(s), but also, potential candidates who can revitalize and further develop the network.*

At the fundamental level, when performing social network analysis, the researcher investigates two overarching concepts: *position* and *role*. In social network analysis, these are interpreted through various procedures

Table 5.5 Network Attributes and Their Measurement[1]

Attributes	Metrics[2]	Description of Metrics
Prominence or Prestige[3]	Degree (input and output)	Number of direct ties to or from an actor
	Authorities and Hubs[4]	*Authorities* are highly relevant pages that are pointed to by numerous good hubs, and *hubs* are pages that point to many relevant pages, i.e., authorities
Brokerage	Betweenness	The extent to which an actor is situated between two other actors
	Structural hole	Connection of nonredundant ties; links that do not exist; latent opportunities

(*Continued*)

Table 5.5 (*Continued*)

Attributes	Metrics[2]	Description of Metrics
Cohesion	Clique and Island	Clique is a fully connected sub-network. Islands are cohesive clusters, where the weights inside clusters must be larger than weights to neighborhood.

[1] There are other attributes, such as *range*, the metrics of which are reachability and geodesic distance. Also, for *cohesion*, metrics include components, cores, and various density measures. For *prominence*, closeness centrality is an additional measure. However, the analysis of all possible attributes is beyond the scope of the current study (Wassermann and Faust, 1994; Hanneman and Riddle, 2005).
[2] Metrics in networking is understood as a set of properties of the communication path.
[3] For undirected networks, the term "centrality" is typically used instead of prestige.
[4] Especially useful for WWW (directed network of homepages).

to uncover structural similarities and patterns of relations among actors in these multirelational networks. Although there is disagreement among social scientists in regards to the interpretation of the notions of social position and role, Wasserman and Faust suggest that, in the context of social network analysis, *position* be interpreted as "a collection of individuals who are similarly embedded in networks of relations," while *role* "refers to the patterns of relations which obtain between actors or between positions."[15]

The most commonly examined attributes of a social network are: prominence, cohesion, brokerage, range, and structural equivalence. Prominence indicates who has power in the network or, more broadly, actors are prominent if they are, directly or indirectly, visible to others in the network. Cohesion, which concerns direct ties, describes attributes of the whole network and shows the presence of strong common relationships among actors, while brokerage indicates bridging connections to other networks.[16] Characteristics that were considered most applicable and relevant to the type of networks investigated in this research are discussed in further detail here, except for the concept of "p-cliques" and "islands," which are reviewed in Appendix E separately.

Prestige: Providing Information (In-degree)

"Both centrality and prestige indices are examples of measures of the prominence or the importance of the actors in a social network."[17] In directed networks, such as the ones investigated in this research, prominence is understood as prestige, rather than centrality. Prestige then can be classified into two categories: For the outgoing arcs or out-degrees it provides a measure of influence, while for the incoming arcs or in-degrees it is acknowledged as a measure of support.[18] Actors with *high out-degree* levels are able to exchange or *disperse information* relatively quickly to others and so they are characterized as influential. Actors with *high in-degree* support the network by *providing information and expertise* so that they are *valuable as sources* for other network members.

Based on the empirical analysis of this research, Figure 5.12 visually represents the input degree partition of the larger and denser transatlantic network, while Figure 5.13 does the same for the sparser S&T sub-network.

There are numerous nodes in both networks, the in-degree value of which is zero. These nodes have no links pointing towards them or referencing them. Top-ranking network-members for this measure are described, in detail, in Table 5.6.

As Table 5.6 indicates, the actor holding the most in-links, consequently, being in the *most prominent position* in both the larger and the science and technology-specific networks, is the *Transatlantic Legislators' Dialogue (TLD)*, an inter-governmental organization, created by the New Transatlantic Agenda. The second prominent actor, also in both types of networks, is the *Science of Collaboratories (SOC)* project, an NSF-sponsored academic/research endeavor. In the broader network, the *Office of Science and Technology Policy, Executive Office of the President (OSTP) and The National Academies (NACA)* are governmental institutions, while the *Center for*

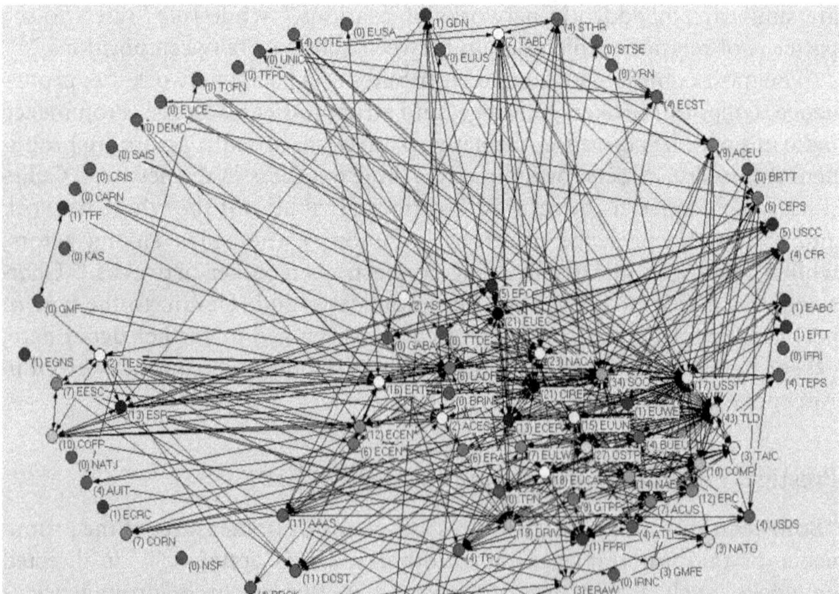

Figure 5.12 Visualization of the In-degree Partitioning of the Transatlantic Network through Direct Links[1]

[1] *We can observe that the majority of the nodes with high in-degree are clustered together towards the bottom right side of the network image.*

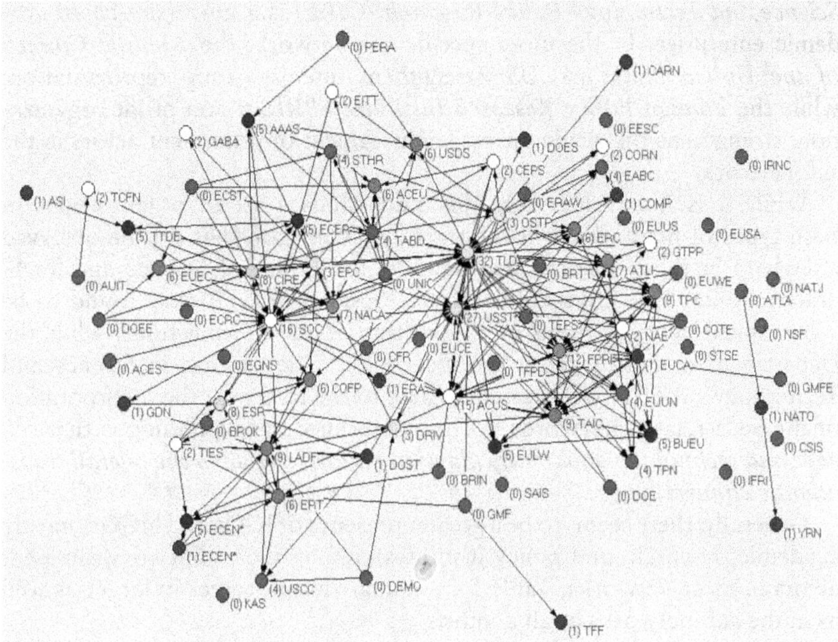

Figure 5.13 Visualization of the In-degree Partitioning of the Transatlantic S&T Sub-network through Direct Links

Table 5.6 Top-Ranking Nodes and Their Values for In-degree

	Name of Organizational Website	Value
"D1"	Transatlantic Legislators' Dialogue (TLD)	43
	The Science of Collaboratories (SOC)	34
	Office of Science and Technology Policy, Executive Office of the President (OSTP)	27
	The National Academies (NACA)	23
	Center for Science and Technology Policy Research (CIRE)	21
	EUROPA, European Commission (EUEC)	21
	Transatlantic Legislators' Dialogue (TLD)	32
	Department of State, US–EU Cooperation in Science and Technology (USST)	27
"d1kw"	The Science of Collaboratories (SOC)	16
	Atlantic Council of the United States (ACUS)	15
	Foreign Policy Research Institute (FPRI)	12

Science and Technology Policy Research (CIRE) is a university-based academic enterprise. In the more specific sub-network, the *Atlantic Council of the United States (ACUS)* strengthens interest group representation, while the *Foreign Policy Research Institute (FPRI)*, a non-profit organization, strengthens the academic-research segment of prominent actors in the sub-network.

While it is nonevident that this study finds a set of organizations in both types of networks, it is a notable phenomenon that can be observed elsewhere in these results. Also of note, the Office of Science and Technology Policy, Executive Office of the President (OSTP) was found to be a prominent actor in terms of overall transatlantic connections, while the Department of State's more specific US–EU Cooperation in Science and Technology's (USST) web-presence came to the fore with the incorporation of the S&T-related keywords.[19] The significance of this finding is that *science and technology apparently plays an important role in the overall transatlantic connections.*

Generally, there seems to be a greater presence of IGOs and NGOs (mostly academic, research, and policy institutes) among those that are prominent actors in these networks. Table 5.7 summarizes in-degrees in larger as well as in the sub-networks at all depths.

Two important patterns are found. First, at "depth2" and "depth3," the same top-ranking nodes emerge in both types of networks; second, nodes with the highest number of in-degrees show more similarities within the S&T sub-network at all depths than they do in the broader network. This more consistent behavior could be attributed to the fact that the character of the network is more policy-specific.

Results, based on the in-degree analysis, indicate that it is the website of the Transatlantic Legislators' Dialogue (TLD), which occupies the most

Table 5.7 Top-Ranking Nodes and Their Values for In-degree at All Depths

D1	**TLD—43**[1] **SOC—34** OSTP—27 NACA—23 CIRE—21 EUEC—21	**d1-kw**	**TLD—32** **USST—27** **SOC—16** **ACUS—15** FPRI—12
D2 and D3	**TLD—62** USST—52 **SOC—49** ACUS—40 ERT—39 DRIV—35	**d2-kw and d3-kw**	**TLD—43** **USST—35** **ACUS—29** **SOC—23** ERC—18

[1] Bold fonts indicate organizations that show similarities in ranking, i.e., they are top-ranking at all "depths."

central position in both the broader as well as the policy-specific sub-network. The TLD, therefore, may be considered the most "prestigious" node. This *underscores the significance of the New Transatlantic Agenda of 1995*, which created this active dialogue. *Another prominent* actor and an NGO, in both types of networks, is the *Science of Collaboratories (SOC) project*, an NSF-sponsored academic/research endeavor. A remarkable pattern that can be observed throughout this study is that *science and technology-related organizations emerge as rather visible actors even before the search is narrowed by including policy-specific key words and key terms*. Another example for this pattern is that the third most prestigious organizational homepage in the broader network belongs to the Office of Science and Technology Policy, Executive Office of the President (OSTP), while the second most prestigious one in the sub-network belongs to the Department of State, US–EU Cooperation in Science and Technology (USST). *Empirical results support* the idea that the *science and technology policy is certainly a key area of concern* among governments as well as private actors.

Overall, two categories seem to stand out: (1) inter-governmental institutions and (2) academic, research, and policy institutes. A few interest groups are actively involved in pursuing connections in these networks, while the same does not seem to hold for think tanks. It is worth noting that while an organization's mission and self-description may not state that it is an official think tank, many of the academic, research, and policy institutes fulfill such function.

Academic and research-oriented entities routinely devise innovative ideas and initiate research and policy action. However, they are in vital need of funds that materialize in the form of NSF-based, or other forms of, governmental resources; hence, the governmental link cannot be ignored here either. Recall that Chapter 4 addressed that, during the early 1940s, research had been declared to be one of the most important national resources of the United States. Considered as such, it becomes evident that mobilization of scientific resources is inherently intertwined with exercising national power and developing and pursuing foreign policies. Also recall that Chapter 2 has discussed the various interpretations of knowledge networks, one of which takes issue with KNET resource-dependencies. Even if we accept that it might constitute a problem, as it was pointed out earlier, the interaction of these so-called KNETs with civil societal actors, and their impact on them, has the potential to legitimate their actions further.

Prestige: Disperse Information (Out-degree)

Another set of central actors are viewed from a slightly different aspect of prestige or prominence. As stated earlier, actors with high out-degree are able to exchange or disperse information relatively quickly to others and so they are characterized as influential (see Figures 5.14 and 5.15 for a depiction of the output-degree partition of "D1" and "d1kw" networks at "depth1").

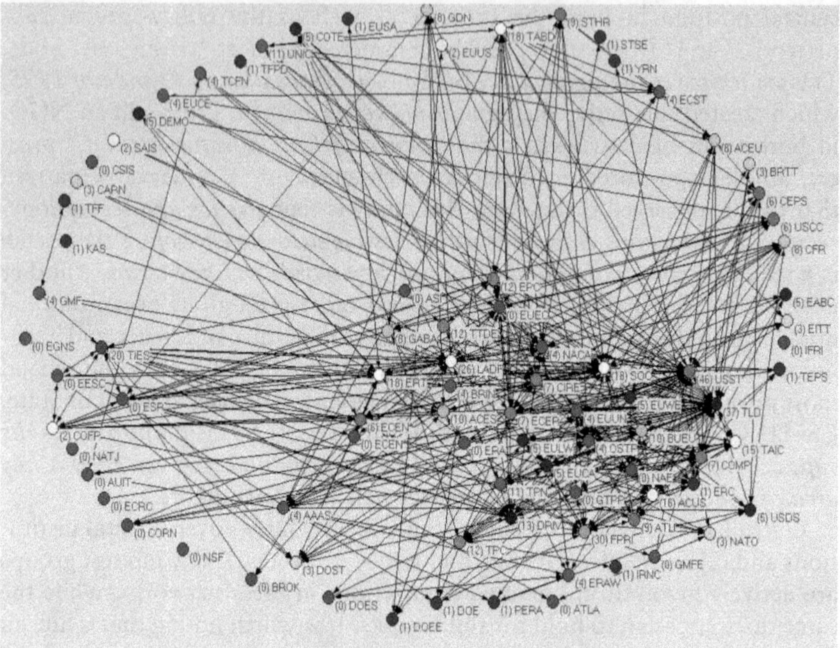

Figure 5.14 Visualization of the Out-degree Partitioning of the Transatlantic Network through Direct Links[1]

[1] *We can observe that the majority of the nodes with high out-degree are clustered together towards the bottom right side of the network image.*

Similar to those results for in-degree partition, several nodes can be found in both networks, the out-degree value of which is zero. These nodes are not referenced by their network members. Top-ranking network-members for the measure of "out-degree" are described for both networks, in detail, in Table 5.8.

This table shows that the network member with the most out-links, consequently in the *most influential* position, in the larger network is the *Department of State's website on US–EU Cooperation in Science and Technology (USST),* while it is the *Transatlantic Legislators' Dialogue (TLD)* in the S&T sub-network. Indeed, the TLD's web presence is the second most influential in regards to exchanging and dispersing information in the broader network as well.

In the larger network, *other influential* actors with high out-degree are the following: the *Foreign Policy Research Institute (FPRI), the Luso-American Development Foundation (LADF), and the Transatlantic Information Exchange System (TIES).* While FPRI is an academic and research-oriented organization, LADF is a private foundation and more of an interest group. TIES, also considered an interest group here, was established with the New

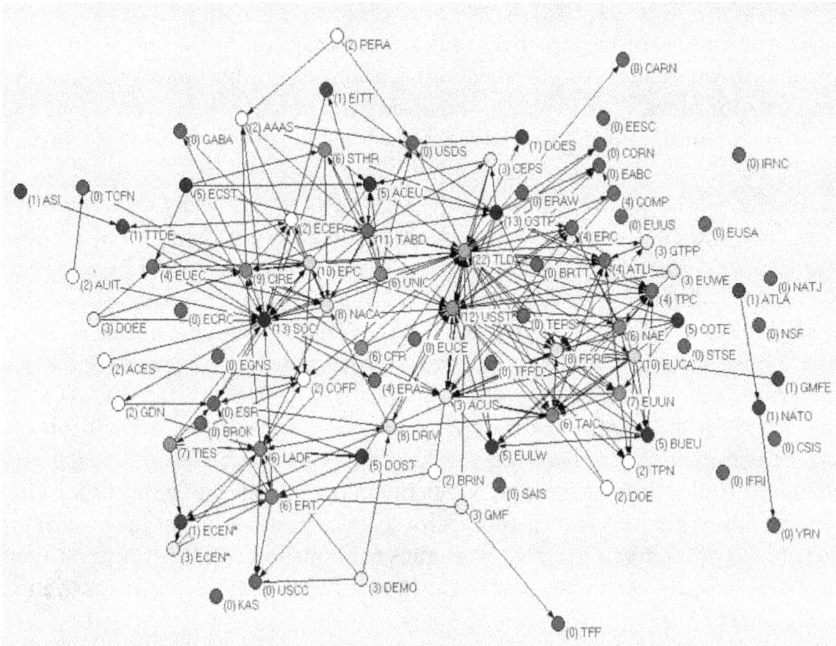

Figure 5.15 Visualization of the Out-degree Partitioning of the Transatlantic S&T Sub-network through Direct Links

Table 5.8 Top-Ranking Nodes and Their Values for Out-degree

	Name of Organizational Website	Value
"D1"	Department of State, US–EU Cooperation in Science and Technology (USST)	46
	Transatlantic Legislators' Dialogue (TLD)	37
	Foreign Policy Research Institute (FPRI)	30
	Luso-American Development Foundation (LADF)	26
	Transatlantic Information Exchange System (TIES)	20
	Transatlantic Legislators' Dialogue (TLD)	22
"d1kw"	The Science of Collaboratories (SOC)	13
	Office of Science and Technology Policy, Executive Office of the President (OSTP)	13
	Department of State, US–EU Cooperation in Science and Technology (USST)	12
	TransAtlantic Business Dialogue (TABD)	11

Transatlantic Agenda, and it is an inter-governmental initiative. As the organization's website informs, "TIES was conceived by a group of European and American NGO leaders and academics, led by Biancheri, founder and current president of the organization, at a conference organized by the European Union and the United States in Washington, D.C. in 1997 as part of the New Transatlantic Agenda."[20]

In the S&T-specific *sub-network TLD* was specified as *most influential,* followed by the Science of Collaboratories; the *Office of Science and Technology Policy, Executive Office of the President (OSTP); Department of State; US–EU Cooperation in Science and Technology (USST); and the TransAtlantic Business Dialogue (TABD)*—in that order. SOC is an NSF-sponsored academic and research institute, OSTP and USST are governmental organizations, while TABD is somewhat different. As it is described on the organization's website, TABD "was conceived to promote closer commercial ties between the U.S. and European Union . . . [it] created the dialogue system as a mechanism to encourage public and civil society input to fostering a more closely integrated transatlantic marketplace . . . [it] includes separate dialogues for consumers, labor, environment and business, and was a key part of the governments' 1995 New Transatlantic Agenda (NTA)."[21]

It can be noted that considering the number of out-degrees, hence influence, fewer similarities were found in these networks. It seems that there is a greater variation in the representation of the various categories of institutions. It is interesting to include those second- and third-depth investigations into the analysis; thus in Table 5.9 the summary results for out-degree for both networks are included (at all depths).

In addition to the TLD two other organizations emerge as influential, which are also part of the New Transatlantic Agenda. These are the Transatlantic Information Exchange System (TIES), a civil societal initiative in the broader network, and the TransAtlantic Business Dialogue (TABD) in the sub-network.

Table 5.9 Top-Ranking Nodes and Their Values for Out-degree at All Depths

D1	**USST—46**	**d1-kw**	**TLD—22**
	TLD—37		**SOC—13**
	FPRI—30		OSTP—13
	LADF—26		USST—12
	TIES—20		TABD—11
D2 and D3	**TLD—52**	**d2-kw and d3-kw**	**TLD—23**
	USST—38		**SOC—20**
	SOC—38		EPC—20
	CIRE—37		**USST—18**
	NACA—36		CIRE—18

Degree versus Node Strength

While we commonly designate the degree of a node as the number of other nodes the node is connected to, the strength of a node is equal to the sum of weights attached to the ties that connect a node to others.[22] Opsahl and others have recently raised the issue of appropriately measuring the strength of ties as a major limitation of methods most frequently used for studying large-scale networks.[23] Although "the strength of a tie is generally operationalized into a weight that is attached to the tie, thereby creating a weighted network," the refinement of a more distinct measurement may depend on the type of services being exchanged among network members.[24] As an innovative example, the cutting-edge research that Opsahl et al. present measures strength as "the average number of messages sent to (received from) others," while others who study telecommunication networks denote line values as call durations.[25] Indeed, the incorporation of the intensity of interaction and relevant measures may hold great promise for future research in any area that employs social network analysis.

Granovetter explained how the strength of ties is impacted by the function the network performs, which is the exchange of information via hyperlink connections in this particular research.[26] In discussing the fundamentals of social network analysis, Wasserman and Faust also illuminate the idea of a "weighted network," in which they define the strength of a tie as the weight attached to it.[27] As Opsahl argues, reinforcing Granovetter's ideas on the significance of the strength of ties, "the measures that scholars typically apply to study networks should be sensitive to tie strength and capture the difference between strong and weak ties. This will ensure that the full richness of the data is retained."[28] While Granovetter made arguments for the strength of weak ties associated with new ideas and innovation, strong ties fulfill certain roles in the network as well. As an early structuralist, Simmel explained strong ties can benefit from the presence of a variety of or diverse ties, weak *and* strong.[29]

In fact, communities with both, *bridging* as well as *bonding* social capital are typically the most effective in organizing for collective action.[30] This, again, supports Simmel's idea on the benefits of being part of a community with multiple and diverse groups.[31] In discussing the benefits gained from high social capital in networked communities, Kavanaugh et al. argue that "[c]ommunities with 'bridging' social capital (weak ties across groups) as well as 'bonding' social capital (strong ties within groups) are the most effective in organizing for collective action."[32] Furthermore, bridging ties in the context of communication media, and, especially e-communication may amplify the effects of actors' capacity to transfer information and knowledge.[33] As Opsahl summarizes the relevant literature he points out that, on the one hand, Krackhardt revealed that strong ties can be useful to reduce uncertainty; Coleman illuminated potential advantages of tradition in social structure, while he also recalls Granovetter's research on the strength of weak ties and their capacity to carry innovative ideas.[34]

Tables 5.10 and 5.11 reveal a comparison of the network analytical results in regards to the degree and strength of the transatlantic network members in both, the broader as well as the S&T-specific sub-networks. Investigating these results in regards to similarities and differences among them allows us to advance our understanding of these networks.

The *incorporation of intensity of connections,* i.e. the in-strength based analysis, *shows that nodal degree and strength are not necessarily congruent. In the broader transatlantic network the Delegation of the European Commission to Canada (EUCA), The National Academies of Engineering (NAE), and the Transatlantic Legislators' Dialogue (TLD) have line values in the hundred thousands, signaling a high intensity of connections. In the policy-specific sub-network, this group that represents high connectivity also includes EUCA and TLD, but it is the US–EU Cooperation in Science and Technology (USST)* that is ranked number one in this group. Considering the nature of the policy, the strength of USST is hardly a surprise.

Next, the other side of prominence is discussed; actors who are able to exchange or disperse information relatively quickly to others, and regarded as influential, are being analyzed. As far as the intensity of connections is concerned, i.e. out-strength, the same actors appear in the broader network regardless of whether we look at the results of out-degree or out-strength. Therefore, the nodes with the most connections sent out are the ones with the highest intensity of those. In the sub-network, *two additional actors, NAE and EUCA, broaden the group of "influentials." While the National Academy of Engineering appears to be a policy-relevant actor, the role of the Delegation of the European Commission to Canada is somewhat puzzling.*

Prestige from Kleinberg's Perspective: Authorities and Hubs

In directed networks, such as the ones analyzed in this book, two of the most frequently used measures for prominence and prestige are Kleinberg's authorities and hubs. These can be considered as formal notions of structural prominence. Authoritative are those that are the most prominent sources of information on a specific issue area.[35] As Kleinberg describes, hubs, however, are "other pages, equally intrinsic to the structure, assemble high-quality guides and resource lists that act as focused *hubs,* directing users to recommended authorities."[36]

In our case, various transatlantic organizations' web pages on transatlantic issues would be such entities that we call authorities. These are the organizational web pages that emerge from the network analysis with high authority scores. There are several pages on the web that link to authoritative pages on a specific topic. As Wassermann and Faust explain, those homepages that are labeled "authorities" describe something potentially useful and/or significant; and because of that, other pages will direct to those.[37]

Table 5.10 In-degree–In-strength Comparison of Top-Ranking Nodes and Their Values at All Depths

	In-degree[1]	In-strength		In-degree	In-strength
D1	TLD—43	EUCA—318,842	d1-kw	TLD—32	USST—182,231
	SOC—34	NAE—253,001		USST—27	TLD—84,010
	OSTP—27	TLD—154,895		SOC—16	EUCA—55,017
	NACA—23	ESR—8,594		ACUS—15	ESR—5,114
	CIRE—21	ACUS—7,167		FPRI—12	ECEN—3,650
	EUEC—21	ERA—5,658			
D2 and D3	TLD—62	USST—378,197	d2-kw and d3-kw	TLD—43	USST—185,709
	USST—52	TLD—290,173		USST—35	TLD—86,273
	SOC—49	EUCA—158,532		ACUS—29	EUCA—55,017
	ACUS—40	ACUS—24,237		SOC—23	ESR—6,480
	ERT—39	ESR—15,047		ERC—18	ECEN—4,024
	DRIV—35	SOC—9,200			

[1] In-degree was defined as the number of ties terminating at a node or vertex (Wasserman and Faust, 1994).

Table 5.11 Out-degree–Out-strength Comparison of Top-Ranking Nodes and Their Values at All Depths

	Out-degree[1]	Out-strength		Out-degree	Out-strength
D1	**USST—46**	**USST—389,319**	**d1-kw**	**TLD—22**	**NAE—176,464**
	TLD—37	**TLD—341,288**		**SOC—13**	**TLD—77,876**
	FPRI—30	**TIES—9,171**		OSTP—13	**EUCA—56,148**
	LADF—26	**ACUS—6,851**		**USST—12**	**USST—8,558**
	TIES—20	**SOC—6,144**		TABD—11	**TIES—5,091**
		FPRI—4,866			
D2 and D3	**TLD—52**	**TLD—265,516**	**d2-kw and d3-kw**	**TLD—23**	**NAE—177,395**
	USST—38	NAE—261,064		**SOC—20**	**TLD—79,258**
	SOC—38	EUCA—165,597		EPC—20	**EUCA—56,512**
	CIRE—37	**USST—82,213**		**USST—18**	**USST—9,298**
	NACA—36	OSTP—24,371		CIRE—18	**TIES—5,981**
		TIES—14,323			
		FPRI—10,965			

[1] Out-degree was defined as the number of ties originating from a node or vertex (Wasserman and Faust, 1994).

Hub pages are not in themselves authoritative sources of topic-specific information. They can be useful to discover those authority pages. They are more of the influential kind of prominent actors. These hub pages are the pages that will emerge with high hub scores during network analysis. Pajek software distinguishes these hubs and authorities as essentially "important vertices." A vertex is considered "a good hub if it points to many good authorities and it is a good authority, if it is pointed to by many good hubs."[38] A "value of one" represents that the vertex is a good authority, a "value of two" signifies that the vertex is a good authority and a good hub at the same time, while a "value of three" means that the vertex is a good hub.

While the "in-degree" "out-degree" dichotomy is one type of distinction of prominence and prestige in social network analysis, Kleinberg's authorities and hubs algorithm measures the same idea. From this perspective, if an organizational homepage is both a good authority and a good hub, it can be considered to be in a great position in the network. Not only is this organization rather influential (an authority), but it is also referenced by the "best" (hubs). Additionally, both measures can be characterized by their weights that show the strength of an organizational web page as an authority or hub, or both.[39] Fortunately for this research, Pajek, developed by Batagelj and Mrvar, adopted Kleinberg's authorities and hubs algorithm; thus, these weights are calculated automatically by the program. The reason for the choice of this software program is to benefit from this advantage and cross-examine the previous result for prestige. Overall, the authority score is a function of the number of occasions it is referenced, and the quality of those websites that reference it. Similarly, the hub score of a web page depends on the number of other sites it points to as well as the quality of those referenced by it.

Figures 5.16 and 5.17 provide visual representations of hubs and authorities in the larger network ("D1") and in the S&T sub-network ("d1kw"), respectively.

Tables 5.12 and 5.13 summarize which actors can be regarded as authorities, or hubs, or both in the broader network as well as in the S&T sub-network.

While the first table shows transatlantic organizations with the highest authority weights, the second one lists the highest scoring hubs. Those network members that are both, good authorities as well as good hubs, are presented in Table 5.14.

Using Kleinberg's authorities, as formal notions of structural prominence, gives us the following results. *Authoritative, or the most prominent, sources of information are: the Delegation of the European Commission to Canada (EUCA), the National Academies of Engineering (NAE), and the Transatlantic Legislators' Dialogue (TLD) in the broader network*, while in the *S&T sub-network the US–EU Cooperation in Science and Technology (USST) has the highest authority score, followed by the Transatlantic Legislators' Dialogue*

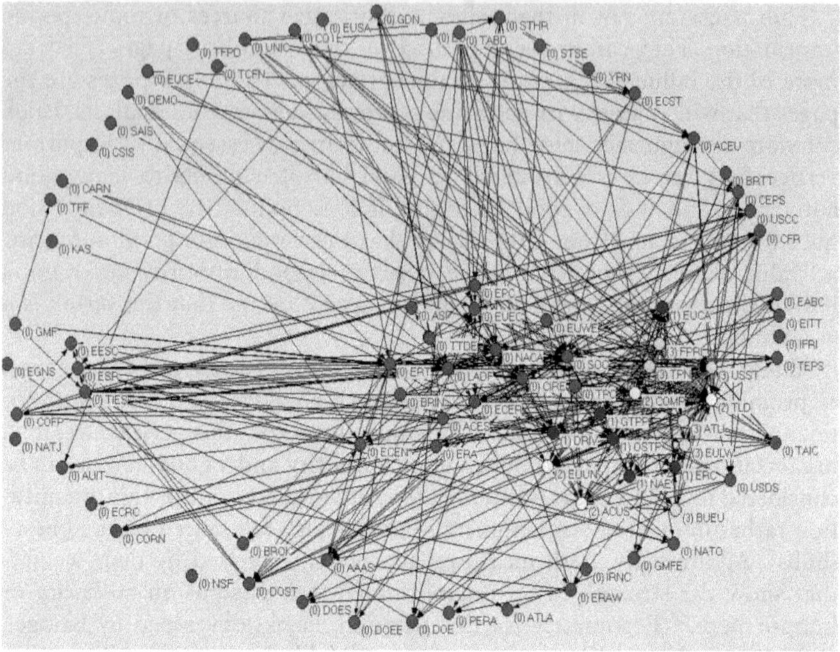

Figure 5.16 Visualization of the Hubs and Authorities Partitioning of the Transatlantic Network

Nodes represent three variations in the roles of organizations in this network: (1) are good authorities, (2) are both good authorities as well as good hubs, while (3) are considered good hubs only. All others are none of those (0).

(TLD) and the Delegation of the European Commission to Canada (EUCA). Interestingly, in the sub-network, those that are both hubs and authorities have higher authority scores than the ones that are solely authorities.

Using *Kleinberg's hubs as a measure of influence*, another set of actors emerge. Those that provide guidance, as well as direct others to resources of information, in the *broader transatlantic network are: the Transatlantic Legislators' Dialogue (TLD) and Department of State's website on US–EU Cooperation in Science and Technology (USST).* These two are substantially more influential in the larger network than others. In the *S&T sub-network, hubs that are most influential* are exactly the same as the ones that the connectivity strength indicators pointed out: *The National Academies of Engineering (NAE), the Transatlantic Legislators' Dialogue (TLD), and the Delegation of the European Commission to Canada (EUCA)*, in decreasing order by their weights. There are a few other organizations that are considered both, but their scores are significantly less, especially their authority scores. Additionally, in Table 5.15, authorities and hubs in both networks, and at all depths, are reported.

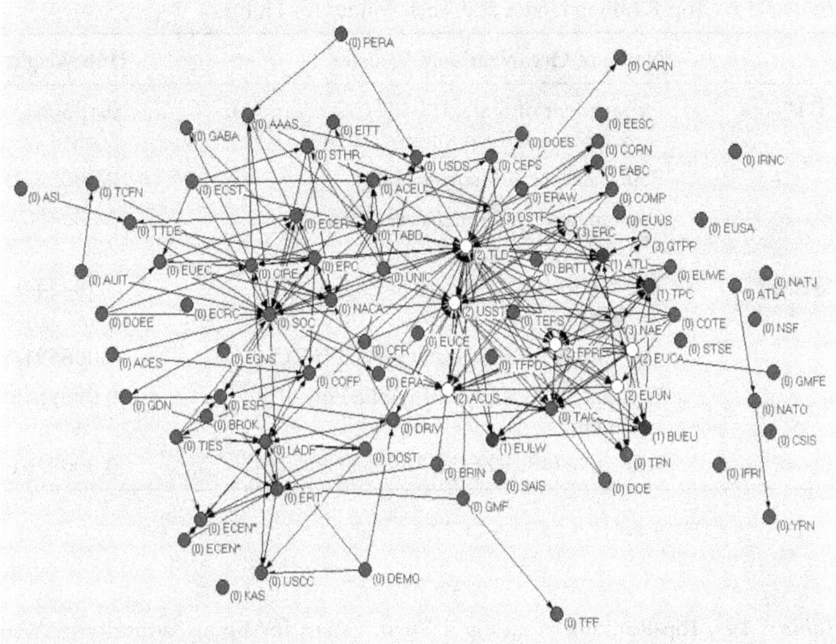

Figure 5.17 Visualization of the Hubs and Authorities Partitioning of the Transatlantic S&T Sub-network

Nodes represent three variations in the roles of organizations in this network: (1) are good authorities, (2) are both good authorities as well as good hubs, while (3) are considered good hubs only. All others are none of those (0).

Table 5.12 Top-Ranking Nodes and Their Values for Authority

	Name of Organizational Website	Authority Weight
"D1"	Delegation of the European Commission to Canada (EUCA)	0.9832737
	The National Academies of Engineering (NAE)	0.1681140
	Georgia Tech, School of Public Policy (GTPP)	0.0042674
	Executive Office of the President (OSTP)	0.0036069
	European Research Council (ERC)	0.0039035
	Digital Repository Infrastructure Vision for European Research (DRIV)	0.0003106
"d1kw"	The Atlantic Initiative (ATLI)	0.0002675
	BUSINESSEUROPE (BUEU)	0.0001944
	EurLex, EU Law (EULW)	0.0001289
	Transatlantic Policy Consortium (TPC)	0.0000779

Table 5.13 Top-Ranking Nodes and Their Values for Hub

	Name of Organizational Website	Hub Weight
"D1"	Department of State, US–EU Cooperation in Science and Technology (USST)	0.1560615
	Policy Research Institute (FPRI)	0.0005216
	Foreign, and the EurLex, EU Law (EULW)	0.0004002
"d1kw"	The National Academies of Engineering (NAE)	0.9887448
	The European Research Council (ERC)	0.0065914
	Georgia Tech, School of Public Policy (GTPP)	0.0009886
	Executive Office of the President (OSTP)	0.0008561

Table 5.14 Top-Ranking Nodes and Their Values for Both: Authority as Well as Hub

	Name of Organizational Website	Authority Weight	Hub Weight
"D1"	Transatlantic Legislators' Dialogue (TLD)[1]	0.0693004	0.9877459
	European Union at the United Nations (EUUN)[2]	0.0070550	0.0000615
	Atlantic Council of the United States (ACUS)[3]	0.0033920	0.0015410
	The Council on Competitiveness (COMP)[4]	0.0001597	0.0001352
"d1kw"	Department of State, US–EU Cooperation in Science and Technology (USST)[2]	0.9918131	0.0051406
	Transatlantic Legislators' Dialogue (TLD)	0.1180246	0.1435284
	Delegation of the European Commission to Canada (EUCA)	0.0487459	0.0412291

1 Higher hub score and a somewhat lower authority score.
2 Much higher authority than hub score.
3 Somewhat higher authority than hub score.
4 Relatively lower scores in both categories.

Table 5.15 Top-Ranking Nodes for Authority and Hub at All Depths

	Authority	Hub		Authority	Hub
D1	**EUCA**	**TLD**	d1-kw	**USST**	**NAE**
	NAE	**USST**		**TLD**	**TLD**
	TLD	**ACUS**		**EUCA**	**EUCA**
	EUUN	**FPRI**		**ATLI**	**ERC**
	GTPP	EULW		**BUEU**	**USST**
	ERC	BUEU		**EULW**	**GTPP**
	OSTP	TPN		**TPC**	**OSTP**
	ACUS	**COMP**			
	DRIV	ATLI			
	COMP	**EUUN**			
D2 and D3	USST	NAE	d2-kw and d3-kw	**USST**	NAE
	EUCA	**TLD**		**TLD**	**TLD**
	TLD	EUCA		**EUCA**	**EUCA**
	ACUS	OSTP		ACUS	**ERC**
	FPRI	**USST**		FPRI	**USST**
	EUUN	**ACUS**		**ATLI**	FPRI
	EULW	**FPRI**		**BUEU**	ACUS
	ERC	**COMP**		**EULW**	**OSTP**
	TAIC	**EUUN**		**EUUN**	**EUUN**
	ATLI	ERC			**GTPP**

It becomes immediately apparent that the vast majority of authorities and hubs, found through analyzing direct links, are identical to those found via secondary and tertiary links. This is true for the S&T sub-network in particular. Results for "influentials" seem more consistent along the various measures, than for those that are regarded as authoritative or prominent sources of information on a specific issue area discussed in the preceding paragraphs.

Overall, for prominence or prestige, the following conclusion could be made. *While this measure can be adequately approximated by in- and out-degree distributions, the use of Kleinberg's measures, authority and hub, provides a more nuanced set of results in regards to which actors are the most prominent in the network.* Note that including node-strength into the investigation gave almost identical results to those obtained by authority/hub measures. This *enhances the validity of the empirical investigations. Four most prominent actors emerge. Out of those, the Transatlantic Legislators' Dialogue (TLD) seems most evident, which confirms that the efforts of the New Transatlantic Agenda of 1995* were, to some extent, already fruitful. The National Academies of Engineering (NAE) appears to be an intriguing finding, unless we look at the details of connectivity. This organization's networking practices indicate that it is not the breadth, but rather the depth of connections that puts this actor in this position. Although well-connected, this organization's significance emerges, almost exclusively, from its connections to two other prominent organizations: the Transatlantic Legislators' Dialogue (TLD) and also the Department of State's US–EU Cooperation in Science and Technology (USST). A similar pattern can be observed in the case of EUCA. The Delegation of the European Commission to Canada (EUCA) gains its prominence solely from pursuing intense virtual connections with the legislators' dialogue (TLD). Lastly, the fourth major actor, USST, although still better connected to its other prominent partners, shows a more diverse set of relations with other network members.

Brokerage: Structural Holes

An important attribute that SNA can highlight is brokerage. This study measures it in two different ways: first, by using Burt's measure "structural holes" or the connection of non-redundant ties, which conceal latent opportunities; and second, by the measure "betweenness," which refers to the extent to which an actor is situated between two other actors.

Burt, in his seminal paper "The Network Structure of Social Capital," showed that there is a robust relationship between network structure and network performance. Before presenting the findings, it is useful to briefly summarize Burt's main ideas on this unique metric, "structural holes," which can be regarded as latent opportunities.[40] Burt's theory of structural holes, which is an extension of social network theory, proposes that there are essentially two types of benefits to be gained in these positions: informational and control benefits.[41] In regards to the former, the quality or relevance of information as well as the speed of diffusion are factors to be considered, while the latter references advantages of being a central actor in a well-connected network. Opportunities for collaboration in all kinds of areas are, potentially, greater for networks that are optimally structured and for their network members in strategically advantageous positions. Information and control benefits are the two broad categories of mechanisms, which account for the relationship between structural holes and performance, as suggested by Burt.[42] He also proposed that information benefits might be further broken down to opportunity recognition and information arbitrage, whereas control benefits include autonomy and competition.

Burt, from an organizational theoretical point of view, explains creativity as a diffusion process, in which "value accumulates as an idea moves through the social structure, each transmission from one group to another having the potential to add value." Therefore, a fifth mechanism, to gain benefits from structural advantage and turn it into performance improvement, is based on the idea that creativity and innovation is rooted in knowledge recombination. Burt describes brokerage "as an engine for productive change."[43] He argues, "[p]eople who have relations that span the structural holes between groups have a vision advantage in detecting and developing good ideas. For their integrative efforts these people receive disproportionate returns" . . . "That vision advantage in detecting and developing good ideas is the mechanism by which brokerage becomes social capital."[44]

Although, some of the aspects of brokerage as social capital were discussed earlier, further clarification of the concept is needed in light of the findings. In discussing the transfer of knowledge from one area of inquiry into another, Bourdieu and Wacquant define social capital as "the sum of the resources, actual or virtual, that accrue to an individual or a group by virtue of possessing a durable network of more or less institutionalized relationships of mutual acquaintance and recognition."[45] Coleman's opposing view asserts that social capital is created by network closure.[46] As Gudmundsson and Lechnerb illuminate, "[t]he opposing view argues that network closure would generate superior 'social capital' and thus superior 'economic rent' as we would have more trust, reputation and cooperation within a closed group with strong internal ties."[47] In their case study on multilateral airline alliances, these authors show that "a combination of opportunities to bridge 'structural holes' as well as a degree of cohesiveness are important in combination but not exclusive of each other."[48] This is in line with Burt's findings that "brokerage across structural holes is a source of value added, but closure can be critical to realizing the value buried in structural holes." Burt sums up the merging of structural hole and social capital theories when he explains, "[c]ast in diverse styles of argument (e.g., Coleman, 1990; Bourdieu and Wacquant, 1992; Burt, 1992; Putnam, 1993), social capital is a metaphor about advantage."[49]

In regards to this metric Batagelj, Mrvar, and Nooy explain, "[t]he higher the aggregate constraint, the less 'freedom' a person has to withdraw from existing ties or to exploit structural holes."[50] Therefore, looking for network members with lower aggregate constraint, hence higher autonomy, which are supposed to perform better, was instrumental to this research. This measure favors nodes that connect a considerable number of powerful, sparsely linked actors with minimal investment in tie strength. Weak ties are preferred over strong ties for two fundamental reasons. First, strong ties are more costly to establish. Second, as Granovetter pointed out, weak ties can be stronger in a sense that they have greater potential to carry new information, hence, being the sources of innovative ideas.[51] Table 5.16 shows top-ranking nodes of the network based on Burt's measure.[52]

First, findings for brokerage from the "structural holes" perspective are discussed. The study finds that actors in the *broader transatlantic network*, which are potential brokers of information and can control benefits, are the following: the *European Roundtable of Industrialists (ERT), the European Commission External Relations (ECER), the Global Development Network (GDN), Trans European Policy Studies Association (TEPS), and the American Association for the Advancement of Science (AAAS)*. Structural

Table 5.16 Top-Ranking Nodes and Their Values for Aggregate Network Constraint (structural holes)

	Name of Organizational Website	Value
"D1"	European Roundtable of Industrialists (ERT)	0.2269690
	European Commission External Relations (ECER)	0.2552764
	Global Development Network (GDN)	0.2556958
	Trans European Policy Studies Association (TEPS)	0.2635591
	American Association for the Advancement of Science (AAAS)	0.2736856
"d1kw"	European Policy Center (EPC)	0.3202118
	Global Development Network (GDN)	0.3337147
	European Institute (EITT)	0.3361601
	The US Department of State (USDS)	0.3371553
	The American Association for the Advancement of Science (AAAS)	0.3486563

holes in the *S&T sub-network are: the European Policy Center (EPC), the Global Development Network (GDN), the European Institute (EITT), the US Department of State (USDS), and the American Association for the Advancement of Science (AAAS).*

Note that from among these network members, the *Global Development Network (GDN) and the American Association for the Advancement of Science (AAAS) play this role in both networks.* Although, at one point, it operated as an independent network of research and policy institutes, the Global Development Network (GDN) is now officially an IGO. Because GDN is an international organization of research and policy institutes, the goal of which is to promote the generation, sharing, and application of multidisciplinary knowledge to policy, this finding of new opportunities can be consequential.

Designated as an academic, research, and policy institute, the American Association for the Advancement of Science could benefit from similar potentials in both network types as well. The AAAS's presence in the group is even more pronounced for two main reasons. First, *AAAS is a more than one and a half centuries old organization, which serves some 162 affiliated societies and academies of science and ten million individuals. Second, GDN is truly a global organization based in Washington, D.C.* Its mission is to "advance science and serve society," hence opportunities not yet capitalized on should be of great interest to AAAS.[53] A recent establishment

Table 5.17 Top-Ranking Nodes for Aggregate Constraint at All Depths

D1	ERT	**d1-kw**	**EPC**
	ECER		GDN
	GDN		EITT
	TEPS		**USDS**
	AAAS		
D2 and D3	**GDN**	**d2-kw and d3-kw**	AAAS
	LADF		BROK
	EPC		**USDS**
	TEPS		GMF
	BROK		**EPC**

of the organizations' Center for Science Diplomacy underscores this interest.

Interest groups, such as the European Roundtable of Industrialists (ERT), a think tank, such as the European Policy Centre (EPC), and research institute types, such as the Trans European Policy Studies Association or the European Policy Center (EPC), also appear in this group. From among governmental agencies, the US Department of State (USDS), and from the group of IGOs, the European Commission External Relations (ECER) belong here as well. This seems like a diverse group with great potentials to facilitate cooperative efforts.

Table 5.17 summarizes structural holes, at all depths, in both the larger network and the smaller sub-network. While the commonality is that, regarding this metric, at "depth2" and "depth3" structural holes are identical, the organizations that emerge as structural holes are somewhat different than the ones at "depth1" in both network systems. This shows that, for structural holes, it matters little whether connections among various web pages occur through just one "hop," or connections are formed through secondary and tertiary page links only. Consequently, a few new nodes become structural holes that might benefit from their position in forming future relations at those levels.

Brokerage: Betweenness

Looking at the results from the "betweenness" measure point of view is next. Recall that, earlier, "betweenness" was described as the extent to which an actor sits between two other actors and, as such, indicates how much a node controls what flows through the network. Actors, which are located strategically on a communication path between two others, hold the power to influence information transmission, whether distorting or withholding it.[54] Results for "betweenness" are shown in Table 5.18.

Table 5.18 Top-Ranking Nodes and Their Values for Betweenness as Brokerage

	Name of Organizational Website	Value
"D1"	Transatlantic Legislators' Dialogue (TLD)	0.0858436
	Department of State, US–EU Cooperation in Science and Technology (USST)	0.0378736
	Science of Collaboratories (SOC)	0.0345195
	European Roundtable of Industrialists (ERT)	0.0264150
"d1kw"	Transatlantic Legislators' Dialogue (TLD)	0.1509891
	Science of Collaboratories (SOC)	0.0760312
	Digital Repository Infrastructure Vision for European Research (DRIV)	0.0388877
	Luso-American Development Foundation (LADF)	0.0318693

Network members that have *high "betweenness" can be regarded as more central* as well as being *able to seize greater opportunities to act as brokers*. The ranking of network actors in both networks indicates that the *Transatlantic Legislators' Dialogue (TLD) has the highest score on this metric. While the Department of State, US–EU Cooperation in Science and Technology (USST) is the second* in regards to "betweenness" in the broader network, *the Science of Collaboratories (SOC) seems to be a key actor in both networks*. Table 5.19 summarizes this metric for both networks (at all depths) and demonstrates that there are a lot of similarities in regards to which organizations score high on "betweenness" as brokerage.

It is important to draw attention to the nuances of the definition of "betweenness" and the difference between this measure and "structural holes" here. Burt investigated this topic and found that "where a structural

Table 5.19 Top-Ranking Nodes for Betweenness at All Depths

D1	TLD USST SOC ERT	d1-kw	TLD SOC DRIV LADF
D2 and D3	TLD USST SOC CIRE	d2-kw and d3-kw	TLD USST SOC CIRE

hole is defined to occur when two people are disconnected, then betweenness is a count of the structural holes to which a person has monopoly access."[55] Although Freeman's "betweenness" measure is an appealing one, there are two issues that Burt raises in regards to the appropriateness of the measure here.[56] "Betweenness," an index, which is "a count of, or ratio of, possible monopoly opportunities for brokerage . . . does not distinguish [between] direct access versus . . . indirect access" opportunities.[57] Burt does not question the measure, but says that he believes we should be cautious in applying this measure to larger networks.[58] The aforementioned ideas confirm that the idea of a structural hole helps us better find the key organizations that have the ability to bridge connections among others. Recognizing Burt's concerns, this study emphasizes the results from the measure that indicated low aggregate constraint in the network, and designates where structural holes or latent opportunities are located.

"Betweenness" is sometimes interpreted as "influence" or the degree of "control of information." Brokers play different roles depending on the group to which they belong. These various types of brokerage roles in these sub-categories are a function of particular combinations of network partitions, thus it requires a calculation and examination of all possible partitions in the network. This can be part of another extensive project; however, it is beyond the scope of this book.

Cohesion

To investigate clustering patterns in these networks, spectral clustering by weighted cuts has been used. This procedure is described in detail in the methodological appendix. This newly discovered clustering method utilizes a technique, which minimizes similarities between clusters, while maximizing similarities within clusters. By maximizing the similarity of nodes to the cluster's geometric center, the cohesion of the cluster emerges.[59] "Cluster cohesion measures how closely related are objects in a cluster."[60] This *cluster analysis reveals that the structure of the network(s) is impacted by a particularly cohesive group of actors within the network*. This cohesiveness shows as a pattern in all of the networks analyzed in this study at all levels.

The first sub-group includes the academic, research, and policy institutes, consisting of the following entities: the United States' Foreign Policy Research Institute, the Trans-Atlantic Initiative on Complex Organizations and Networks based both in Boston and Zurich, and the Atlantic Initiative based in Berlin. Also in this group are: the Transatlantic Policy Consortium, which includes both American and European scholars and university professionals; the US university-based Center for Research on Collaboratories and Technology Enhanced Learning Communities; and the Georgia Tech School of Public Policy.

The second sub-group includes inter-governmental institutions represented by EurLex, the European Union's legal site, and the Transatlantic Legislators' Dialogue, which was a result of the New Transatlantic Agenda of 1995. A few others belong to this sub-group as well, such as the European Union's mission at the United Nations; the Delegation of the European Commission to Canada; EUROPA, the European Union's official website; and the European Research Council. The third sub-group consists of government agencies, such as the US Department of State's US–EU Cooperation in Science and Technology homepage, the Office of Science and Technology Policy: Executive Office of the President, and The National Academy of Engineering in the United States. In the fourth sub-group there are a few interest groups, such as the Transatlantic Policy Network, which has grown from a group of transatlantic legislators to a much broader and diverse group of EU and US politicians, corporate leaders, think tanks, and academics. Also in this sub-group is the Atlantic Council of the United States, which is an international network of citizens' associations; BUSINESSEUROPE, which provides policy-access to industrial federations; and the US Council on Competitiveness.

This diverse set of actors consists of governmental organizations (mostly IGOs), academic, research, and policy institutes, as well as a few interest groups. Two other patterns stand out. First, transatlantic entities, created by the New Transatlantic Agenda of 1995, belong in this group. Second, *science-oriented institutions are well-represented, regardless of which network we look at, the broader network or the S&T sub-network. These findings indicate that the New Transatlantic Agenda did create institutions that demonstrate an active presence through their virtual networking practices. It should be pointed out that S&T polices seem to have an enhanced role in overall transatlantic collaborative practices.*

CATALYSTS OF KNOWLEDGE: NGOS VERSUS THE STATE/GOVERNMENT

As it was argued earlier in this book, this research builds on the work of Ikenberry, Keohane, Nye, Slaughter, and others in the discipline. In addressing the changing nature of our complex, interdependent world and the resulting issues, these authors emphasize the importance of a greater diversity of actors, state or non-state. As previously discussed, another significant aspect this research accounts for is the role of technology, which is increasingly pronounced and transforms the modes of interactions among these diverse actors. Charnovitz explains that the last decade of the 20th century has already seen a dramatic increase in the participation of various non-governmental organizations in transnational activities.[61] The role and impact of NGOs in relation to access to information and knowledge-diffusion is intimately intertwined with the technology-driven information boom that characterizes the 21st century. Cogburn, and other scholars of Internet governance and "multi-stakeholderism," also assert that we are seeing the emergence of less state-centric approaches to governance due to the failure of traditional state-centered solutions to resolve complex transnational problems.[62]

Distribution of Types of Institutions in the Transatlantic Network(s)

The findings demonstrate that, in these network(s), the web-presence and *hyperlinking practices of transatlantic organizations varies based on which category they belong to.* There are certain types of organizations that stand out as network members, based on their distinct attributes measured by social network analysis. In the broader network, inter-governmental organizations as well as academic, research, and policy institutes, as a category, each represent 27.9% within the transatlantic network examined in this book. Government agencies can claim 16.3%, interest groups 15.1%, and think tanks 12.8% of the overall membership in this network. Looking closely at the *S&T sub-network,* a reduction of the network to 71 members can be observed. Out of these network members, it is inter-governmental organizations that hold the greatest share, 29.6%. The second largest group, representing 25.4%, consists of academic, research, and policy institutes. The third main group is constituted by interest groups with an 18.3% presence in the network. The fourth and the fifth categories are government agencies and think tanks constituting 15.5% and 11.3% of the membership, respectively.

From among the *15* organizations that were network members in the broader transatlantic network, but are not part of the S&T sub-network, it is the academic, research, and policy institutes that show the greatest decrease (40%). It is, perhaps, attributable to the fact that some of these institutes in this category have a mission or profile that cannot be associated with S&T policy at all. Inter-governmental organizations constitute 27% of these 15, while government agencies and think tanks each showed a 20% decrease in their numbers in the sub-network. The number of interest groups in the sub-network, however, remained the same as it was in the broader transatlantic network. This, in fact, shows a proportionally greater representation of this category in the S&T-specific network.

A *main goal* of this research has been to *unravel innovative ways of forging more dynamic and successful transatlantic communication and cooperation.* This book aimed to achieve this by *revealing the fine structure of transatlantic networks* not only in terms of network attributes, but also in terms of the *types of actors* that all interact in these networks. As discussed earlier, networks were analyzed from this theoretically important perspective by dividing network members into five categories.[63] Results indicate that academic, research, and policy institutes, as well as inter-governmental organizations, have the greatest share (28% each) in the broader network; whereas in the S&T policy-specific sub-network, inter-governmental (30%) organizations have the greatest share from all five categories, and the share of academic, research, and policy institutes is somewhat decreased (26%). In regards to the presence of two other organization types, government agencies and think tanks, the following can be argued. Although the number of government agencies is slightly greater than that of think tanks, the drop in their numbers is proportional to the size of the sub-network. Intriguingly, interest group representation remains unchanged after narrowing down the broader network to S&T policy-specific sub-network. This implies that interest groups are somewhat better represented in this sub-network.

Results also indicate that there is a variety of actors actively involved in these transatlantic virtual networks. *While state actors are not invisible, they are not predominant actors in these networks; inter-governmental organizations have a significant share.* Academic, research, and policy institutes are represented in greater numbers in the broader network, but they seem to be actively involved in the sub-network also. Nonetheless, when combined with the category of "think tanks," arguing that these all have an intellectual commitment to expert knowledge that is grounded in scientific, codified forms of knowledge, these results can be interpreted somewhat differently. Under this scenario, the *combined weight of academic, research, and policy institutes and think tanks proves to be predominant* in the networks (*41% in the larger network and 37% in the S&T sub-network*). The fact that these *epistemic community-like entities* represent a significant share in both networks *refutes the third hypothesis*. This is because *although they do play important roles in S&T* policy, which is an area characterized by complexity and technical uncertainty, *their roles are just as important in the broader network*. This is most probably because *complexity and technical uncertainty impacts all policy areas* in our information-driven societies.

In *Think Tanks and Civil Societies,* McGann and Weaver explain that there are several roles that think tanks fulfill, but they perform different varieties of these tasks defined by these authors. Additionally, *the boundaries of this category are not entirely clear; there may be an overlap in the functions of think tanks on the one hand, and academic, research, and policy institutes* on the other hand.[64] In *agreement with the first hypothesis,* these underscore the validity of liberal IR theory and the role of non-state actors in cooperation and policy-coordination. Additionally, results further indicate that non-state actors, NGOs as well as IGOs, emerge as the most prominent actors in the network corroborated by the social network analysis. This *further confirms the first hypothesis* that these can be regarded as the "communicative linchpin" that catalyzes transatlantic cooperation.

Lastly, an important premise of this book is that the role of science and technology is especially pronounced in regards to the future development of transatlantic relations. As indicated earlier, an important pattern emerged from the empirical analysis: *science and technology-related organizations, or organizations whose mission is tied to science and technology promotion, emerge as rather visible actors even before the search is narrowed and policy-specific key words and key terms are incorporated into the search.* This *proves the validity of the second hypothesis* that these types of organizations have a significant role in finding policy solutions to increasingly complex foreign policy problems in transatlantic relations.

As discussed earlier, this book explores inter-organizational links within the science and technology policy domain of transatlantic relations. Addressing transnational challenges requires formal and informal collaboration among actors as their successes are increasingly intertwined. The communities and organizations that participate in such activities are more likely to stimulate cooperative action under conditions of high issue complexity and technical uncertainty.[65] Specifically, this study investigates policy areas in which the EU–US Agreement for Scientific and Technological Cooperation is active. This dynamic cooperative action is also confirmed by the agreement, which indicates that, along with a few other areas, it is policies that concern biotechnology, alternative energy resources, and nanotechnology where the most active cooperation takes place.[66,67]

Conclusion

Taken together, these findings shed new light on the nature of transatlantic cooperative relationships. As the constantly evolving novel experiment that we call European integration progresses and the EU's supranational institutions develop, both partners of the transatlantic relationship are in great need of forging innovative ways to cooperate. Just within the past few years, there have been tremendous changes in terms of both American as well as European foreign policy perspectives. The fact that the Lisbon Treaty has been signed signifies a major step forward towards an EU Common Foreign and Security Policy. On the other side of the Atlantic, the direction of foreign policy has also changed with the new administration in place. Most Europeans, perhaps with the exception of "Euroskeptics," believe that the chances of creating stronger ties and more successful cooperation between the EU and the US have increased. This is evidenced by recent communications such as the following: "Obama's vision must be ultimately understood . . . as a new vision of international relations based on an awareness in Europe and the United States, and indeed in many other parts of the world, of the realities and consequences of globalization and the concomitant emergence of an international civil society." In fact, in his first UN speech, President Obama quoted Roosevelt as he spoke about our shared humanity and shared goals and problems we need to address collectively.[68]

As Louis Pasteur once wrote, "science knows no country, because knowledge belongs to humanity, and is the torch which illuminates the world."[69]

In the current era of global turbulence, scholars of international relations seek to better understand and overcome challenges spurred by intensified global communication and interchange; and while the unprecedented scientific and technological progress of the past several decades has the potential to enable us to tackle complex problems, it looks as though the human capacity to cope with these changes and our ability to capitalize on the empowerment brought about by scientific progress are lagging behind.

Scholars of international relations do not seem to have been engaged in an intense discourse on the role of research and development policies in economic and foreign polices. This study aims to fill that gap. *This book argues that scientific and technological cooperation is an especially fruitful policy area for three reasons. First,* a regular dialogue between researchers and practitioners can provide a platform for further developing "low politics" issues to cooperate in "high politics." *Second,* social impacts and determinants of intensified scientific and technological change are becoming more salient for the general public, which should motivate policy-makers to address issues such as alternative energy resources more intensively. *Third,* science, technology, and their interaction with international politics make foreign policy decision-making rather complex; old actors with altered interests, as well as new actors and their impact on social and political structures provide an entirely different context.

Improving communication among and between scientists, policy-makers, and the general public is more important in a world in which science and technology is central to all critical global challenges. As this book has shown, through the case study of transatlantic relations, complexity and technical uncertainty impacts policy areas more extensively today than it did in the past. This trend, which is not expected to be different in the coming decades, is manifested in the active networking roles of organizations with a S&T-related mission. As this study supports, through empirical evidence, these types of organizations have a significant role in finding policy solutions to increasingly complex foreign policy problems in transatlantic relations. Combined with the findings on the considerable role that various non-governmental organizations, especially epistemic community-like organizations, play in transatlantic and, potentially, other transnational politics and policies, this research suggests that policy-makers should capitalize on the potentials of virtual communication more extensively. It also suggests that R&D and innovation policies should be at the forefront of foreign policy.

Additionally, findings indicate that transnational agreements, such as the S&T cooperation between the US and the EU or the New Transatlantic Agenda are not unfruitful endeavors in that some of the most actively networking organizations, e.g., the Transatlantic Legislators' Dialogue, originated from such cooperative arrangements. An interesting finding of this research is that these networks demonstrate preferential attachment. The fact that connectivity is concentrated to a number of actors has policy implications for transatlantic cooperation. This book recommends that researchers and policy practitioners consider addressing this issue when planning on further enhancing transatlantic cooperation and look for organizations that are so-called "structural holes" in these networks. *Organizations, such as the American Association for the Advancement of Science (AAAS) or the Global Development Network (GDN), which were found to be fulfilling such roles in the broader as well as in the S&T-specific sub-network, hold latent opportunities to expand the network and enhance network activity.* These have the potential to improve transatlantic networking practices and broaden the network via connecting to and incorporating others. This is especially true for the S&T sub-network, which demonstrates an even stronger centralization.

NOTES

1. Vannevar Bush, *Science the Endless Frontier: A Report to the President on a Program for Postwar Scientific Research* (Washington, D.C., 1945), http://nsf.gov/od/lpa/nsf50/vbush1945.htm.
2. To help categorization, we used the organizational web pages' mission statement. In regards to think tanks, we did the same, but used McGann and Weaver's (2006) list of think tanks and modified the think tank categorization accordingly. James McGann and R. Kent Weaver. *Think Tanks and Civil Societies: Catalysts for Ideas and Action* (New Brunswick: NJ: Transaction Publishers, 2006).
3. Mark A. Pollackand Gregory C. Shaffer (Eds). *Transatlantic Governance in the Global Economy.* (Lanham, MD: Rowman and Littlefield Publishers, Inc., 2001).
4. At "depth1" the shortest path distance is a direct link or one "hop," at "depth2" it can be considered a secondary link or two "hops," while at "depth3" we consider it to be a tertiary link or three "hops" for the crawler.
5. D. Fuhry, Personal communication, January 13, 2010.
6. Viv Cothey, "Web-crawling Reliability," *Journal of the American Society for Information Science and Technology* 55, no. 14 (2004): 1228–1238.
7. While the analysis reported in this study is based on excluding loops, i.e., self-references, we find it essential to note that, based on the broader analysis that showed all loops present, some of the most active organizations' hyperlinking practices demonstrated that their self-references can be in the millions. As an example, Transatlantic Legislators' Dialogue has over one million hyperlinks as loops.
8. We identify the overall transatlantic network through *primary* links as "D1" through *secondary* links "D2" and *tertiary* links "D3."
9. The "kw" references that the S&T sub-networks are potential knowledge networks in a particular policy area.
10. These secondary and tertiary connections were uncovered during the data analyses.
11. Stanley Wasserman and Katherine Faust, *Social Network Analysis. Methods and Applications* (Cambridge, MA: Cambridge University Press, 1994).
12. "Curve fitting is the process of constructing a curve, or mathematical function, that has the best fit to a series of data points" (Wikipedia.com).

13. "A variety of complex systems share an important property: some nodes have a tremendous number of connections to other nodes, whereas most nodes have just a handful . . . In this sense the network appears to have no scale" so there is no typical size of the nodes. Albert L. Barabási and Eric Bonabeau. "Scale-Free Networks." *Scientific American* 288 (May 2003): 52.
14. Soumen Chakrabarti, *Mining the Web: Discovering Knowledge from Hypertext Data* (San Francisco: CA: Morgan Kaufmann Publishers, 2003), 243.
15. Wasserman and Faust, *Social Network Analysis. Methods and Applications*, 348.
16. Ronald S. Burt, *Structural Holes: The Social Structure of Competition*. (Cambridge: Harvard University Press, 1992); Caroline Haythornthwaite, "Social Network Analysis: An Approach and Technique for the Study of Information Exchange." *Library and Information Science Research* 342 (1996): 323–342.
17. Wasserman and Faust, *Social Network Analysis. Methods and Applications*, 170.
18. Wasserman and Faust, *Social Network Analysis. Methods and Applications*.
19. The prominence of OSTP was established in the broader network even *without* incorporating science and technology specific search words into the network analysis.
20. "Transatlantic Information Exchange System (TIES)," http://tiesweb.org/about_ties/history.htm.
21. "TransAtlantic Business Dialogue," http://tabd.com/.
22. The weight attached to ties here is understood as the frequency of interactions among actors that are connected.
23. Tore Opsahl et al., "Prominence and Control: The Weighted Rich-Club Effect," *Physical Review Letters* (2008): 1–4.
24. Wasserman and Faust, *Social Network Analysis. Methods and Applications*.; Opsahl et al., "Prominence and Control: The Weighted Rich-Club Effect."
25. Tore Opsahl, "Tore Opsahl Personal Web Log," 2010, http://toreopsahl.com/.; Angela Bohn et al., "Social Network Analysis of Weighted Telecommunications Graphs," ePub WU Institutional Repository, (March 2009), http://epub.wu.ac.at/708/.
26. Mark S. Granovetter, "The Strength of Weak Ties." *American Journal of Sociology* 78, no. 6 (1973): 1360–1380.
27. Wasserman and Faust, *Social Network Analysis. Methods and Applications*.
28. Opsahl, "Tore Opsahl Personal Web Log."; Opsahl et al., "Prominence and Control: The Weighted Rich-Club Effect."
29. Georg Simmel, *The Sociology of Georg Simmel* (New York, NY: Free Press, 1950).
30. Granovetter, "The Strength of Weak Ties."; Robert D. Putnam, *Bowling Alone: The Collapse and Revival of American Community* (New York, NY: Simon & Schuster, 2000).
31. Simmel was a German sociologist and a structuralist in that he viewed society as a complex system with interrelated ties.
32. Andrea L. Kavanaugh et al., "Weak Ties in Networked Communities," *The Information Society* 21, no. 2 (April 2005): 119.
33. Kavanaugh et al., "Weak Ties in Networked Communities."
34. David Krackhardt, "The Strength of Strong Ties: The Importance of Philos in Organizations," in *Networks and Organizations: Structure, Forms, and Action*, ed. Nitin Nohria and Robert G. Eccles (Boston, MA: Harvard Business School Press, 1992), 216–239.; James S. Coleman, "Social Capital in the Creation of Human Capital," *American Journal of Sociology* 94 (1988): S95–S120; Granovetter, "The Strength of Weak Ties."; Opsahl, "Tore Opsahl Personal Web Log."

35. Jon M. Kleinberg, "Authoritative Sources in a Hyperlinked Environment," in *SODA '98 Proceedings of the Ninth Annual ACM-SIAM Symposium on Discrete Algorithms, Journal of the ACM (JACM)*, 1999, 668–677.
36. Ibid., 3.
37. Wasserman and Faust, *Social Network Analysis. Methods and Applications.*
38. Vladimir Batagelj and Andrej Mrvar, "PAJEK—Program for Analysis and Visualization of Large Networks," Ljubljana, Slovenia, 2009, 28, http://vlado.fmf.uni-lj.si/pub/networks/pajek/doc/pajekman.pdf.
39. These "weights are defined recursively. A higher authority weight occurs if the page is pointed to by pages with high hub weights. A higher hub weight occurs if the page points to many pages with high authority weights" (http://math.cornell.edu/).
40. Ronald S. Burt, "The Network Structure of Social Capital," *Research in Organizational Behavior* 22 (2000): 345–423.
41. Burt, *Structural Holes: The Social Structure of Competition.*
42. Ibid.; Burt, *The Network Structure of Social Capital.*
43. Ronald S. Burt, "Structural Holes and Good Ideas," *American Journal of Sociology* 110, no. 2 (2004): 349–399.
44. Ibid., 37.
45. Pierre Bourdieu and Loïc J.D. Wacquant, *An Invitation to Reflexive Sociology*, (Chicago, IL: University of Chicago Press, 1992), 119.
46. Coleman, "Social Capital in the Creation of Human Capital."; James S. Coleman, *Foundations of Social Theory*, (Cambridge, MA: Harvard University Press, 1990).
47. Sveinn Vidar Gudmundsson and Christian Lechner, "Multilateral Airline Alliances: Balancing Strategic Constraints and Opportunities," *Journal of Air Transport Management* 12, no. 3 (May 2006): 153.
48. Ibid., 154.
49. Ronald S. Burt, "Structural Holes Versus Network Closure as Social Capital," in *Social Capital: Theory and Research*, eds. R. S. Burt, K. Cook, N. Lin (New York, NY: Aldine de Gruyter, 2001), 1.
50. Wouter Nooy, Andrej Mrvar, and Vladimir Batagelj, *Exploratory Social Network Analysis with Pajek* (New York, NY: Cambridge University Press, 2005), 148.
51. Granovetter, "The Strength of Weak Ties."
52. Those with lower values of aggregate constraint are ranked higher.
53. "The American Association for the Advancement of Science," http://aaas.org/aboutaaas/.
54. Alex Bavelas, "A Mathematical Model for Group Structure," *Human Organizations* 7 (1948): 16–30.; Marvin E. Shaw, "Group Structure and the Behavior of Individuals in Small Groups," *The Journal of Psychology* 38, no. 1 (July 1954): 139–149; Wasserman and Faust, *Social Network Analysis. Methods and Applications.*
55. Ronald S. Burt, "The Social Capital of Structural Holes," in *New Directions in Economic Sociology*, eds. Mauro F. Guillén et al. (New York, NY: Russel Sage Foundation, 2005), 156.
56. Linton C. Freeman, "A Set of Measures of Centrality Based on Betweenness," *Sociometry* 40, no. 1 (1977): 35–41; L.C. Freeman, "Centrality in *Social Networks*: I. Conceptual Clarification.," Social Networks 1 (1979): 215–239.
57. Burt, "The Social Capital of Structural Holes," 156.
58. Burt interprets larger networks in this regards as those with more than five members.
59. "The center of a cluster is often a centroid, the average of all the points in the cluster, or a medoid, the 'most representative' point of a cluster." Michael

Steinbach, Levent Ertoz, and Vipin Kumar, "The Challenges of Clustering Highy Dimensional Data," in *New Directions in Statistical Physics: Econophysics, Bioinformatics, and Pattern Recognition,* ed. Luc T. Ville (Berlin, Germany: Springer, 2004), 278.

60. Pang-Ning Tan, Michael Steinbach, and Vipin Kumar, "Data Mining Cluster Analysis: Basic Concepts and Algorithms," 2004, 24, www-users.cs.umn.edu/~kumar/dmbook/dmslides/chap8_basic_cluster_analysis.pdf.
61. Steve Charnovitz, "Participation of Non-governmental Organizations in the World Trade Organization," *University of Pennsylvania Journal of International Economic Law* 17 (1996): 331–357.
62. Derrick L. Cogburn, "In Whose Name?: A Multimodal Exploration of Transnational Deliberative Democratic Practices in Multistakeholder Global Information Policy Formulation Processes" (San Diego, CA: International Studies Association, 2006), 8, http://allacademic.com/meta/p100585_index.html.
63. See Appendix B.
64. James McGann and R. Kent Weaver, *Think Tanks and Civil Societies: Catalysts for Ideas and Action* (New Brunswick: NJ: Transaction Publishers, 2006).
65. Emanuel Adler, "The Emergence of Cooperation: National Epistemic Communities and the International Evolution of the Idea of Nuclear Arms Control," *International Organization* 46, no. 1 (1992): 101–145.
66. Paula J. Dobriansky, "Science, Technology, and Foreign Policy: The Essential Triangle," 2003, http://2001–2009.state.gov/g/rls/rm/2003/20250.htm.
67. "OSTP Press Release" (Office of Science and Technology, 2004), http://ostina.org/index2.php?option=com_content&do_pdf=1&id=414.
68. Álvaro de Vasconcelos and Marcin Zaborowski, eds., "The Obama Moment: European and American Perspectives," *Intereconomics* (European Union Institute for Security Studies, January 29, 2009), 11–12, http://iss.europa.eu/uploads/media/The_Obama_Moment__web_A4.pdf.
69. Louis Pasteur, "Quotationspage.com," accessed March 02, 2007, http://quotationspage.com/quote/27258.html.

6 Conclusion

An invasion of armies can be resisted, but not an idea whose time has come.

—Victor Hugo, 1852[1]

Summing up, this book has investigated cooperative arrangements between transatlantic partners, the European Union and the United States, and their online communication via hyperlink network analysis. This research has argued that detecting online networking practices in these political networks, either governmental or non-governmental, and determining their structure, which characterizes them, can be helpful in the appraisal of transatlantic connections. This book also asserted that individual websites of transatlantic organizations form hyperlink affiliations with others, for the purpose of strengthening relationships and inter-organizational trust. In the networks described and investigated in this book, just as in any type of network, one can uncover the presence of potentially significant and interesting groups of actors inside the network, based on their unique characteristics, by using structural analysis.[2] As explained earlier, several indicators might be used to understand the influence of knowledge network participants, such as key players and listserv and website dominance, as well as publications in, or citation of, academic journals.[3] This book builds on this suggestion. A major purpose of the book has been to unravel the structure of existing transatlantic networks in general, and those that have an influence on cooperative action within the science and technology policy domain, specifically. Links among web pages have the ability to reveal prominent sites and densely knit communities, as well as other characteristics described, in detail, in the earlier chapters. These are typically either computed or otherwise measured.

Furthermore, as emphasized throughout the book, the complex nature of transnational communication and cooperation, coupled with the complex problems that we need to address collectively, require more efficient and proactive responses. As the connection was made earlier, rational knowledge and ideas are the foundation for our intellectual capital and human potential, which enable us to address change. Therefore, ideas as "agents of change" are at the heart of policy learning and policy change.[4] Without making the connection, transnational policy change cannot be realized. Based on the premise that ideas are regarded as "agents of change," *this book proposes that the virtual networking practices of knowledge network members be regarded as "conduits of change."* This is in line with networked governance researcher Lazer's suggestion that the international system is best understood as an informational network, where linkages among sovereign "units in the system are conduits for information."[5]

The question may still arise: Why is this important and how does it connect to studying networks from a political scientist's point of view? An important link here might be the various "faces of power" that provide forceful explanations to social and political phenomena.[6] In social network analysis, structural determinants of power acquisition are strongly related to the concept of centrality, prominence, and prestige, discussed in detail in the previous chapters.[7] Recall that the review of the literature emphasized that putting knowledge into practice requires that two basic conditions be met. First, one must have access to relevant information. Second, once acquired, knowledge needs to be internalized. However, as Lucas points out, to be able to innovate by communication, we need to be aware of this resource's empowering capacities.[8] As organizational theorists, Pfeffer and Salancik argue, the gathering and transmission of information are powerful political resources. As such, these can be regarded as incentives to induce cooperative action among organizations, as well as a means to further legitimize the organization itself.[9]

RESEARCH CONTRIBUTION

This book draws together insights from various theoretical approaches and disciplines and adds to the existing literature in several ways. *First,* it *provides empirical evidence to the theoretical framework* described in Chapter 2, with special regards to the networked modes of governance. To attain this goal, the transatlantic network-system and the specific policy area of scientific and technological cooperation serve as a case study. This way, the *potentials* of the various KNET-influences to create and disseminate knowledge can be mapped. Ideally, the understanding gained from this research, in regards to networking patterns and network capacity, can further assist in developing knowledge-based solutions to address common issues of transnational significance. As one of the transatlantic organizations, the German Marshall Fund, illuminates, "the focus of the Cold War agenda was Europe . . . the focus of the transatlantic agenda is global."[10]

Second, this book contributes to the understanding of the complex nature of transnational communication and cooperation from a network perspective by connecting and synthesizing ideas developed within the various theories and disciplines described in the relevant literature. Embracing multiple dimensions of knowledge helps us enhance our capabilities of understanding the world in which we live. An important task for researchers is to be able to generate synergy among methodological, theoretical, or even empirical skills that can contribute to the success of their research. Also, theories that reflect diverse approaches may capitalize on their complementarities. These ideas are supported by Hall and Taylor's writing on "the three new institutionalisms." Hall and Taylor argue that there is hope for better theories if those theories speak to each other, learn from one another and, perhaps, attempt to pursue an integration of some sort.[11] These theoretical lenses already inspired a number of collaborative efforts across disciplines, such as economics, sociology, psychology, computer science, mathematics, statistics, physics, and to a certain extent, political science. Nonetheless, it seems that *political science, and international relations especially, needs more empirical research using network analysis* to assess the role of virtual networks as facilitators of cooperative arrangements. Overall, the book aims to fill *a still existing gap between the network perspective and the study of international relations in the specific area of transatlantic cooperation.*

Third, this book corroborates Pollack and Shaffer's suggestion that there is a gap in the literature on what constitutes the communicative "linchpin" in transatlantic cooperative relations and that it can be found in the networking practices of transatlantic think tanks, policy research institutes, academics, research analysts and other experts and professionals.[12] *Fourth,* this study aims to find innovative ways to enhance the weakened transatlantic partnership by examining virtual networking practices of transatlantic organizations using state-of-the-art techniques. To my knowledge, *no other research to date has used social network analytical tools and visualization techniques to investigate transatlantic cooperation.*

This book is unique in a number of ways. First, it is one of the few studies that takes on an interdisciplinary endeavor attempting to induce some level of synergy among various theoretical approaches, as well as among various disciplines. This research includes a collaborative effort with Professor Ruoming Jin and his team at the Computer Sciences Department at Kent State University. This represents an innovative approach in political science and, especially, in the subfield of international relations (IR). It is because, in general, IR scholars have not yet benefited from either network theory or from the powerful tools of social network analysis. As Lake and Wong observe, "[d]espite considerable interest in political networks, especially transnational advocacy networks (TANs), political scientists have imported few insights from network theory into their studies."[13] However, "[w]ith respect to *inter-organizational networks* . . .

social network analysis" is of common usage in the literature on alliances in organizational management studies.[14] Network analysis typically requires more of an interdisciplinary investigation by its nature that those who are engaged in networked governance research are beginning to discover.

Second, a key argument of the book is that the behavior and performance of transatlantic organizations can be more fully understood by examining their virtual network of relationships using social network analytic tools. These techniques are proliferating in numerous disciplines, as they prove useful to identifying opinion leaders in an organizational or social system. In agreement with the first and third hypotheses, *this research was not only able to uncover a broader transatlantic network configuration, but also a policy-specific sub-network that exists within the transatlantic community, based on empirical evidence.* This research considered how different network features affect communication and potential knowledge transfer. These virtual networks, which facilitate the exchange and diffusion of information and knowledge, create an environment that is conducive to the generation of new ideas and innovation by communication. In our 21st-century complex environment, communication in the global public, as well as private, spheres via virtual networks might be comparatively more powerful than mass communication through the media.

Third, structural characteristics of these networks, explained and illustrated graphically in Figures 5.10 through 5.13, show remarkable properties. Notably, and *in line with the fourth hypothesis,* this research was able to show, based on empirical evidence, that *these networks constitute scale-free networks, commonly found in virtual social networks, which follow the power-law distribution popularized by Barabási.*[15] However, an *additional finding* that does not exactly conform to the initial expectations might be just as noteworthy. It is the fact that the strength of node connections describes exponential decrease, which shows even *stronger centralization* than the power-law that describes the behavior of the degree of connections. This is because, according to my best knowledge, this has never been found in the literature, which usually describes only the degree of connections without considering their strength. The closest that comes to this is in the research of Opsahl et al. who found a positive and significant "*correlation coefficient between average out-strength (in-strength) and out-degree (in-degree) . . . [which] signals that hubs spend more time and resources with each of their contacts than the less connected users.*"[16] There is no mention of exponential distribution, however.

Fourth, the book addresses the idea of *brokerage as social capital* with the goal of contributing to research on advancing the transatlantic partnership. To my knowledge, *this exact combination of research perspectives cannot be found in the relevant literature.* Previously, this study established that the analysis uncovered transatlantic organizations that qualify as structural holes in the network. This is *in accordance with the fifth hypothesis* that it is possible to locate and point out potential future brokers in the networks. Using structural holes as a measure of brokerage, Burt argues that the brokering of connections between *disconnected network segments creates opportunities* which, in turn, have the ability to generate social capital.[17] From an organizational performance perspective, Nooy, Mrvar, and Batagelj illuminate, "[p]eople or organizations with low aggregate constraint are hypothesized to perform better."[18] Therefore, exploring organizations, labeled as "structural holes," which are network members with low aggregate constraint, hence high autonomy, was an integral part of the research. The expectation is that these network members perform better as brokers. In light of the need for strengthening the transatlantic partnership, the significance lies in the potential brokering roles of these organizations or, using Burt's term, the idea that they can be the "engine[s] for productive change."[19] Recall that from among network members, the *Global Development Network (GDN) and the American Association for the Advancement of Science (AAAS)* have the *potential to play brokering roles* in both networks. Both organizations have strong foundations to advance academic and research endeavors in addition to the fact that they operate with globally extensive reach. Consequently, *the fact that the brokering roles of these organizations as potential focus points are revealed here has significant policy implication for those who aim to enhance the potentials of the transatlantic partnership.*

Fifth, this study addresses whether institutions created by the New Transatlantic Agenda of 1995 fulfill important roles by building bridges across the Atlantic via networking. Although Pollack researched the NTA's performance extensively, the research perspective developed in this book enables us to uncover the particulars of virtual networking practices of transatlantic organizations.[20] This, to my knowledge, has not been previously performed in this context. This study finds that some of these organizations, indeed, play an active role in promoting the partnership, while some others do not. A *major finding* is that the *Transatlantic Legislators' Dialogue (TLD) is one of the most prominent and well-connected members* of the transatlantic networks in *almost every category* of measurement. This dialogue reflects the European Parliament and the US Congress' commitment to the NTA's goal of enhancing parliamentary ties between the European Union and the United States. Two other organizations emerge from among those created by the NTA. These are the *Transatlantic Information Exchange System* (TIES) and the *TransAtlantic Business Dialogue* (TABD). Unlike TLD, however, these are solely prominent in terms of being influential in the network. Hence, they are *not as much sources of information on specific issues, but rather they direct others to sources* and have the ability to exchange or disperse information relatively quickly. TIES is a unique NGO type in the network. TIESWeb was launched by Franck Biancheri, the founder of Newropeans, a uniquely pan-European party. TIESWeb was the first transatlantic web portal dedicated to dialog between European and American civil societies.

Unfortunately, with the recent passing of Biancheri in 2012, it seems that the future of this web portal is uncertain. *TABD* is, in essence, a dialogue system, which includes several interest groups for consumers, labor, environment, and business. This organization is rather active and has been a stable participant in transatlantic relations.

POSITIONING THE RESEARCH IN THE DISCIPLINE

Social network analysis can prove useful in unraveling what types of network structures function well for what kinds of tasks. It is also valuable for uncovering patterns, such as the *impact of structural characteristics on the overall network*. As an example, Leenders and Uzzi found that the "density of connections has [an] inverse U relationship with performance in creative settings."[21] "There are, however, compelling reasons to believe that network structure does affect informational factors that, in turn, affect systemic success."[22] On the individual/node-level analysis of outcomes, the "impact of being in a particular place in the network (e.g., impact of centrality: degree, reachability . . . benefit of brokering between other actors)" could be determined.[23] A key insight is that the network structure of interactions puts constraints on system dynamics through information flow control, and by creating patterns of interaction among network members or components.

Social network analysis not only enables us to *identify key players* in the network, but also permits analysis of various other organizational phenomena. As Weare et al. affirm, both "density and centralization, serve to describe the structure of social networks and are related to the cohesion and democratic character of associations, which are important factors to their performance."[24] Furthermore, *cohesiveness* not only *affects organizational capacity*, but also facilitates information-diffusion, which, again, enhances capacity.[25] Other SNA tools, such as measures of centrality, for example "degree," can refer to prestige or influence of actors in the network; "closeness" may facilitate the ability to effectively communicate; and "betweenness" can point out who the brokers or gatekeepers might be who control information flows in the network.[26]

Even though this research differs in its theoretical focus and argument from other research that uses similar methodology, there are a few studies that employ various forms of social network analysis that are not dissimilar from what this study entails. Some examples from political science are: Carpenter's inquiry into the variations of issue emergence in transnational advocacy networks, Krebs' "Mapping Networks of Terrorist Cells," Schneider et al.'s comparison of networks in the National Estuary Program, and Fischer et al.'s examination of the case of Swiss immigration policy.[27] Other examples from information studies to criminal justice studies to education are: Mueller et al.'s analysis of organizational capacity through the example of Campaign for Communication Rights in the Information Society, Natarajan's investigation of the structure of drug distribution networks, and Song and Miskel's "policy actors' influence on state reading policy."[28] Additionally, Lake and Wong's book chapter on Amnesty International and the emergence of human rights norms represents research that tries to combine insights of network theorists and political scientists. Using network theory, these authors show "the implications of network structure (i.e., quantity and quality of connections) on the emergence of human rights norms."[29]

Although much research has been done on the idea of social networks' transferring information to individuals, research on systemic network structure and systemic-level success and "how network structure affects overall system performance, and in particular, collective problem solving" is, at best, scarce.[30] This book will, hopefully, add to the research on systemic network structure within the transatlantic domain. This research can be placed into the framework of an emerging, yet broader, body of knowledge—the role of information and communication networks in collaborative knowledge production and diffusion in the context of transnational cooperation. This is closely related to the idea of networked and Internet governance, which was elaborated on in the theoretical chapter. Scholars of networked governance like Lazer "conceptualize the international system as an informational network—where the sovereign units in the system produce and process information, and linkages among units in the system are conduits for information."[31]

In addressing new forms of governance and the re-configuration of authority, scholars of international relations engage in exploring the various levels of institutionalization of the policy decision-making process. The role of public and private networking modes of operation is at the core of these scholarly endeavors. Investigating computer-mediated communication (CMC) practices of transnational civil society organizations, Cogburn finds significant civil society participation in global policy networks.[32] Levinson explores knowledge transfer processes in regards to the Internet Governance Forum (IGF), which was "created as a non-decision-making and multi-stakeholder entity as an outcome of the United Nation's World Summit on the Information Society . . . [and] . . . represents an innovation in the complex, nuanced internet governance policy space."[33] As mentioned in Chapter 2, these authors combine global Internet governance with inter-organizational learning, collaboration, knowledge-transfer, and the roles of epistemic community-like entities as they explore different types of multilevel or multi-stakeholder governance. These tie well with the *reciprocal relationship between communication technology and society and, in a broader sense, science, technology, and society, which is an important aspect of this book.*

A notable Europeanist, Sbragia, also investigates multilevel governance from the EU's perspective. She argues that, in this regional organization, the still existing presence of nation-states visibly creates a division between "institutions of nonterritorial politics," such as the European Commission or the European Parliament, as well as "institutions of territorial politics," such as the Council of the European Union.[34] This confirms that the nature of policy has an impact on the modes of governance and the sharing of authority.

THEORETICAL IMPLICATIONS

Addressing the changing nature of our complex, interdependent world, Ikenberry, Keohane, Nye, Slaughter, and others emphasize the importance of a greater diversity of actors, state or non-state. Based on the empirics, this research is able to *support the validity of liberal IR theories and the neoliberal institutionalist approach regarding change in transnational relations.* At the same time, this book also stresses the role of networks that, in general, are more on the informal scale of institutions, as well as it investigates the power of shared ideas and communication through networking patterns. As Risse points out, global governance cannot be separated from the diverse discourses and communication processes that take place as part of this governance process. He further explains that a

> Habermasian perspective on discourse as reasoning introduces transformative potential into the alleged inevitability of globalization . . . if we treat global governance as a political response to globalization to enhance the legitimacy and problem-solving capacity of multilateral institutions, social constructivism helps us to critically examine some of the claims put forward by proponents of deliberative democracy on a global scale . . . [and] allows to discuss some of the trade-offs involved in making global governance more legitimate and more effective.[35]

While Risse's main goal does not appear to be the molding of social constructivism with other approaches to IR, he, nevertheless, draws attention to a powerful idea: the idea that various aspects of globalization, specifically, and, the fast-paced change of the current era, generally, demand that scholars reevaluate their theoretical lenses on a regular basis. Scholars need to become more innovative and initiate more dialogues if their goal is to achieve "a synthetic and genuinely global interdiscipline of international studies."[36] As Hellmann explains, "academic work evaluating and integrating literature is ever more necessary to cope with the explosion of information now facing us." He suggests that scholars invest more in dialogue and synthesis than in debate and pluralism.[37] At the same forum, Moravcsik advocates for a theoretical synthesis when he discusses the need for a "coherent understanding of international relations as a progressive and empirical social science."[38] As this book takes on an interdisciplinary endeavor attempting to induce some level of synergy among various theoretical approaches, as well as among various disciplines, it strives to contribute to the dialogue between neoliberal institutionalists and constructivists.

POLICY IMPLICATIONS

As stated in the introductory section, *this book aims to reveal and draw attention to innovative ways of forging more dynamic and successful transatlantic cooperative arrangements*. This research has future policy implications, especially in light of the fact that the extensive literature on transatlantic relations constantly brings up the dilemma of the weakened transatlantic partnership. In agreement with the majority of these transatlantic scholars, this book also regards the transatlantic partnership as a core element of the international system.

The primary implications of this research reside in finding an emerging network among websites of transatlantic significance, describing the structural patterns of cooperation/affiliation network, and *exploring what the structural characteristics suggest in terms of cooperative power, information access, and knowledge dissemination*. Additionally, attempting to predict in what direction these networks are able to, or will, evolve has important implications for policy.[39] The fact that *these networks demonstrate preferential attachment has policy implications for transatlantic organizations*. If connectivity is concentrated to a number of actors who seem to collaborate among themselves and only slowly reach out to less active network-members, then researchers and policy practitioners need to consider addressing this issue when planning on further enhancing transatlantic cooperation. This also confirms the idea that there can be an *enormous role for* network members that are considered to be *structural holes* in the network. These have the potential to improve transatlantic networking practices and broaden the network via connecting to and incorporating others. The *fact that the S&T sub-network demonstrates an even stronger centralization than the power-law makes us believe that this network has not reached its full potential yet*. At the same time, this feature might give those "shakers and movers" in the network a greater chance to initiate concentrated policy responses.

This study also reflects an effort to combine new findings and results in the various disciplines that already benefited from network theory, and apply it to political science phenomena. This research wants to demonstrate how knowledge networks are enabled by the web and how policy theorists and practitioners could benefit from understanding and capitalizing on this 21st-century resource. Networking modes of operation can be, at a minimum, complementary to the efforts of international regimes or intergovernmental organizations, due to their unique ability to benefit from their less formal network-type influences. *International policy coordination is becoming increasingly difficult and complex; therefore, it calls for new, innovative approaches*. In delivering global public goods, all traditionally applied methods seem to have failed or have been rejected. This suggests that new, innovative ways of thinking and cooperation need to be considered."Today, increasingly complex societies force public officials to develop new governance models."[40] Traditional, hierarchical models of governance might not address 21st-century complex challenges adequately. The communication revolution and widespread reliance on the Internet, in all facets of our political and social lives, necessitate that organizational boundaries be transcended. To create new governance models as responses to these challenges, we witness the emergence of forms of networked governance or governing by networks.[41] Writing about complex systems, Henshaw explains,

> [a]s science has begun to ask where the enduring features of nature come from and how they work, the answer seems to be "complex systems" . . . As the science has advanced, and as the modern problems of [various policy] conflicts emerge, a new kind of science is emerging that requires . . . using all the tools and combining all the related perspectives of others, to develop complex knowledge systems matching the variety of the complex system problems they respond to.[42]

From the book's research perspective, it is important that *complexity is highly sensitive to changes in network topology.*[43] *The link between network structure and dynamics represents one of the most promising areas of complexity research.*

FUTURE DIRECTIONS

Future directions in this research should be guided by a multidimensional approach and, as such, it should be a more interdisciplinary endeavor. Knowledge of the communication context has significant implications for network research. Consequently, networks that operate in the political sphere, and within the transnational context, require that researchers exploit the tools that network research has recently afforded us and, simultaneously, they call for a thorough investigation within the discipline.

First, a comprehensive analysis of how these transatlantic networks, investigated in this study, evolve over time requires that a temporal analysis over a period of several years be pursued. Therefore, this book suggests that this project, which ought to involve a broad exploration of the lifecycle of these hyperlink networks and its implications for political, social, and cultural phenomena, be carried on. Although patterns of organizational networking practices change slowly, progressing this way gives us greater potential for unraveling long-term changes in online structures. Such investigations might further clarify in what particular ways these networking patterns catalyze or constrain future cooperative action in transatlantic relations. As a result, various questions such as the following can be answered. How does the KNET evolve, and how is this process coupled with policy adoption? How can we use the characteristics of KNET structure to predict policy change or vice versa? Are there distinct hyperlink network lifecycles and, if so, how stable or durable are those? What are the implications of those for the success of distinct policies? What are the implications for resource acquisition and allocation?

A *second* future direction lies in a detailed content analysis of all websites in the networks analyzed in this research. Although an enormous undertaking, this could unravel the specifics of the information and knowledge that is being transmitted among network members, and even beyond the network. These investigations could help us answer several questions: Can successes and failures be attributed to, at least to some extent, these communities or networks? Do they contribute to policy change and the emergence of certain regimes? As Haas suggests, "some regimes stem from communities of shared knowledge and not simply from domestic or transnational interest groups."[44]

The *third* suggestion for future directions is to unravel how these networks, investigated in this research, influence global civil societal advocacy networks or transnational advocacy networks (TANS). These TANS are another manifestation of networks of people with more of an activist and policy-advocate, rather than academic, orientation.[45] Further research might reveal the interplay of more civil society-based "unofficial" dialogues, which can prove to be vital elements of the network-system. As Pollack and Shaffer state, the New Transatlantic Agenda created a number of official dialogues as well as initiated several "unofficial," or non-government-supported, dialogues and initiatives that "seek to include a broad spectrum of stakeholders" and make better use of private foundations. Hence the legitimating role of these stakeholders can be uncovered.[46]

As a *fourth* potential future direction, the inclusion of Canadian relations into the transatlantic framework is suggested. Recall that the European Union's delegation to Canada emerged as a significant actor in these transatlantic networks. This should constitute an interesting research direction not yet explored. *Lastly,* another interesting question for future research is to investigate the relationship between institutionalization and networked modes of operation within the transatlantic partnership.

While the first and the last direction involve a rather extensive temporal analysis and visualization of the transatlantic networks, these might be considered ideal for pointing out the progression of the hypothesized communication network among transatlantic network-members. This goal can only be achieved through repeated data-mining and social networks analysis on the same networks over the course of several years. Organizational hyperlinking practices, quite unlike individual social networking habits, are such that they normally demonstrate change over the course of years rather than months, weeks, or daily. Therefore, this temporal analysis should be considered a much larger project, which is a future goal of the author. In regards to these directions, important questions can be answered: What makes these links/networks work? How do their structural characteristics and patterns change over time?[47] To what extent can it be measured? What is it that keeps networks together? Is it mostly power, value homophily, or other phenomena?[48] These recommendations can further address the future development of a transatlantic partnership based on shared knowledge, norms, and understandings.

NOTES

1. Victor Hugo, *History of a Crime (Histoire D'un Crime)*, 2005 reprint (Mondial, 1852).
2. Vladimir Batagelj, "Algorithms for Analysis of Large Networks" (University of Ljubljana, FMF, Dept. of Mathematics; and IMFM Ljubljana, Dept. of Theoretical Computer Science Math/Chem/Comp, Summer school IUC Dubrovnik, June, 16–22, 2008), http://pajek.imfm.si/lib/exe/fetch.php?media=slides:mcc08.pdf.
3. Donald E. Abelson, *Do Think Tanks Matter? Assessing the Impact of Public Policy Institutes* (CA: McGill-Queens University Press, 2002); Peter Hayes, "The Role of Think Tanks in Defining Security Issues and Agendas," 2004, http://nautilus.org/wp-content/uploads/2011/12/1021_Hayes1.pdf; Diane Stone and Andrew Denham, *Think Tank Traditions, Policy Research and the Politics of Idea* (Manchester, UK: Manchester University Press, 2004).
4. Steven W. Hook, "Ideas and Change in U.S. Foreign Aid: Inventing the Millennium Challenge Corporation," *Foreign Policy Analysis* 4, no. 2 (April 2008): 148.
5. D. Lazer, "Regulatory Capitalism as a Networked Order: The International System as an Informational Network," *The ANNALS of the American Academy of Political and Social Science* 598, no. 1 (March 1, 2005): 52.
6. P. Bachrach and M. S. Baratz, "Two Faces of Power," *American Political Science Review* 56, no. 4 (1962): 947–952.
7. Stanley Wasserman and Katherine Faust, *Social Network Analysis. Methods and Applications* (Cambridge, MA: Cambridge University Press, 1994).
8. Chris Lucas, "Synergy and Complexity Science," *Complexity & Artificial Life Research Concept for Self-Organizing Systems,* CALResCo, 2006. www.calresco.org/wp/synergy.htm.
9. Jeffrey Pfeffer and Gerald R. Salancik, *The External Control of Organizations: A Resource Dependence Perspective* (New York, NY: Harper and Row, 1978).
10. The German Marshall Fund of the United States, *Framing a Transatlantic Agenda for a Global Era, Discussion Panel at the Brussels Forum: Transatlantic Challenges in a Global Era* (Brussels, Belgium, 2006), http://gmfus.org/doc/ProgramBrochure_inside.pdf.
11. A. Hall and C. R. Taylor, "Political Science and the Three New Institutionalisms," *Political Studies* 44, no. 5 (1996): 936–957.
12. Mark A. Pollack and Gregory C. Shaffer, *Transatlantic Governance in the Global Economy*, ed. Mark A. Pollack and Gregory C. Shaffer, (Lanham, MD: Rowman and Littlefield Publishers, 2001).
13. David Lake and Wendy H. Wong, "The Politics of Networks: Interest, Power, and Human Rights Norms," in *Networked Politics: Agency, Power, and Governance*, ed. Miles Kahler (Ithaca, NY: Cornell University Press, 2009), 1–2.
14. Ines Mergel and T. Langenberg, "What Makes Online Ties Sustainable? A Research Design Proposal to Analyze Online Social Networks," *Harvard Program on Networked Governance* (2006), 6, http://hks.harvard.edu/netgov/files/png_workingpaper_series/PNG06-002_WorkingPaper_MergelLangenberg.pdf.

15. Albert L. Barabási and Eric Bonabeau, "Scale-Free Networks," *Scientific American* 288 (May 2003): 60–69.
16. Tore Opsahl et al., "Prominence and Control: The Weighted Rich-Club Effect," *Physical Review Letters* (2008): 1–4.
17. Ronald S. Burt, "Structural Holes Versus Network Closure as Social Capital," in *Social Capital: Theory and Research,* eds. R.S. Burt, K. Cook, N. Lin. (New York, NY: Aldine de Gruyter, 2001).
18. Wouter Nooy, Andrej Mrvar, and Vladimir Batagelj, *Exploratory Social Network Analysis with Pajek* (New York, NY: Cambridge University Press, 2005), 148.
19. Burt, "Structural Holes and Good Ideas," 36.
20. Mark A. Pollack, "The New Transatlantic Agenda at Ten: Reflections on an Experiment in International Governance," *JCMS: Journal of Common Market Studies* 43, no. 5 (December 2005): 899–919.
21. Roger Th.A.J Leenders, Jo M.L van Engelen, and Jan Kratzer, "Virtuality, Communication, and New Product Team Creativity: a Social Network Perspective," *Journal of Engineering and Technology Management* 20, no. 1–2 (June 2003): 69–92; Brian Uzzi and J. Spiro, "Collaboration and Creativity: The Small World Problem1," *American Journal of Sociology* 111, no. 2 (2005): 447–504; David Lazer, "An Introduction to Social Network Analysis," 2007, 11, http://hks.harvard.edu/netgov/files/sna/dg.O_2007_SNA_Tutorial_DLazer.pdf.
22. David Lazer and Allan Friedman, "The Tragedy of the Network," in *American Sociological Association, Montreal Convention Center* (Montreal, Quebec, Canada, 2006), 2, http://citation.allacademic.com/meta/p105078_index.html.
23. Lazer, "An Introduction to Social Network Analysis," 11.
24. Christopher Weare, W.E. Loges, and N Oztas, "Email Effects on the Structure of Local Associations: A Social Network Analysis," *Social Science Quarterly* 88, no. 1 (2007): 223.
25. James S. Coleman, "Social Capital in the Creation of Human Capital," *American Journal of Sociology* 94 (1988): S95–S120; James S. Coleman, *Foundations of Social Theory* (Cambridge, MA: Harvard University Press, 1990); Burt, *The Network Structure of Social Capital.*; N. S. Contractor and P.R. Monge, "Managing Knowledge Networks," *Management Communication Quarterly* 16, no. 2 (November 1, 2002): 249–258; E.M. Rogers, *Diffusion of Innovations*, 5th ed. (New York, NY: Free Press, 2003).; John Scott, *Social Network Analysis: A Handbook*, 2nd ed. (Thousand Oaks, CA: Sage Publications Ltd., 2000).; Weare, Loges, and Oztas, "Email Effects on the Structure of Local Associations: A Social Network Analysis."
26. Kelvin Chan and Jay Liebowitz, "The Synergy of Social Network Analysis and Knowledge Mapping: A Case Study," *International Journal of Management and Decision Making* 7, no. 1 (2006): 19–35.
27. R. Charli Carpenter, "Setting the Advocacy Agenda: Theorizing Issue Emergence and Nonemergence in Transnational Advocacy Networks," *International Studies Quarterly* 51 (2007): 99–120; V.E. Krebs, "Mapping Networks of Terrorist Cells," *Connections* 24, no. 3 (2002): 43–52; Mark Schneider and John Scholz, "Building Consensual Institutions: Networks and the National Estuary Program," *American Journal of Political Science* 47, no. 1 (January 2003): 143–158; Andreas Fischer, Sarah Nicolet, and Pascal Sciarini, "Europeanisation of a Non-EU Country: The Case of Swiss Immigration Policy," *West European Politics* 25, no. 4 (2002): 143–170.
28. Milton L. Mueller, Brenden N. Kuerbis, and Christiane Pagé, "Democratizing Global Communication? Global Civil Society and the Campaign for Communication Rights in the Information Society," *International Journal of*

Communication 1 (2007): 267–296; Mangai Natarajan, "Understanding the Structure of a Large Heroin Distribution Network: A Quantitative Analysis of Qualitative Data," *Journal of Quantitative Criminology* 22, no. 2 (June 9, 2006): 171–192; M. Song, "Who Are the Influentials? A Cross-State Social Network Analysis of the Reading Policy Domain," *Educational Administration Quarterly* 41, no. 1 (February 1, 2005): 7.

29. Lake and Wong, "The Politics of Networks: Interest, Power, and Human Rights Norms," 138.
30. Lazer and Friedman, "The Dark Side of the Small World: How Efficient Information Diffusion Drives Out Diversity and Lowers Collective Problem Solving Ability," 4.
31. Lazer, "Regulatory Capitalism as a Networked Order: The International System as an Informational Network."
32. Derrick L. Cogburn, "Diversity Matters, Even at a Distance: Evaluating the Impact of Computer-Mediated Communication on Civil Society Participation in the World Summit on the Information Society," *Information Technologies and International Development* 1, no. 3 (2004): 15–40.
33. Nanette S. Levinson, "Unexpected Allies in Global Governance Arenas? Cross-Cultural Collaborative Knowledge Processes & the Internet Governance Forum," Paper Presented at the Annual Meeting of The International Studies Association's Annual Convention." In *"Theory vs. Policy? Connecting Scholars and Practitioners."* New Orleans: International Studies Association, 2010, www.allacademic.com/meta/p413163_index.html.
34. Alberta M. Sbragia, "Thinking About the European Future: The Uses of Comparison," in *Euro-Politics. Institutions and Policymaking in the "New" European Community*, ed. Alberta M. Sbragia (Washington, D.C.: The Brookings Institution, 1992).; Alberta M. Sbragia, "The European Community: a Balancing Act," *Publius: The Journal of Federalism* 23, no. 3 (1993): 23–38.
35. Thomas Risse, "Social Constructivism Meets Globalization," In *Globalization Theory: Approaches and Controversies,* eds. Anthony McGrew and David Held (Cambridge, UK: Polity Press, 2007).
36. Thomas J. Biersteker, "Eroding Boundaries, Contested Terrain," *International Studies Review* 1, no. 1 (June 1999): 4–5; Hellmann, "THE FORUM Are Dialogue and Synthesis Possible in International Relations?," *International Studies Review* 5 (2003): 123–153.
37. Ibid., 123.
38. Andrew Moravcsik, "Theory Synthesis in International Relations: Real Not Metaphysical," *International Studies Review* 5 (2003): 131.
39. Recall that structural holes fulfill brokerage roles that help us determine future directions of network development.
40. William D. Eggers and Stephen Goldsmith, *Governing by Network: The New Shape of the Public Sector* (Washington, D.C.: Brookings Institution Press, 2004).
41. Ibid.
42. P. F. Henshaw (Lead Author) and Mark McGinley (Topic Editor), "Complex Systems," in *Encyclopedia of Earth*, ed. Cutler J. Cleveland (Washington, D.C.: Environmental Information Coalition, National Council for Science and the Environment, 2009), 1, http://eoearth.org/view/article/151405.
43. O. Sporns, G. Tononi, and G. M. Edelman, "Theoretical Neuroanatomy: Relating Anatomical and Functional Connectivity in Graphs and Cortical Connection Matrices," *Cerebral Cortex* 10, no. 2 (February 2000): 127–41.

44. Peter M. Haas, "Do Regimes Matter? Epistemic Communities and Mediterranean Pollution Control," *International Organization* 43, no. 3 (Summer 1989): 377.
45. Margaret E. Keck and Kathryn Sikkink, *Activists Beyond Borders: Advocacy Networks in International Politics* (Ithaca, NY: Cornell University Press, 1998).
46. Pollack and Shaffer, *Transatlantic Governance in the Global Economy*, 274.
47. Structural characteristics can be clustering, degree distribution, or some others.
48. "Similarity breeds connection. This principle—the homophily principle—structures network ties of every type, including marriage, friendship, work, advice, support, information transfer, exchange, comembership, and other types of relationship. The result is that people's personal networks are homogeneous with regard to many sociodemographic, behavioral, and intrapersonal characteristics. Homophily limits people's social worlds in a way that has powerful implications for the information they receive, the attitudes they form, and the interactions they experience" (McPherson, Smith-Lovin, and Cook, 2001, p. 415).

Appendix A
Research Appendix—Methodology

DATA AND DATA COLLECTION

As mentioned before, the data gathered and analyzed in this study, are *network data*. The major difference between conventional and network data is that conventional data focus on actors and attributes, while network data focus on actors and relations; hence, network analysis considers "data on ties among the units."[1] The unit of analysis used to designate structural connections in the potential knowledge network (KNET) is an Internet hyperlink from one network member to another. The members, or "nodes," are comprised of organizations engaged in the New Transatlantic Agenda.[2]

Using hyperlink network analysis and data-mining techniques, this study first identified websites (URLs) of 87 core organizations that were considered most salient in pursuing transatlantic relations. First, a manual search was performed to specify these initial "nodes" by utilizing the Google search engine and keyword analysis. Key words and terms were used, such as "EU–US," "transatlantic relations," "transatlantic connections," "EU–US cooperation," and "transatlantic cooperation." In the initial stage of this research a web crawler, developed by the Department of Computer Science at Kent State University, was used and configured to stop after it crawled all pages.[3] The crawler found that those specified 87 URLs link directly to approximately 4,300 pages or websites at "depth1."[4] "Depth1" involves direct links from one website to another, while "depth2" represents the network through secondary connections, i.e. two "hops" from page to page to reach these nodes, while "depth3" represents tertiary links in this network. These sites, in turn, link to approximately 70,000 pages at "depth2."[5] Those 4,300 "depth1" pages link to about 70,000 distinct pages not yet included in the seed URLs' pages or other "depth1" pages.[6]

The next step was to determine connectivity values for these pages, therefore all hyperlinks out of those pages of interest were followed as well. As Borgatti explains, key players in the network, in other words opinion leaders in a social network, could be pointed out using network centrality values. The higher the value, the more it is likely that these actors are indeed key players whose activities are significant in inducing changes in policy.[7] After identifying network properties, such as connectivity, the web crawler moved onto "depth3."[8] It continued by following the hyperlinks out of those 70,000 pages. This revealed 1.2 million new pages, which we call "depth3" pages.[9] This is equivalent to an initial analysis of 1.2 million pages of material on this topic.

To summarize the procedure briefly, each depth refers to a web page's shortest distance path length to any of those 87 core sites or URLs.[10] The path length is the number of hyperlinked pages that needs to be traversed to get from one page to another.[11] It might be interpreted as the number of "clicks" one needs to make to get to the destination page from the homepage.

This process, called "web crawling" or "spidering," during which a crawler that is essentially a computer program iteratively and automatically downloads web pages. The crawler is supplied by the initial seed home pages and then downloads the rest of the site, or it could "also perform additional calculations during the crawl in order to identify pages judged relevant to the crawl or to reject pages as duplicates of ones previously visited."[12] In sum, "the hyperlinks contained on those pages are identified and subsequently crawled . . . [and this] process continues until the crawler is stopped."[13]

The extensive search by the data-mining technique resulted in the discovery of a few additional websites judged relevant by the program. These are reported in detail when the findings are being discussed. What this research has found is that this boundary refinement produced only a few links that are noteworthy for the intensity of their connections. Even some of those, which emerged as significant, were typically closely related to one of those 87 seeds. There were only two corporate websites and a few others present that have most certainly nothing to do with transatlantic relations, but, rather, their presence has to do with the nature of the web.

DATA CODING

The core transatlantic network is constituted by organizations of various types, as noted earlier. For practical purposes, these organizations are coded using three- or four-letter acronyms (see Appendix B for full names, abbreviations, and websites of these organizations). To implement the sub-network specification, a list of key words and key terms was created, illustrated in Table A.1, which were additionally fed into the WebCrawler. To make a sound selection of search words and terms key terms that frequently appear in the wording of the *EU–US Agreement for Scientific and Technological Cooperation* were used.

Table A.1 Key Words Used for a Web Crawl to Generate and Specify a Science and Technology Specific Sub-network

Keywords	Key terms
science/scientific	alternative energy resources
technology/technological	science and technology
research	science and technology policy
innovation	research and development
energy	
renewable	
NSF/National Science Foundation	
R&D	
knowledge	
collaboration	
alternative	
biotechnology	
nanotechnology	

DATA ANALYZING TECHNIQUES

The best known role for web crawlers is to uncover sources conventional search engines cannot see and, also, to collect and update data in the search engine's index.[14] These crawlers run continuously and extract digital links unobtainable through manual data-gathering techniques. Data-mining, a form of knowledge-discovery in databases, involves automatically searching large stores of data for meaningful or interpretable patterns.[15] It is especially suited for analyzing structural/relational data, because "[t]he structural approach emphasizes the value of network analysis for uncovering deeper patterns beneath the surface of empirical interactions."[16] "Relations reflect emergent dimensions of complex social systems that cannot be captured by simply summing or averaging its members' attributes."[17] Therefore, the network perspective provides an approach that is better suited to investigate 21st-century social complexities.

Since social networks are best represented by graphs, a remark is in order about recent developments in this area. A sub-area of data-mining, known as Graph Mining, which focuses on graph analysis, and large graphs in particular, is becoming more prevalent.[18] Research on social network analysis within the computer science discipline, in data-mining specifically, is fairly new and received more attention only in recent years. As Chakrabarti and others observe, research on social network analysis in the data-mining community now includes clustering analysis, link prediction, PageRank, and Hub-Authority, as well as classification.[19] Recently, more extensive research has been conducted on complex social relationships. This includes both data-mining and social network analysis. Therefore, integrating the two seems to be rather promising in uncovering the structure and the underlying relationships in complex systems. As a case study by Yang et al. on terrorism asserts, networked data-mining holds sufficient promise for future research.[20]

Social network analysis and, more broadly, the network perspective seem to have attracted considerable interest in the various disciplines, the social sciences being no exception. Wasserman and Faust argue that an undeniable advantage of the network perspective is that it provides additional leverage to address social scientific research questions. Wasserman and Faust further explain that SNA does so by exploring patterns of relationships among social entities and "by giving precise formal definition to aspects of the political, economic, or social structural environment . . . [through] finding the presence [or absence] of regular patterns in relationships as *structure.*"[21]

The network perspective seems to be nearing its apex, in no small part, due to the scholarly desire to disentangle the growing number of complex phenomena in nature and society. Social and political structures are, in themselves, complex systems, and the combination of those with virtual communication structures requires that researchers increasingly take a more interdisciplinary approach to studying these. Combining the aforementioned idea with Wasserman and Faust's description of social network analysis as inherently interdisciplinary makes it intuitive that researchers in the various disciplines could benefit greatly from collaboration using the network perspective.[22]

Kenis and Schneider argue that the "network perspective conveys its own picture of the world, its particular epistemological background . . . implies a new perception of causal relations in social processes." Examining the social world from this new perspective, social organization and governance become more decentralized concepts in which coordination of action emerges from the deliberate interaction of network members. As Kenis and Schneider further explain, the network "perspective—like the older perspectives, too—is shaped by time and by the information age, and thus is more or less influenced by information and communication theory."[23,24]

This study employs exploratory social network analysis, the purpose of which is to detect and interpret meaningful patterns that are not previously specified. As Nooy, Mrvar, and Batagelj explain, the four elements of exploratory social network analysis can be specified as the "definition of the network, network manipulation, determination of structural features, and visual inspection."[25] In social network analysis, the unit of observation is typically actors or a set of actors, which can be collective social units and/or relational ties or events. Wasserman and Faust assert that the power of SNA lies "in the ability to model the relationships among systems of actors."[26] In this research, the units of observation are transatlantic organizations, identified as network members. As Wasserman and Faust describe, "relation refers to the collection of ties of a given kind measured on pairs of actors from a specified actor set."[27] Relational quantification may uncover two significant properties: whether relations are directional or nondirectional and whether they are dichotomous or valued. If relations are valued, then the strength, frequency, and intensity of those ties can all be defined and analyzed.[28]

In regards to evaluating social relations, Wasserman and Faust emphasize three dimensions: direction, strength, and content. They define direction as an indication of who the sender and the receiver are in the relation. A distinction between "edges" and "arcs" should be pointed out.[29] These established linkages among actors are called edges or unordered pairs of vertices if those lines are undirected, while arcs are what we call ordered pairs of vertices or directed lines.[30] The networks in this study are directed, and the direction shows which transatlantic organization references the other via hyperlinking. Direction also shows who sends information to whom. When the direction of the resource flow is irrelevant, the relation among actors or nodes is considered to be undirected. In such cases, there is no information on either the sender or the receiver. The World Wide Web is an example of a directed graph. The files are the vertices, while links among files are the directed edges or arcs. Strength of ties is defined as the frequency of interactions, or communication frequency among actors. In this research, strength denotes how often two organizations are referencing one another via hyperlinks. Lastly, content defines the kind of resources being exchanged.[31]

In order be able to identify the most important or prominent actors in the network, prominence could be further divided into centrality and prestige, which, in turn, helps us clarify the concept.[32] Centrality refers to the actor's connection with or to other actors in the network and is usually used for undirected graphs. Centrality then denotes a dichotomous relation between each pairs of actors, i.e., a relationship is either present or absent.[33] In directed networks, however, such as the ones investigated in this research, prominence is understood as prestige. Wasserman and Faust illuminate that "the notion of prestige . . . can only be quantified by using relations for which we can distinguish 'choices' sent from choices received by the actors." Prestige, then, indicates who has power in the network or who is "in charge." In the case of directed networks, such as our case, degree centrality can be divided into two distinct measures: "in-degree" and "out-degree."[34] Degree is the number of direct connections an actor has with other actors in the network. Hanneman and Riddle explain that "[a]ctors who have more ties have greater opportunities because they have choices. This autonomy makes them less dependent on any specific other actor, and hence more powerful."[35] A network actor, which is the recipient of numerous ties, has a higher value of in-degree. This indicates higher prestige or prominence, whereas actors with high out-degree are able to exchange or disperse information relatively quickly to others and so they are characterized as influential.

"Betweenness," an additional measure of centrality as well as an "aspect of a structurally advantaged position," provides certain actors with "the capacity to broker contacts among other actors—to extract 'service charges' and to isolate actors or prevent contacts."[36] As Wassermann and Faust explain, "betweenness" is the extent to which an actor sits along the communication path between nodes, or pairs of nodes, that are not connected.[37,38] By having a strategic location on a communication path between two others, a node essentially holds power to influence information flow; it may even withhold or distort information. "Betweenness" can be regarded as a measure of the degree to which a node serves as a bridge that can essentially act as a bottleneck to information flow.[39] High "betweenness" indices refer to higher levels of brokerage power for actors. Wassermann and Faust use Padgett and Ansell's classic analysis on elite networks to demonstrate that the Medici had higher "betweenness" centralization indices than their competitors.[40] Padgett and Ansell's research on the family and business relations of Florentine families during the early Renaissance is often used as an example in the relevant literature, because their study ultimately explains the rise of the Medici.[41]

In directed networks, such as these transatlantic networks and their subnetworks examined in this study, we can usually identify two types of important vertices: hubs and authorities. These are distinct measures of prestige, which seem especially useful in the case of directed networks of homepages on the World Wide Web where the direction is an important measure of the relationship. As Mrvar and Batagelj explain, "[e]ach home page describes something (is an authority) and because of that other pages point to it. But on the other hand, each page points to some other pages (is a hub)."[42] Following Kleinberg's definition on those important measures, authorities are highly relevant pages that are pointed to by numerous "good" hubs, while hubs are pages that point to many relevant pages, i.e., authorities. In sum, a good authority is a page with several in-links, authoritative or otherwise valuable content on a certain topic, which others trust and link to.[43] A page is considered a good hub if it has numerous out-links and it serves as "an organizer of the information on a particular topic and points to many good authority pages on the topic."[44] Hassel adds, "authorities and hubs have a mutual reinforcement relationship."[45] In terms of prestige, it becomes intuitive that a good authority is highly prestigious, while a good hub has high-reflected prestige.[46,47] In conclusion, prestige refers to the fact that an actor is the recipient of other actors' connection, and it is typically used for directed graphs. Prestige is especially relevant for analyzing and predicting organizational behavior.

Recall from earlier in this study that brokerage measures the extent of bridging connections, and a bridge is defined as a tie, the removal of which splits off the community, increasing the number of components. Bridges have the ability to act as bottlenecks to information flow that, quite evidently, affords control.[48] Brokerage can be measured by betweenness and structural holes. The introduction of the term "structural hole" is attributed to Burt, who argued that an essential part of a social structure is through links that do not exist.[49] "By systematically exploring the absence of useful relation of individuals," and/or organizations of any given community, competitive advantages could be gained and capitalized on.[50] These structural holes or connections of nonredundant contacts, using Burt's description, conceal opportunities ready to be exploited and link together disparate network segments via brokers and weak ties.[51] As an example, an emerging relationship between the director of a professional association and an industrial company's CEO seeking customers who belong to this professional association is a structural hole. Gaining access is a key in such relationships, and the head of the association can fulfill the role of a broker helping the company to gain access to its members.

The way Pajek handles locating structural holes is that it computes proportional strength of relations: both dyadic constraints and aggregate constraints for all vertices.[52] While the former can be defined as a constraint between two nodes or actors in the network, the latter is the sum of all dyadic constraints of any given node or actor. The lower the constraint, the greater the freedom of action and success in being able to exploit the position; and the higher the constraint, the less freedom actors will have to either withdraw from existing ties or to be able to exploit the opportunities that come with being a structural hole.[53]

Additional social network analytical measures, such as cliques and islands, measure network cohesiveness. Wasserman and Faust explain the term cliques as fully connected sub-networks or a "maximal complete sub-graph of three or more nodes."[54] Intuitively, a clique with more actors would be considered more cohesive. A "clique is a maximal complete subgraph . . . with "k" possible vertices and all possible [connections] edges [or arcs] among them."[55] A clique may be strictly defined by those subgroups whose only connection is to other members, known as "p-cliques." A unique kind of partition of the vertices to cohesive clusters according to weights of vertices is called "islands." To determine these involves the partition of the vertices of the network with values on lines, or weights, to cohesive clusters, where the weights inside clusters must be larger than weights to neighborhood.[56] Here "the height of a vertex (vector) is defined as the maximum weight of the neighbor lines."[57] To sum up, it is the network type and application that will best direct the researcher towards what measures to make use of from the numerous available ones for network analysis.

Network analysis can be employed to examine the interactions between nodes, i.e., actors, groups, or institutions. Additionally, it intends to measure information or other resource flows between nodes. Investigating network interactions on the World Wide Web lends itself to gathering what is called relational data or ties and connections among agents that constitute a larger relational system.[58] The specific form of social network analysis performed in this study is hyperlink analysis, which is, essentially, SNA applied to cyberspace.[59]

Such linking practices work on the analogy of social connections. This allows for empirically mapping networks of common meaning and purpose as represented by online linking practices.[60] Barabási suggested that the assumption is that hyperlinks connecting websites function as citations, hence they represent both a membership in a common ideational community as well as a form of acknowledgement of authority. In other words, they demarcate associational space.[61] This way, the mapping of network elements and boundaries can be realized.

As Chakrabarti illuminates, "[t]he World Wide Web is the largest and most widely known repository of hypertext. Hypertext documents contain text and generally embed hyperlinks to other documents distributed across the Web."[62] Although Chakrabarti traces the origins of hypertext specifically, and the idea of citation in general, to the beginnings of written language and the Talmud's annotations, he admits that in modern times it was Vannevar Bush's 1945 work on a computing device called "Memex," and also Nelson's proposed Xanadu hypertext system, that brought the idea of hypertext to the fore.[63,64] Bush's intuition about the exponential expansion and the need for summing up, storing, and being able to track the human experience has proved true. Nelson on the other hand is credited with coining the term "hypertext," although he defined it as "non-sequential writing," and later the term became limited to computers only.[65]

There are a number of statistical algorithms frequently used to uncover patterns[66] and similarities among actors in networks as well as facilitate classification.[67] Cluster analysis is such a statistical algorithm devised to reveal sub-groups or clusters of actors tied together, but not tied to other groups.[68] In more general terms, clustering is used to partition a set of data so that objects in the same cluster are more similar to one another than they are to objects in other clusters. There are other kinds of substructures, for example cliques that I discussed previously. As Hanneman and Riddle explain, "[t]his view of social structure focuses attention on how solidarity and connection of large social structures can be built up out of small and tight components: a sort of "bottom up" approach."[69]

In this research, spectral clustering has been used to perform cluster analysis. There are many different ways of clustering data, but recently spectral clustering has become the most popular technique used for cluster analysis. A technique and/or approach that is based on the idea of weighted graph partitioning is described, in detail, in Meilă and Pentney's paper, "Clustering by weighted cuts in directed graphs."[70] For the purposes of this study, it is not necessary to go into the details of this data-mining technique, but the basic idea is that the researcher cuts "a weighted graph into a number of disjoint pieces, i.e. clusters, such that the intra-cluster weights or similarities are high and the inter-cluster weights are low."[71] Additionally, clustering by weighted cuts, as described by Meilă and Pentney, has an advantage over other methods, because networks that are asymmetric need to be symmetrized before applying clustering. In this case, some of the clustering present in the original asymmetric network might disappear, or at least, becomes invisible. Overall, spectral clustering outperforms other, traditional partition-based clustering algorithms such as "k-means" in efficiency and accuracy.[72]

VISUAL REPRESENTATION WITH PAJEK

Although there are several computer programs for social network analysis, the software programs used for analyzing the emerging network in this particular project were "GraphViz" and mainly "Pajek." The data collected cannot only be analyzed, but can also be visually represented as a network using Pajek.[73] GraphViz is an open source graph drawing tool for laying out connectivity graphs. It is a "way of representing structural information as diagrams of abstract graphs and networks. Automatic graph drawing has many important applications in software engineering, database and web design, in networking and in visual interfaces for many other domains."[74] This software is different from the other software, Pajek, in various ways, but most importantly it does not perform analysis or collect or create data. It is fundamentally a graph-drawing tool to connect nodes and edges and visualize the resulting graph in the two-dimensional space.[75] GraphViz proved useful in the initial mapping of the networks.

Pajek, which means "spider" in Slovenian, is a program run on Windows suitable for the analysis and visualization of large networks.[76] This freely available software for noncommercial purposes was developed by Batagelj and Mrvar. This program, along with others in the same category, has been used to visualize a wide variety of networks, such as biological phenomena or communication networks. The program's main goals are as follows. The first is to support the forming of a general concept by extracting common features from specific examples via factorization or partitioning the larger network into its elementary parts, i.e., smaller networks.[77] This facilitates the dissecting and scrutinizing of those smaller sub-networks and units with greater precision. The second goal is to provide a visualization tool, and the third is to select "efficient algorithms for analysis of large networks." In order to achieve these goals "Pajek provides an interface for graph visualization and implements many algorithms for network and graph analysis such as paths, flows, clustering, generalizations, partitions, and decompositions."[78] It is a great resource for Pajek users to be able to manipulate their networks by extracting a part of their network to inspect based on particular criteria, for example the strength of connections between entities that are beyond or above a certain value.[79]

These analytical procedures do not alter the original network; rather, they provide better visualization for the researcher on parts of a network or sub-networks. As Nooy, Mrvar, and Batagelj argue, within social network analytical techniques "some measures pertain to the entire network, whereas others summarize the structural position of a sub-network or a single vertex."[80] To optimize the graph layout iteratively, the Kamada-Kawai spring layout algorithm was used, where all nodes are connected by springs with a resting length proportional to the length of the shortest path between them.[81]

In a network, nodes are connected by lines that represent relationships. I established earlier that the networks in this research should be regarded as directed, so the graphs generated by Pajek represent and visualize them as such. An additional step was needed during the exploratory analysis with the software. This is because loops or self-lines that are interpreted as self-references were deleted. Loops have importance when evaluating the total number of events, but loops are arcs to themselves that should not be regarded as interaction if we want to uncover what information, and potential knowledge, flows through links among actors.

NOTES

1. Stanley Wasserman and Katherine Faust, *Social Network Analysis. Methods and Applications* (Cambridge, MA: Cambridge University Press, 1994), 21.
2. A node can be any entity in a network: a person, system, group, or organization.
3. A web crawler is a computer program that browses and gathers information on the web in a methodical, automated manner.
4. URL refers to a Uniform Resource Locator, i.e., a unique address for a file, document, or other resource that is accessible on the World Wide Web. A site links to another page if the web page or its sub-pages contain a hyperlink, which directs the user to an outside page. An outside page is considered to be at "depth 1" away from the original URL, when the aforementioned original site or its immediate sub-pages link *directly* to that outside page (D. Fuhry, personal communication, January 13, 2010).
5. Those 4,300 outside pages may themselves link to other pages of interest. We call these newly identified pages "depth 2" pages (D. Fuhry, personal communication, January 13, 2010).
6. Personal communication with D. Fuhry, January 13, 2010.
7. Stephen P. Borgatti, "Identifying Sets of Key Players in a Social Network," *Computational and Mathematical Organization Theory* 12, no. 1 (April 2006): 21–34.
8. This means that we repeat the process for the third time and follow all hyperlinks out of those 70,000 pages, which were not already included in seed URLs or depth 1 or depth 2 pages (D. Fuhry, personal communication, January 13, 2010).
9. Personal communication with D. Fuhry, January 13, 2010.
10. At "depth 1" the shortest path distance is a direct link or one "hop," at "depth 2" it can be considered a secondary link or two "hops," while at "depth 3" we consider it to be a tertiary link or three "hops" for the crawler.
11. Personal communication with D. Fuhry January 13, 2010.
12. M. Thelwall, "A Web Crawler Design for Data Mining," *Journal of Information Science* 27, no. 5 (October 01, 2001): 319.

13. Personal communication with D. Fuhry January 13, 2010.
14. Ibid.
15. Soumen Chakrabarti, *Mining the Web: Discovering Knowledge from Hypertext Data* (San Francisco: CA: Morgan Kaufmann Publishers, 2003).
16. David Knoke and Song Yang, *Social Network Analysis, Quantitative Applications in the Social Sciences Series*, 2nd ed., (London, UK: Sage Publications, 2008), 3.
17. Ibid., 7.
18. Data mining is essentially an umbrella term used in a wide variety of contexts, and there seems to be no consensus in the scholarly literature where data mining ends and social network analysis begins or what is their common domain. In fact, the two fields are becoming increasingly related.
19. Chakrabarti, *Mining the Web: Discovering Knowledge from Hypertext Data.*
20. Yu-Bin Yang, Ni Li, and Yao Zhang, "Networked Data Mining Based on Social Network Visualizations," *Journal of Software* 19, no. 8 (October 22, 2008): 1980–1994.
21. Wasserman and Faust, *Social Network Analysis. Methods and Applications*, 3, 3. Emphasis in original.
22. Wasserman and Faust, *Social Network Analysis. Methods and Applications.*
23. "According to Krippendorf (1989: 443), the science of control and communication (i.e., cybernetics) 'is fundamentally concerned with . . . how organization emerges and becomes constituted by networks and communication processes, and how wholes behave as a consequence of the interaction among the parts.'" Patrick Kenis and Volker Schneider, "Policy Networks and Policy Analysis: Scrutinizing a New Analytical Toolbox," in *Policy Networks: Empirical Evidence and Theoretical Considerations*, ed. Bernd Marin and Renate Mayntz (Frankfurt am Main: Campus Verlag, 1991), 26–27.
24. Patrick Kenis and Volker Schneider, "Policy Networks and Policy Analysis: Scrutinizing a New Analytical Toolbox," in *Policy Networks: Empirical Evidence and Theoretical Considerations*, ed. Bernd Marin and Renate Mayntz (Frankfurt am Main: Campus Verlag, 1991), 26–27.
25. Wouter Nooy, Andrej Mrvar, and Vladimir Batagelj, *Exploratory Social Network Analysis with Pajek* (New York, NY: Cambridge University Press, 2005), 6.
26. Wasserman and Faust, *Social Network Analysis. Methods and Applications*, 19.
27. Ibid., 20.
28. Directional, as opposed to nondirectional, means having an origin and destination. Dichotomous simply refers to the presence or absence of a relationship, while valued relationship can be further qualified.
29. Wasserman and Faust, *Social Network Analysis. Methods and Applications.*
30. Nooy, Mrvar, and Batagelj, *Exploratory Social Network Analysis with Pajek.*
31. Wasserman and Faust, *Social Network Analysis. Methods and Applications.*
32. Ronald S. Burt and David Knoke, "Prominence," in *Applied Network Analysis: A Methodological Introduction*, ed. R. S. Burt and M. J. Minor (Beverly Hills, CA: Sage Publications, 1983), 195–222.; Wasserman and Faust, *Social Network Analysis. Methods and Applications.*
33. This dichotomous relation then will be assigned a value "1" for being present and a value "0" if absent in a sociomatrix.
34. Ibid., 169–170.
35. Robert A. Hanneman and Mark Riddle, *Introduction to Social Network Methods* (Riverside, CA: University of California, Riverside, published in digital form, 2005), 146. http://faculty.ucr.edu/~hanneman/.
36. Ibid., 147.

37. The term in SNA used for these "non-connected" nodes is nonadjacent nodes.
38. Wasserman and Faust, *Social Network Analysis. Methods and Applications.*
39. Nooy, Mrvar, and Batagelj, *Exploratory Social Network Analysis with Pajek.*
40. Wasserman and Faust, *Social Network Analysis. Methods and Applications.*
41. J.F. Padgett and C.K. Ansell, "Robust Action and the Rise of the Medici, 1400–1434," *American Journal of Sociology* 98, no. 6 (1993): 1259–1319.
42. Andrej Mrvar and Vladimir Batagelj, "Pajek Workshop," in Sunbelt XXIX, San Diego, March 10–15, 2009, 46, http://pajek.imfm.si/lib/exe/fetch.php.?id=download&cache=cache&media=dl:wsxxixa.pdf.
43. Kleinberg, "Authoritative Sources in a Hyperlinked Environment," In *SODA '98 Proceedings of the Ninth Annual ACM-SIAM Symposium on Discrete Algorithms, Journal of the ACM (JACM),* (1999): 668–677.
44. Martin Hassel, "Resource Lean and Portable Automatic Text Summarization" (KTH, Stockholm, 2007), 29, doi: ISBN-978-917178-704-0.
45. Ibid., 31.
46. These ideas merged from the research of Kleinberg and Page (1996), who tried to "remedy the 'abundance problem' inherent in broad [information] queries" (Chakrabarti, 2003, p. 209). They ultimately came up with two new algorithms to rank web pages based on links: PageRank and HITS (Hyperlink Induced Topic Search), the latter of which uses a query to select a sub-graph from the web and then identifies hubs and authorities in that sub-graph (Chakrabarti, 2003).
47. Soumen Chakrabarti and Ganesh Ramakrishnan, "Mining the Web," 2002. PowerPoint presentation, www.authorstream.com/Presentation/aSGuest87226-848737-intro/
48. Wasserman and Faust, *Social Network Analysis. Methods and Applications.*
49. Ronald R. Burt, *Structural Holes: The Social Structure of Competition* (Cambridge: Harvard University Press, 1992).
50. Brian Uzzi and Michael Schwartz, "Book Review of 'Holy Theory': The Social Structure of Competition (1992) by Ronald S. Burt," *Contemporary Sociology* 22 (1993): 155.
51. Burt, *Structural Holes: The Social Structure of Competition.*
52. Pajek is a freely available software suitable for the analysis and visualization of large networks developed by Batagelj and Mrvar (http://vlado.fmf.uni-lj.si/pub /networks/pajek/). Pajek uses the term "aggregate constraint" to interpret structural holes as a measure.
53. Nooy, Mrvar, and Batagelj, *Exploratory Social Network Analysis with Pajek.*
54. Wasserman and Faust, *Social Network Analysis. Methods and Applications,* 254.
55. Vladimir Batagelj, "Algorithms for Analysis of Large Networks," University of Ljubljana, FMF, Dept. of Mathematics; and IMFM Ljubljana, Dept. of Theoretical Computer Science Math/Chem/Comp, Summer school IUC Dubrovnik, June 16–22, 2008, 19, http://pajek.imfm.si/lib/exe/fetch.php?media=slides:mcc08.pdf.
56. Vladimir Batagelj and Andrej Mrvar, "PAJEK—Program for Analysis and Visualization of Large Networks," Ljubljana, Slovenia, n.d., http://vlado.fmf.uni-lj.si/pub/networks/pajek/doc/pajekman.pdf.
57. Ibid., 23.
58. John Scott, *Social Network Analysis: A Handbook,* 1st ed. (Newberry Park, CA: Sage Publications Ltd., 1991).
59. H.W. Park, "Hyperlink Network Analysis: A New Method for the Study of Social Structure on the Web," *Connections* 25, no. 1 (2003): 49–61.
60. Wasserman and Faust, *Social Network Analysis. Methods and Applications.*

61. Albert L. Barabási and Eric Bonabeau, "Scale-Free Networks," *Scientific American* 288 (May 2003): 60–69.
62. Chakrabarti, *Mining the Web: Discovering Knowledge from Hypertext Data*, 1.
63. Memex refers to memory extension.
64. Chakrabarti, *Mining the Web: Discovering Knowledge from Hypertext Data*.; Vannevar Bush, *Science the Endless Frontier: A Report to the President on a Program for Postwar Scientific Research*, Washington, D.C., 1945. http://nsf.gov/od/lpa/nsf50/vbush1945.htm; Theodor Nelson, "Computers, Creativity and the Nature of the Written Word," 1965, http://faculty.vassar.edu/mijoyce/MiscNews_Feb65.html.
65. Chakrabarti, *Mining the Web: Discovering Knowledge from Hypertext Data*.
66. These patterns are interaction patterns in our case.
67. Algorithm references a procedure, process, or a set of rules that lead to solving a particular problem used in mathematics and computer science specifically.
68. Hanneman, Robert A. Riddle, *Introduction to Social Network Methods*.
69. Ibid., 170–171.
70. M. Meilă and William Pentney, "Clustering by Weighted Cuts in Directed Graphs," in *SIAM Conference on Data Mining (SDM)*, 2007, http://citeseerx.ist.psu.edu/viewdoc/download?doi=10.1.1.80.2833&rep=rep1&type=pdf.
71. Ulrike Luxburg, "A Tutorial on Spectral Clustering," *Statistics and Computing* 17, no. 4 (August 22, 2007): 395–416.; Gregor Hörzer, "An Introduction to Spectral Clustering" (Computational Intelligence Seminar E, Institute for Theoretical Computer Science, Graz, University of Technology, 2007), 4, http://igi.tugraz.at/lehre/seminarE/SS07/hoerzer.pdf.
72. Meilă and Pentney, "Clustering by Weighted Cuts in Directed Graphs."
73. Nooy, Mrvar, and Batagelj, *Exploratory Social Network Analysis with Pajek*.
74. "Graphviz—Graph Visualization Software," 2009, http://graphviz.org.
75. Personal communication with D. Fuhry, January 13, 2010.
76. Batagelj and Mrvar, "Networks/Pajek, Program for Large Network Analysis."
77. Alain Bouchard, "Link Analysis & Visualization," A product review and technical memorandum by Valcartier: Defence R&D Canada, 2004), http://cradpdf.drdc-rddc.gc.ca/PDFS/unc45/p522560.pdf.
78. Ibid., 47.
79. Nooy, Mrvar, and Batagelj, *Exploratory Social Network Analysis with Pajek*.
80. Ibid., 12.
81. Tomihisa Kamada and Satoru Kawai, "A Simple Method for Computing General Position in Displaying Three-Dimensional Objects," *Computer Vision, Graphics, and Image Processing (CVGIP)* 41, no. 1 (1988): 43–56.

Appendix B
Transatlantic Connections—KNETs

Table B.1 Transatlantic Connections—KNETs

Node #	Name of Organization	Acronym	Website
1.	The German Marshall Fund	GMF	www.gmfus.org/template/index.cfm
2.	Transatlantic Policy Network	TPN	www.tpnonline.org
3.	Foreign Policy Research Institute	FPRI	www.fpri.org/about
4.	TAICON: The Trans-Atlantic Initiative on Complex Organizations and Networks	TAIC	www.icr.ethz.ch/taicon
5.	The Konrad-Adenauer-Stiftung	KAS	www.kas.de/wf/en
6.	BRINT Institute, The Knowledge Creating Company	BRIN	www.brint.org
7.	The Transnational Foundation for Peace and Future Research	TFF	www.transnational.org/index.html
8.	The Carnegie Endowment for International Peace	CARN	www.carnegieendowment.org
9.	SAIS Center for Transatlantic Relations, Johns Hopkins University	SAIS	http://transatlantic.sais-jhu.edu/index.htm

(*Continued*)

Table B.1 (*Continued*)

Node #	Name of Organization	Acronym	Website
10.	Center for Strategic and International Studies	CSIS	www.csis.org/index.php
11.	The Atlantic Initiative	ATLI	www.atlantic-initiative.org/root/index.php?page_id=90
12.	Transatlantic Policy Consortium	TPC	www.spea.indiana.edu/tac/ moved to www.indiana.edu/~idsspea/tpc
13.	Demos, Network for Ideas and Action	DEMO	www.demos.org/home.cfm
14.	The Network of European Union Centers of Excellence	EUCE	www.unc.edu/euce
15.	GABA German American Business Association	GABA	www.gabanetwork.org/index.php?option=com_frontpage&Itemid=1
16.	Transatlantic Community Foundation Network	TCFN	www.tcfn.efc.be/whats_new.php
17.	Transatlantic Foreign Policy Discourse	TFPD	www.tfpd.org/index.html
18.	The Transatlantic Information Exchange System (TIESWeb)	TIES	www.tiesweb.org/about_ties/history.htm
19.	United Nations Information and Communication Technologies Task Force	UNIC	www.unicttaskforce.org/ (UNIC) also: www.unicttf.org/, currently: www.un-gaid.org
20.	The Center for Research on Collaboratories and Technology Enhanced Learning Communities	COTE	www.cotelco.net/Default.aspx
21.	Global Development Network	GDN	www.gdnet.org/middle.php

(*Continued*)

Table B.1 (*Continued*)

Node #	Name of Organization	Acronym	Website
22.	The European Union Studies Association	EUSA	www.eustudies.org
23.	The American Consortium on EU Studies	ACES	http://transatlantic.sais-jhu.edu/Who_We_Are/ACES
24.	EU, Delegation to the EU to the US, European Union Centers of Excellence in the US	EUUS	www.eurunion.org/infores/eucenter.htm
25.	TransAtlantic Business Dialogue	TABD	www.tabd.com
26.	Committee on Science and Technology, US House of Representatives	STHR	http://science.house.gov/default.aspx
27.	Science, Technology, and Innovation Subcommittee of the Unites States Senate Committee on Commerce, Science, and Transportation	STSE	http://commerce.senate.gov/public/index.cfm?FuseAction=Subcommittees.Subcommittee&Subcommittee_ID=c29924b6-6f75-4c33-b0a1-20cac0bfbceb
28.	Think Tank Directory Europe	TTDE	www.eu.thinktankdirectory.org
29.	The Aspen Institute	ASI	www.aspeninstitute.org
30.	Young Researchers Network project	YRN	www.yrn2007.com/component/option,com_frontpage/Itemid,1
31.	The Luso-American Development Foundation	LADF	www.flad.pt/?no=0000002#
32.	Official Journal of the European Communities, AGREEMENT for S&T Cooperation between the EU and the US	ECST	http://eur-lex.europa.eu/LexUriServ/site/en/oj/1998/l_284/l_28419981022en00370044.pdf

(*Continued*)

Table B.1 (*Continued*)

Node #	Name of Organization	Acronym	Website
33.	US Dept. of State on US-EU Cooperation in Science and Technology	USST	www.state.gov/p/eur/rls/fs/42549.htm
34.	EUROPA, Gateway to the European Union, European Commission	EUWE	http://ec.europa.eu/index_en.htm
35.	AmCham EU	ACEU	www.amchameu.be
36.	The Atlantic Council of the United States	ACUS	www.acus.org/
37.	BRUEGEL, Brussels European and Global Economic Laboratory	BRTT	www.bruegel.org/Public/WebSite.php?ID=2
38.	Centre for European Policy Studies	CEPS	www.ceps.be/index3.php (new site: www.ceps.eu/home)
39.	Chamber of Commerce of the United States	USCC	www.uschamber.com/default
40.	Council on Foreign Relations	CFR	www.cfr.org
41.	European Policy Centre	EPC	www.epc.eu/home.asp
42.	The European Round Table of Industrialists	ERT	www.ert.be/home.aspx
43.	European-American Business Council	EABC	www.eabc.org
44.	European Institute in the US	EITT	www.europeaninstitute.org
45.	Institut Francais des Relations Internationales	IFRI	www.ifri.org/frontDispatcher
46.	Trans European Policy Studies Association	TEPS	www.tepsa.be/index.asp
47.	BUSINESSEUROPE	BUEU	www.businesseurope.eu/Content/Default.asp

(*Continued*)

Table B.1 (*Continued*)

Node #	Name of Organization	Acronym	Website
48.	US Council on Competitiveness	COMP	www.compete.org
49.	EurLex, EU Law	EULW	http://eur-lex.europa.eu/en/index.htmn
50.	Transatlantic Legislators' Dialogue	TLD	www.europarl.europa.eu/intcoop/tld/default_en.htm
51.	EU at the UN	EUUN	www.europa-eu-un.org
52.	Delegation of the European Commission to Canada	EUCA	www.delcan.ec.europa.eu/en
53.	US Department of State	USDS	www.state.gov
54.	North Atlantic Treaty Organization	NATO	www.nato.int
55.	European Commission External Relations	ECER	http://ec.europa.eu/external_relations/us/index_en.htm
56.	Digital Repository Infrastructure Vision for European Research project of the EU, EC	DRIV	www.driver-repository.eu
57.	The German Marshall Fund of the United States, Climate and Energy Program	GMFE	www.gmfus.org/climate/index.cfm
58.	The Science of Collaboratories project	SOC	www.scienceofcollaboratories.org
59.	European Research Area NSF's	ERA	http://ec.europa.eu/research/era/index_en.html
60.	International Research Network Connections	IRNC	www.startap.net/translight
61.	Center for Science and Technology Policy Research	CIRE	http://sciencepolicy.colorado.edu/about_us

(*Continued*)

Table B.1 (*Continued*)

Node #	Name of Organization	Acronym	Website
62.	The European Research Area "ERAWATCH"	ERAW	http://erawatch.jrc.es/public/welcome.htm
63.	The Atlanticc Alliance	ATLA	www.atlanticcalliance.org
64.	The Georgia Tech School of Public Policy	GTPP	www.spp.gatech.edu
65.	PRIME Network of Excellence, a.k.a. pre-ERA	PERA	www.prime-noe.org
66.	The US Department of Energy	DOE	www.doe.gov
67.	US Department of Energy's Energy Efficiency and Renewable Energy program	DOEE	www.eere.energy.gov
68.	US Department of Energy, Office of Science	DOES	www.er.doe.gov/index.htm
69.	US Department of Energy, Science and Technology	DOST	www.doe.gov/sciencetech/index.htm
70.	Brookings Institution, The Hamilton Project, science and diplomacy program	BROK	www.brookings.edu/projects/hamiltonproject.aspx
71.	The American Association for the Advancement of Science	AAAS	www.aaas.org
72.	The Office of Science and Technology Policy, Executive Office of the President	OSTP	www.ostp.gov/cs/about_ostp/history
73.	The National Academies	NACA	www.nationalacademies.org

(*Continued*)

Table B.1 (*Continued*)

Node #	Name of Organization	Acronym	Website
74.	National Science Foundation	NSF	www.nsf.gov
75.	European Commission, Energy, Innovation and technological development in energy	ECEN[i]	http://ec.europa.eu/energy/res/legislation/res_directive_en.htm
76.	European Commission, Energy, Innovation and technological development in energy	ECEN	http://ec.europa.eu/energy/res/setplan/communication_2007_en.htm
77.	European Research Council	ERC	http://erc.europa.eu/index.cfm
78.	CORDIS, the Community Research and Development Information Service for Science, Research and Development	CORN	http://cordis.europa.eu/news/home_en.html
79.	Joint Research Centre	ECRC	http://ec.europa.eu/dgs/jrc/index.cfm
80.	The National Academy of Engineering	NAE	www.nae.edu/nae/naehome.nsf
81.	Federal Ministry for Transport, Innovation and Technology, Austria	AUIT	www.bmvit.gv.at/en/index.html
82.	Nature Publishing Group, Nature	NATJ	www.nature.com/index.html
83.	CORDIS, Community Research and Development Information Service for Science, FP7	COFP	http://cordis.europa.eu/fp7/home_en.html

(*Continued*)

Table B.1 (*Continued*)

Node #	Name of Organization	Acronym	Website
84.	European Global Navigation Satellite System Supervisory Authority	EGNS	www.gsa.europa.eu
85.	European Economic and Social Committee	EESC	http://eesc.europa.eu
86.	AthenaWeb, European Science Research	ESR	www.athenaweb.org
87.	European Commission	EUEC	http://ec.europa.eu/index_en.htm

[i] This organization has shown activity on two websites simultaneously, the second one being http://ec.europa.eu/energy/res/setplan/communication_2007_en.htm.

Appendix C
Transatlantic Connections by Types of Organization—Transatlantic Network

Table C.1 Transatlantic Connections by Types of Organization—Transatlantic Network

Academic, Research & Policy Institute	Government Agency	International Organization (IGO)	Think Tank	Interest Group
GMF[1]	DOST	UNIC	KAS[2]	TPN[3]
FPRI[4]	STHR	GDN[5]	TFF[6]	GABA[7]
TAIC[8]	STSE	NATO	CARN[9]	TCFN[10]
BRIN[11]	DOES	EUUS	BRTT	TIES[12]
SAIS[13]	USST	EUEC	CEPS[14]	TABD[15]
ATLI[16]	DOEE	ESR[17]	EPC[18]	LADF[19]
TPC[20]	NSF[21]	EESC	BROK[22]	ACEU
TFPD[23]	OSTP	COFP	CSIS[24]	ACUS[25]
COTE[26]	USDS	EGNS[27]	CFR[28]	USCC
EUSA[29]	AUIT	CORN[30]	DEMO[31]	ERT
ACES	DOE	ERC	TTDE	EABC
CIRE[32]	NACA	ERAW		BUEU[33]
ASI[34]	IRNC	ECER		COMP
CIRE[35]	NAE	DRIV[36]		
YRN[37]		ERA[38]		
EITT[39]		ECRC		
IFRI[40]		ECEN		
EUCE[41]		PERA[42]		
NATJ[43]		TLD		
AAAS		EULW		
GMFE		EUWE		

(*Continued*)

Table C.1 (*Continued*)

Academic, Research & Policy Institute	Government Agency	International Organization (IGO)	Think Tank	Interest Group
SOC[44]		ECST		
GTPP		EUUN		
ATLA[45]		EUCA		

1 A nonpartisan American public policy and grant making institution.
2 European think tank and consulting agency.
3 A multi-party group of EU and US politicians, corporate leaders, think tanks, and academics.
4 A non-profit organization devoted to bringing the insights of scholarship to develop policies that advance US national interests.
5 An international organization of research and policy institutes.
6 An independent think tank.
7 A non-profit organization that fosters transatlantic knowledge-sharing and networking among German-American and Californian business and tech communities.
8 A transatlantic community active in the areas of social networks and complexity, based at Harvard and the Swiss Federal Institute of Technology.
9 A private, non-profit organization dedicated to advancing cooperation between nations and promoting active international engagement by the United States.
10 Participants represent 17 countries in Europe and North America, forming a multinational network of community foundation leaders, researchers, and thinkers.
11 Its goal is to bridge the gaps between business and technology, data and knowledge, and theory and practice.
12 Initiated by European and American NGO leaders and academics in 1997 as part of the New Transatlantic Agenda.
13 As one of a select number of EU Centers of Excellence, it engages international scholars and students with government officials, journalists, business executives, and other opinion leaders from both sides of the Atlantic.
14 It is among the most experienced and authoritative think tanks operating in the European Union.
15 A dialogue system to encourage public and civil society input to fostering a more closely integrated transatlantic marketplace. It includes separate dialogues for consumers, labor, environment, and business; it was a part of New Transatlantic Agenda.
16 A nonpartisan, non-profit organization dedicated to furthering transatlantic cooperation based in Berlin.
17 A video portal and workspace for European audiovisual communication professionals in the areas of science and scientific information.
18 An independent, not-for-profit think tank, committed to making European integration work.
19 A private, independent Portuguese institution. Its main goal is to provide financial and strategic support for innovative projects and cooperation between Portuguese and American civil society.
20 Its goal is to strengthen relationships between European and American scholars and professionals in the field of public policy analysis and education.
21 An independent federal agency created by Congress in 1950 to promote scientific progress as well as advance the overall well-being of the nation.
22 Involves the Brookings in general and its science and diplomacy program.
23 A project of The German Institute for International and Security Affairs, which is an independent scientific establishment that conducts practically oriented research.

[24] It provides strategic insights and policy solutions to decision-makers in government, international institutions, the private sector, and civil society; bipartisan, non-profit.
[25] An international network of citizens' associations created in 1954 with the creation of the Atlantic Treaty Association.
[26] A social science research center in the School of Information Studies at Syracuse University, an affiliated center of the Burton Blatt Institute, Centers of Innovation on Disability.
[27] EUEC research.
[28] A nonpartisan and independent membership organization. CFR has promoted understanding of foreign policy and America's role in the world since its founding in 1921.
[29] It is the premier scholarly and professional association focusing on the European Union, the ongoing integration process, and transatlantic relations.
[30] Part of EUEC.
[31] A nonpartisan public policy research and advocacy organization.
[32] Within the Cooperative Institute for Research in Environmental Sciences (CIRES) at the University of Colorado—Boulder.
[33] Original aims included uniting the central industrial federations, encouraging a Europe-wide competitive industrial policy, and acting as a spokesperson body to the European institutions.
[34] A set of seminars and policy programs that recruit executives to multi-day discussions.
[35] Within the Cooperative Institute for Research in Environmental Sciences (CIRES) at the University of Colorado—Boulder.
[36] An EU, EC program.
[37] The European Studies Program at the University of Victoria strengthening Canadian-Transatlantic relations.
[38] EU, EC.
[39] A Washington-based public-policy organization devoted to transatlantic affairs.
[40] France's leading independent international relations center dedicated to policy-oriented research and analysis of global political affairs.
[41] Includes 10 research universities in the US.
[42] PRIME gathers 51 institutions representing 65 research groups from 19 countries.
[43] Their goal is to serve scientists through prompt publication of significant advances in any branch of science, to provide a forum, and to provide rapid dissemination to the public.
[44] Driven by researchers at the University of Michigan and Howard University, and is sponsored by the National Science Foundation.
[45] Tripartite alliance between Imperial College London, Georgia Institute of Technology, and Oak Ridge National Laboratory.

Appendix D
Transatlantic Connections by Types of Organization—Transatlantic S&T Sub-Network

Table D.1 Transatlantic Connections by Types of Organization—Transatlantic S&T Sub-network

Academic, Research & Policy Institute	Government Agency	International Organization (IGO)	Think Tank	Interest Group
GMF[1]	DOST	UNIC	TFF[2]	TPN[3]
FPRI[4]	STHR	GDN[5]	CARN[6]	GABA[7]
TAIC[8]	DOES	NATO	CEPS[9]	TCFN[10]
BRIN[11]	USST	TLD	EPC[12]	TIES[13]
ATLI[14]	DOEE	EUEC	BROK[15]	TABD[16]
TPC[17]	OSTP	ESR[18]	CFR[19]	LADF[20]
COTE[21]	USDS	EUWE	DEMO[22]	ACEU
ACES	AUIT	COFP	TTDE	ACUS[23]
CIRE[24]	DOE	ECST		USCC
ASI[25]	NACA	CORN[26]		ERT
YRN[27]	NAE	ERC		EABC
EITT[28]		ERAW		BUEU[29]
EUCE[30]		ECER		COMP[31]
AAAS		DRIV[32]		
GMFE		ERA[33]		
SOC[34]		EULW		
ATLA[35]		ECEN		
GTPP		PPERA[36]		
		EUUN		

(*Continued*)

Table D.1 (*Continued*)

Academic, Research & Policy Institute	Government Agency	International Organization (IGO)	Think Tank	Interest Group
		EUCA		
		EGNS[37]		

[1] Nonpartisan American public policy and grant-making institution.
[2] Independent think tank.
[3] A multi-party group of EU and US politicians, corporate leaders, think tanks, and academics.
[4] A non-profit organization devoted to bringing the insights of scholarship to develop policies that advance US national interests.
[5] An International Organization of research and policy institutes.
[6] A private, non-profit organization dedicated to advancing cooperation between nations and promoting active international engagement by the United States.
[7] A non-profit organization that fosters transatlantic knowledge-sharing and networking among German-American and Californian business and tech communities.
[8] A transatlantic community active in the areas of social networks and complexity, based at Harvard and the Swiss Federal Institute of Technology.
[9] It is s among the most experienced and authoritative think tanks operating in the European Union.
[10] Participants represent 17 countries in Europe and North America, forming a multinational network of community foundation leaders, researchers, and thinkers.
[11] Its goal is to bridge the gaps between business and technology, data and knowledge, and theory and practice.
[12] An independent, not-for-profit think tank, committed to making European integration work.
[13] Initiated by European and American NGO leaders and academics in 1997 as part of the New Transatlantic Agenda.
[14] A nonpartisan, non-profit organization dedicated to furthering transatlantic cooperation based in Berlin.
[15] Involves the Brookings in general and its science and diplomacy program.
[16] A dialogue system to encourage public and civil society input to fostering a more closely integrated transatlantic marketplace. It includes separate dialogues for consumers, labor, environment, and business; it was a part of New Transatlantic Agenda.
[17] Its goal is to strengthen relationships between European and American scholars and professionals in the field of public policy analysis and education.
[18] A video portal and workspace for European audiovisual communication professionals in the areas of science and scientific information.
[19] A nonpartisan and independent membership organization. CFR has promoted understanding of foreign policy and America's role in the world since its founding in 1921.
[20] A private, independent Portuguese institution. Its main goal is to provide financial and strategic support for innovative projects and cooperation between Portuguese and American civil society.
[21] A social science research center in the School of Information Studies at Syracuse University, an affiliated center of the Burton Blatt Institute, Centers of Innovation on Disability.
[22] A nonpartisan public policy research and advocacy organization.
[23] An international network of citizens' associations created in 1954 with the creation of the Atlantic Treaty Association.
[24] Within the Cooperative Institute for Research in Environmental Sciences (CIRES) at the University of Colorado—Boulder.

[25] A set of seminars and policy programs that recruit executives to multi-day discussions.
[26] EUEC.
[27] The European Studies Program at the University of Victoria strengthening Canadian-Transatlantic relations.
[28] A Washington-based public-policy organization devoted to transatlantic affairs.
[29] Goals include uniting the central industrial federations, encouraging competitive industrial policy, and acting as a spokesperson body to the EU institutions.
[30] Includes 10 research universities in the US.
[31] NGO.
[32] An EU, EC program.
[33] EU, EC.
[34] Driven by researchers at the University of Michigan, and Howard University, and is sponsored by NSF.
[35] Tripartite alliance between Imperial College London, Georgia Institute of Technology, and Oak Ridge National Laboratory.
[36] PRIME gathers 51 institutions representing 65 research groups from 19 countries.
[37] EUEC research.

Appendix E
Additional Key Findings Based on Network Attributes

P-CLIQUES

Network partitions according to strong "p-cliques," or densely connected sub-groups, were generated in Pajek for networks "D1" as well as for "d1-kw" at all levels. Pajek includes a special p-clique procedure, which results in a network partition of nodes into clusters, such that the vertices have at least proportion "p" (number between 0 and 1) neighbors inside the cluster.[1] Figure E.1 visualizes the strong p-clique partition of the larger transatlantic network (D1), while Figure E.2 depicts these in the S&T sub-network (d1-kw).

As shown in Table E.1, there are three strong p-cliques identified using Pajek in the "D1" network. The distribution makes it clearly visible that the majority of these nodes form a strong clique, clique number 5, in the "D1" network. Therefore, this clique in the broader transatlantic network seems rather cohesive. In network "D2" there are four strong p-cliques. Most of those belong to clique #7, except for one organization in #1, three organizations in #2, and 15 in #5. Network "D3" characteristics, in this regard, look identical to those of the "D2" network.

In the sub-network "d1-kw," as summarized in Table E.2, there are more groups that are cohesive; among these, group #7 stands out. It is remarkable that there are a lot of similarities between this cohesive sub-group and cluster #8 analyzed previously. At the other two levels or depths, d2-kw and d3-kw have fewer p-cliques, i.e., cliques 8 and 9 are missing, while NATO constitutes clique #4 by itself. Otherwise, the patterns are similar to that of network d1-kw; therefore, it unnecessary to represent these visually in this research.

Several similarities can be observed, in regards to what organizations constitute the most cohesive group in the partitioning into eight clusters. This holds for the partitioning of both the broader and the policy-specific transatlantic sub-network, as well as for the densely connected sub-groups measured by Pajek's strong p-clique metrics. This similarity is pronounced in the "d1-kw" sub-network, in clique 7.[2] All of those organizations that cluster together into one cluster in all networks at all levels, described in the

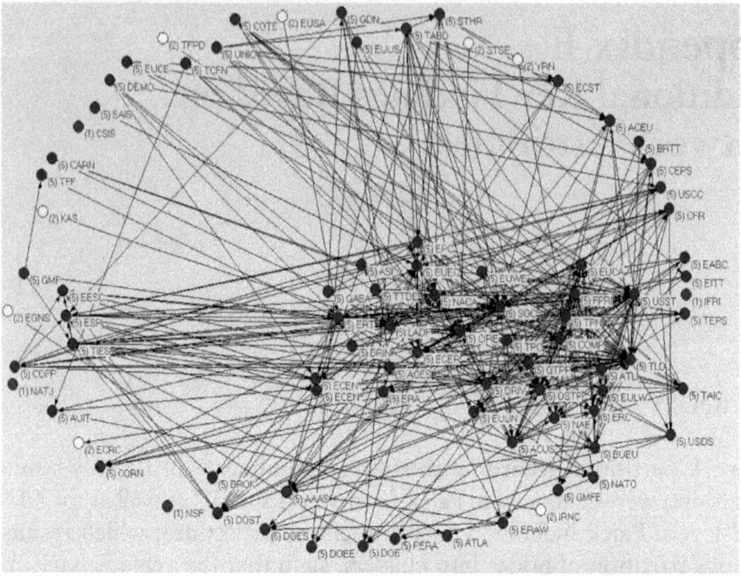

Figure E.1 Visualization of Strong P-cliques Partition of the Transatlantic Network

Nodes correspond to the three strong cliques observed in this network. The most extensive clique is designated as "clique 5" by Pajek.

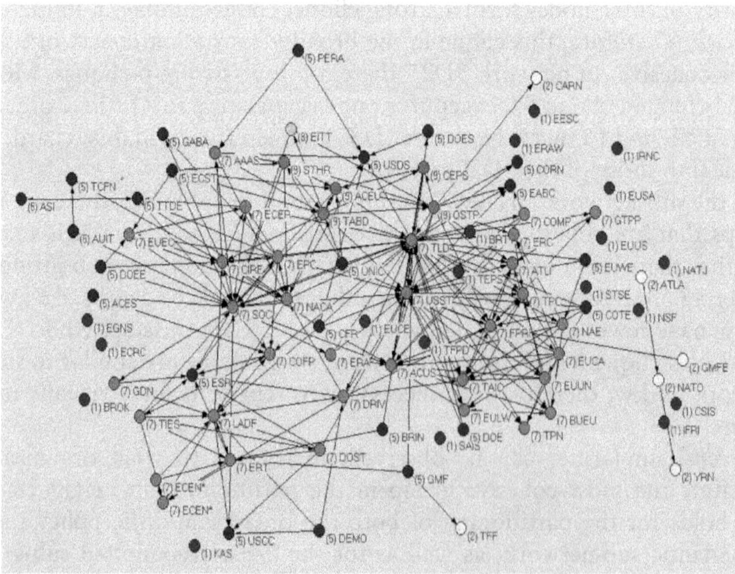

Figure E.2 Visualization of Strong P-cliques Partition of the Transatlantic S&T Sub-network

Six strong p-cliques were generated by Pajek.

Table E.1 Strong P-cliques in the Transatlantic Network at All Depths

D1			D2 and D3				
1	2	5	1	2	5		7
CSIS	KAS	All Others	NSF	IFRI	GMF	BRTT	All Others
IFRI	TFPD			NATJ	BRIN	EABC	
NSF	EUSA			EGNS	TFF	IRNC	
NATJ	STSE				CSIS	ATLA	
	YRN				TFPD	ECRC	
	IRNC				EUSA	EESC	
	ECRC				STSE	ESR	
	EGNS				ECST		

Table E.2 Strong P-cliques in the Transatlantic S&T Sub-network

1	2	5		7		8	9
CSIS	TFF	**GMF**	**DOES**	TPN	DRIV	EITT	TABD
KAS	CARN	**BRIN**	**CORN**	FPRI	SOC		STHR
SAIS	YRN	**DEMO**	**AUIT**	TAIC	ERA		ACEU
EUCE	NATO	**GABA**	**ESR**	ATLI	CIRE		CEPS
TFPD	GMFE	**TCFN**		TPC	GTPP		OSTP
EUSA	ATLA	**UNIC**		**TIES**	DOST		
EUUS		**COTE**		**GDN**	AAAS		
STSE		**ACES**		**LADF**	NACA		
BRTT		**TTDE**		**USST**	ECEN		
IFRI		**ASI**		ACUS	ERC		
TEPS		**ECST**		**EPC**	**NAE**		
IRNC		**EUWE**		**ERT**	COFP		
ERAW		**USCC**		**BUEU**	EUEC		
BROK		**CFR**		**COMP**			
NSF		**EABC**		**EULW**			
ECRC		**USDS**		**TLD**			
NATJ		**PERA**		**EUUN**			
EGNS		**DOE**		**EUCA**			
EESC		**DOEE**		**ECER**			

previous paragraph, are also members of the cohesive clique, except for three: the Center for Research on Collaboratories and Technology Enhanced Learning Communities; EUROPA, the European Union's official website; and the Office of Science and Technology Policy: Executive Office of the President.

ISLANDS

Last, but not least, this study considers a unique kind of partition of vertices to cohesive clusters according to the weights of vertices. These are called "islands," which Pajek calculates and visualizes. This involves the partition of the vertices of the network with values on lines, or weights, to cohesive clusters, where *the weights inside clusters must be larger than weights to neighborhood.*[3] "The height of a vertex (vector) is defined as the maximum weight of the neighbor lines."[4]

The significance of these islands lies in their ability to quickly point out a few groupings of network members that are well-connected to one another, i.e., among themselves only. In Figures E.3 and E.4, we can see that in both types of networks, the broader, as well as the S&T sub-network, the *four most well-connected network members form two cohesive pairs.*

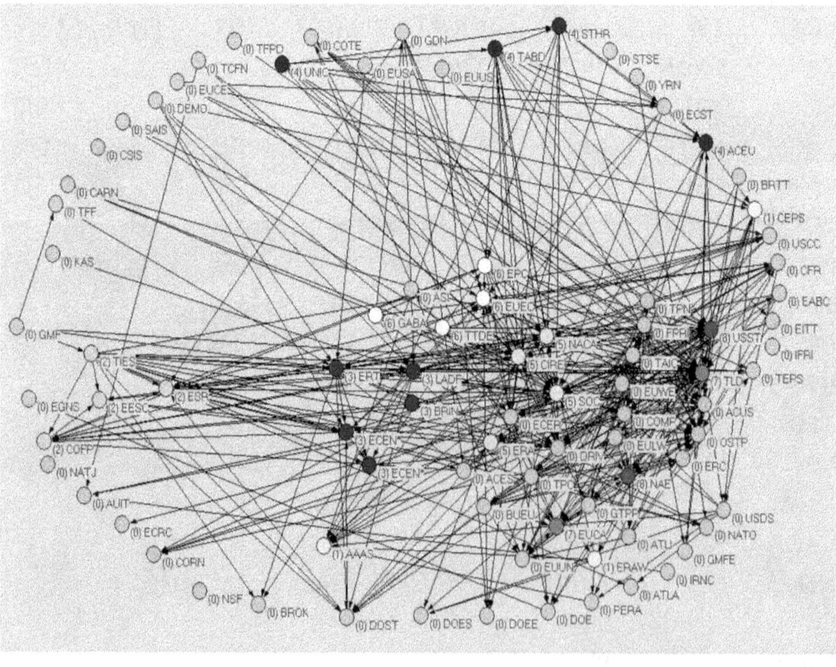

Figure E.3 Visualization of Islands Partition of the Transatlantic Network
Eight islands were generated by Pajek.

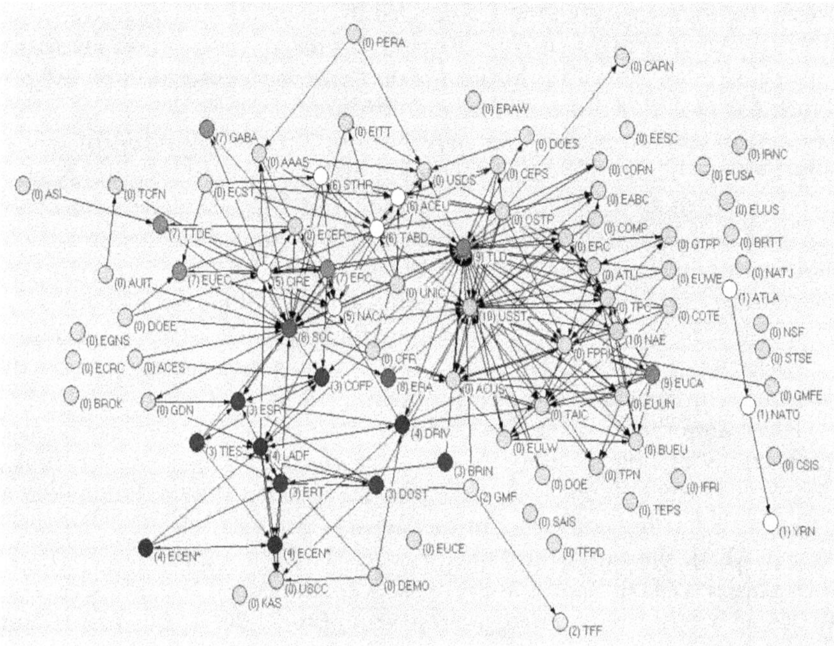

Figure E.4 Visualization of Islands Partition of the Transatlantic S&T Sub-network
Ten islands were generated by Pajek.

The US–EU Cooperation in Science and Technology (USST) web page—National Academies of Engineering (NAE) web page is pursuing virtual connections with the highest frequency between themselves.[5] This finding has significant implications for the sharing of scientific knowledge and ideas on technological advancement among the transatlantic partners. S&T policy seems to be a priority policy area in transatlantic relations after all, at least considering virtual networking patterns.

The second pair with the most frequent virtual interactions is the Transatlantic Legislators' Dialogue (TLD)—Delegation of the European Commission to Canada (EUCA).[6] It is inspiring to see, at least from the justification of the NTA's perspective, that this dialogue, created by the New Transatlantic Agenda of 1995, actively seeks connections. It is interesting, however, that TLD's main partner in virtual connections is the Delegation of the European Commission to Canada, as opposed to another network member within the US's institutional domain. The third pair is the Science of Collaboratories (SOC)—the European Research Area (ERA).[7] SOC is a unique kind of NSF-sponsored project, driven by researchers at the University of Michigan and Howard University. SOC investigates and aims to identify as well as codify the broad underlying technical and social elements that lead to successful collaboratories.[8] In 2000, the EU decided to create the European Research Area (ERA), which was an effort to create a unified research area all across Europe. Closely related to this idea is the "free movement of knowledge," which has recently been coined as the fifth freedom in the EU. In the spirit of the Lisbon Strategy, the "free movement of knowledge" is regarded as a priority to respond to the challenges of globalization and transform the EU into 'a truly modern and competitive economy. [9] It "enable[s] researchers to move and interact seamlessly, benefit from world-class infrastructures and work with excellent networks of research institutions."[10] Looking at the numbers, which indicate the hyperlink activity within this pair, makes it clear that their virtual interaction is more than 10 times greater in the S&T sub-network. This seems like a reasonable finding, considering the strictly policy-specific nature of these two entities.

There are other "islands," or cohesive groups, with somewhat intense connections among themselves, but their shared number of hyperlinks decreases sharply, so only two examples are mentioned here. First, we can distinguish a group consisting of the German American Business Association (GABA), the European Policy Centre (EPC), the Think Tank Directory Europe (TTDE), and the European Commission (EUEC).[11] Although GABA is a business-oriented interest group and EPC is an independent think tank, EPC's main goal is to foster the European integration process. Their connection to the EU Commission shows a policy-coherent response. Second, an organizational triad among the TransAtlantic Business Dialogue (TABD), Committee on Science and Technology, the US House of Representatives (STHR), and the AmCham EU, (ACEU) is seen. It shows that these two broad interest groups, the business dialogue and the chamber of commerce, maintain relations with the policy-specific committee in the US legislature.[12] They maintain the intensity of connections in both types of networks.

NOTES

1. Wouter Nooy, Andrej Mrvar, and Vladimir Batagelj, Exploratory Social Network Analysis with Pajek (New York, NY: Cambridge University Press, 2005).
2. The specific number given to each cluster holds no particular significance; it was generated by the clustering technique. What matters is the similarity of clustering patterns or groupings in each network.
3. Vladimir Batagelj and Andrej Mrvar, "PAJEK—Program for Analysis and Visualization of Large Networks," Ljubljana, Slovenia, 2009. http://vlado.fmf.uni-lj.si/pub/networks/pajek/doc/.
4. Ibid., 23.
5. The USST-NAE pair has 235,796 as their line value in the D1 network, while they have 159,483 as their line value in the d1-kw sub-network, indicating the frequency of interactions or number of hyperlinks shared between them.
6. The TLD-EUCA pair has 160,495 as their line value in D1 the network, while they have 56,062 as their line value in the d1-kw sub-network, indicating the frequency of interactions or number of hyperlinks shared between them.

7. The SOC-ERA pair has 191 as their line value in D1 network, while they have 2,366 as their line value in the d1-kw sub-network, indicating the frequency of interactions or number of hyperlinks shared between them.
8. The term "collaboratory" refers to the use of a variety of communication and computational technologies available for long-distance collaboration to support geographically dispersed collaborative research (www.scienceofcollaboratories.org).
9. EUEC, "European Council Summit," March 17, 2008, http://euractiv.com/en/science/summit-backs-fifthfreedom-eu-scientists/article-170989.
10. "European Research Area," http://ec.europa.eu/research/era.
11. The GABA-EPC-TTDE-EUEC group has 790 as their line value in D1 network, while they have 775 as their line value in the d1-kw sub-network, indicating the frequency of interactions or number of hyperlinks shared between them.
12. The TABD-STHR-ACEU group has an identical number, 141, as their line value in both the D1 network and in the d1-kw sub-network. This number refers to the frequency of interactions or number of hyperlinks shared between them.

Bibliography

AAAS. *2009–2010 Annual Review*, 2010. http://diplomacy.aaas.org/files/CSD_YIR_Year2_Web.pdf.

———. *2009–2010 Year in Review*, 2010.

Aaron, David L., Ann M. Beauchesne, Frances G. Burwell, C. Richard Nelson, K. Jack Riley, and Brian Zimmer. "The Post-9/11 Partnership: Transatlantic Cooperation Against Terrorism," 2004. http://scholar.google.com/scholar?hl=en&btnG=Search&q=intitle:The+Post+9+/+11+Partnership+:+Transatlantic+Cooperation+against+Terrorism#2.

Abelson, Donald E. *Do Think Tanks Matter? Assessing the Impact of Public Policy Institutes*. Montreal, Canada: McGill-Queens University Press, 2002.

Adewoye, Omonyi. "Leadership and the Dynamics of Reform in Africa." In *Reflections on Leadership in Africa. Forty Years after Independence*, edited by Haroub Othman, 39–48. Brussels, Belgium: VUB University Press, 2000.

Adler, Emanuel. "The Emergence of Cooperation: National Epistemic Communities and the International Evolution of the Idea of Nuclear Arms Control." *International Organization* 46, no. 1 (1992): 101–145.

Almond, Gabriel A., and Sidney Verba. *The Civic Culture: Political Attitudes and Democracy in Five Nations*. Princeton, NJ: Princeton University Press, 1963.

American Association for the Advancement of Science. http://aaas.org/aboutaaas/.

American Society of International Law. "Postal Agreement with Great Britain." *The American Journal of International Law* 2, no. 4 (1908): 849–853.

Angell, Norman. *The Great Illusion*. Cosimo Classics, 2007.

Armitage, David, and Michael J. Braddick. *The British Atlantic World, 1500–1800*. New York, NY: Palgrave Macmillan, 2002.

Ash, Timothy G. *Free World: America, Europe, and the Surprising Future of the West*. New York, NY: Random House, 2004.

Avery, John. *Space-Age Science and Stone-Age Politics*. e-book. Copenhagen: Danish Pugwash Group, 2005. Lulu.com.

Bachrach, P, and M.S. Baratz. "Two Faces of Power." *American Political Science Review* 56, no. 4 (1962): 947–952.

Bacon, Francis. "Religious Meditations, of Heresies, 1597." In *The Essays of Sir Francis Bacon*. Limited Sl. New York, NY: The Heritage Press, 1944.

Banchoff, Thomas. "Value Conflict and US–EU Relations: The Case of Unilateralism." *ACES Working Paper Series* (June 2004). www1.american.edu/aces/Work ing Papers/2004[1].3.pdf.

Barabási, Albert L. *Linked: How Everything Is Connected to Everything Else and What It Means for Business, Science, and Everyday Life*. Cambridge, MA: Perseus Publishing, 2002.

Barabási, Albert L., and Eric Bonabeau. "Scale-Free Networks." *Scientific American* 288 (May 2003): 60–69.
Barth, Kai-Henrik. "Catalysts of Change: Scientists as Transnational Arms Control Advocates in the 1980s." In *Global Power Knowledge. Science and Technology in International Affairs,* edited by John Krige and Kai-Henrik Barth. Chicago, IL: University of Chicago Press, 2006.
Batagelj, Vladimir. "Algorithms for Analysis of Large Networks." University of Ljubljana, FMF, Dept. of Mathematics; and IMFM Ljubljana, Dept. of Theoretical Computer Science Math/Chem/Comp, Summer school IUC Dubrovnik, June 16–22, 2008. http://pajek.imfm.si/lib/exe/fetch.php?media=slides:mcc08.pdf.
Batagelj, Vladimir, and Andrej Mrvar. "Networks/Pajek, Program for Large Network Analysis," 2005. http://vlado.fmf.uni-lj.si/pub /networks/pajek/.
———. "PAJEK—Program for Analysis and Visualization of Large Networks." Ljubljana, Slovenia, 2009. http://vlado.fmf.uni-lj.si/pub/networks/pajek/doc/.
Bavelas, Alex. "A Mathematical Model for Group Structure." *Human Organizations* 7 (1948): 16–30.
Beck, Ulrich. *Risk Society: Towards a New Modernity.* London, UK: Sage Publications Ltd., 1992.
———. *Reflexive Modernization: Politics, Tradition and Aesthetics in the Modern Social Order.* Stanford, CA: Stanford University Press, 1995.
Berejikian, Jeffrey, and J.S. Dryzek. "Reflexive Action in International Politics." *British Journal of Political Science* 30, no. 2 (2000): 193–216.
Biersteker, Thomas J. "Eroding Boundaries, Contested Terrain." *International Studies Review* 1, no. 1 (June 1999): 3–9.
BILAT USA 2.0. "EU-US S&T Agreement," 2013. http://euussciencetechnology.eu/content/eu-us-st-agreement.
Blanpied, William A. "Science and Public Policy: The Steelman Report and the Politics of Post-World War II Science Policy." In *AAAS Science and Technology Policy Yearbook of 1999*: 305–320.
Boekholt, P., J. Edler, P. Cunningham, and K. Flanagan. "Drivers of International Collaboration in Research." *Final Report* (2009). http://eurosfaire.prd.fr/7pc/doc/1266832886_drivers_of_international_cooperation_in_research.pdf.
Bohn, Angela, Norbert Walchhofer, Patrick Mair, and Kurt Hornik. "Social Network Analysis of Weighted Telecommunications Graphs." *ePub WU Institutional Repository* (March 2009). http://epub.wu.ac.at/708/.
Bollyky, Thomas J., and Anu Bradford. "Getting to Yes on Transatlantic Trade." *Foreign Affairs* (July 10, 2013). http://foreignaffairs.com/articles/139569/thomas-j-bollyky-and-anu-bradford/getting-to-yes-on-transatlantic-trade?page=show.
Borgatti, Stephen P. "Identifying Sets of Key Players in a Social Network." *Computational and Mathematical Organization Theory* 12, no. 1 (April 2006): 21–34.
Borrás, Susanna. *The Innovation Policy of the European Union: From Government to Governance.* Cheltenham, UK: Edward Elgar Publishing, 2003.
Bouchard, Alain. "Link Analysis & Visualization." A product review and technical memorandum by Valcartier: Defence R&D Canada, 2004. http://cradpdf.drdc-rddc.gc.ca/PDFS/unc45/p522560.pdf.
Bourdieu, Pierre, and Loïc J.D. Wacquant. *An Invitation to Reflexive Sociology.* Chicago, IL: University of Chicago Press, 1992.
Bradford, Colin I. "Global Governance Reform for the 21st Century," 2005. http://brookings.edu/~/media/research/files/papers/2005/10/24globaleconomics bradford/20051024bradford.pdf.
Braun, Dietmar. "New Governance for Innovation—Keynote Presentation." In *Workshop Held at the Occasion of the 30th Anniversary of the Fraunhofer Institute for Systems and Innovation Research (ISI).* Karlsruhe, Germany, 2002.

Brookings Institute. "A Compact Between the United States and Europe." Brookings Institute, 2005. http://brookings.edu/fp/cuse/analysis/USEUCompact.pdf.

Burt, Ronald S. *Structural Holes: The Social Structure of Competition.* Cambridge: Harvard University Press, 1992.

———. "The Network Structure of Social Capital." *Research in Organizational Behavior* 22 (2000): 345–423.

———. "Structural Holes Versus Network Closure as Social Capital." In *Social Capital: Theory and Research,* edited by R.S. Burt, K. Cook, and N. Lin. New York, NY: Aldine de Gruyter, 2001.

———. "Structural Holes and Good Ideas." *American Journal of Sociology* 110, no. 2 (2004): 349–399.

———. "The Social Capital of Structural Holes." In *New Directions in Economic Sociology,* edited by Mauro F. Guillén, Randall Collins, Paula England, and Marshall Meyer, 148–193. New York, NY: Russel Sage Foundation, 2005.

Burt, Ronald. S., and David Knoke. "Prominence." In *Applied Network Analysis: A Methodological Introduction,* edited by R.S. Burt and M.J. Minor, 195–222. Beverly Hills, CA: Sage Publications, 1983.

Bush, Vannevar. *Science the Endless Frontier: A Report to the President on a Program for Postwar Scientific Research.* Washington, D.C., 1945. http://nsf.gov/od/lpa/nsf50/vbush1945.htm.

Calabresi, Massimo. "Hillary Clinton and the Rise of Smart Power." *Time Magazine,* November 7, 2011. http://content.time.com/time/magazine/article/0,9171,2097973,00.html.

Carayannis, Elias G., and David F.J. Campbell. *Mode 3 Knowledge Production in Quadruple Helix Innovation Systems.* New York, NY: Springer New York, 2012.

Carpenter, R. Charli. "Setting the Advocacy Agenda: Theorizing Issue Emergence and Nonemergence in Transnational Advocacy Networks." *International Studies Quarterly* 51 (2007): 99–120.

Castells, Manuel. *The Information Age, Volumes 1–3: Economy, Society and Culture (Information Age Series).* Chichester, West Sussex: Wiley-Blackwell, 1999.

Chakrabarti, Soumen. *Mining the Web: Discovering Knowledge from Hypertext Data.* San Francisco: CA: Morgan Kaufmann Publishers, 2003.

Chakrabarti, Soumen, and Ramakrishnan, Ganesh. "Mining the Web," 2002. PowerPoint Presentation, www.authorstream.com/Presentation/aSGuest87226-848737-intro/

Chan, Kelvin, and Jay Liebowitz. "The Synergy of Social Network Analysis and Knowledge Mapping: A Case Study." *International Journal of Management and Decision Making* 7, no. 1 (2006): 19–35.

Charnovitz, Steve. "Participation of Non-Governmental Organizations in the World Trade Organization." *University of Pennsylvania Journal of International Economic Law* 17 (1996): 331–357.

Cogburn, Derrick L. "In Whose Name?: A Multimodal Exploration of Transnational Deliberative Democratic Practices in Multistakeholder Global Information Policy Formulation Processes." San Diego, CA: International Studies Association, 2006. http://citation.allacademic.com/meta/p_mla_apa_research_citation/1/0/0/5/8/p100585_index.html.

Cogburn, D.L. "Diversity Matters, Even at a Distance: Evaluating the Impact of Computer-Mediated Communication on Civil Society Participation in the World Summit on the Information Society." *Information Technologies & International Development* 1, no. 3 (2004): 15–40.

Coleman, James S. *Foundations of Social Theory.* Cambridge, MA: Harvard University Press, 1990.

Coleman, James S. "Social Capital in the Creation of Human Capital." *American Journal of Sociology* 94 (1988): S95–S120.

Commission, European. "23–24 May 2013—The Atlantic: A Shared Resource." European Commission, 2013. http://ec.europa.eu/research/iscp/index.cfm?lg=en&pg=usa.
Commission of the European Communities, *Communication from the Commission to the Council, the European Parliament, the European Economic and Social Committee and the Committee of the Regions: On the Progress Made Under the 7th European Framework Programme for Research*. Brussels, 2009. http://eur-lex.europa.eu/LexUriServ/LexUriServ.do?uri=SEC:2009:0589:FIN:EN:PDF.
Contractor, N.S., and P.R. Monge. "Managing Knowledge Networks." *Management Communication Quarterly* 16, no. 2 (November 1, 2002): 249–258.
Corning, P.A. "Synergy, Cybernetics and the Evolution of Politics." *International Political Science Review* 17, no. 1 (1996): 91–119.
Cothey, Viv. "Web-crawling Reliability." *Journal of the American Society for Information Science and Technology* 55, no. 14 (2004): 1228–1238.
Council to the European Union. *EU Presidency Conclusion*. Vol. 2005. Brussels, 2005. http://consilium.europa.eu/uedocs/cms_data/docs/pressdata/en/ec/84335.pdf.
Cox, James. "Transcript of Interview with Andrew Moravcsik 'The World This Weekend.'" UK: BBC, 2002. http://princeton.edu/~amoravcs/library/bbc.pdf.
Cronbach, L.E.E.J. "Beyond the Two Disciplines of Scientific Psychology." *American Psychologist* 30 (February 1975): 116–127.
CRS Report for Congress, *Science and Technology Policymaking: A Primer*, by Stine, Deborah D., 2009. http://fas.org/sgp/crs/misc/RL34454.pdf.
Daalder, I.H. "The End of Atlanticism." *Survival* 45, no. 2 (June 2003): 147–166.
Dehgan, Alex, and E. Colglazier, William. "Development Science and Science Diplomacy." *Science and Diplomacy*, 2012. http://sciencediplomacy.org/print/100.
Dewey, John. *The Public and Its Problems*. New York, NY: Holt, 1927.
Dobriansky, Paula J. "Science, Technology, and Foreign Policy: The Essential Triangle," 2003. http://2001-2009.state.gov/g/rls/rm/2003/20250.htm.
Drezner, Daniel. "Lost in Translation: The Transatlantic Divide Over Diplomacy." In *Growing Apart: America and Europe in the 21st Century*, edited by Jeffrey. Kopstein and Sven Steinmo. Cambridge, MA: Cambridge University Press, 2007.
Dryzek, John S. *Discursive Democracy: Politics, Policy, and Political Science*. New York, NY: Cambridge University Press, 1990.
———. "Transnational Democracy in an Insecure World." *International Political Science Review/ Revue Internationale de Science Politique* 27, no. 2 (April 1, 2006): 101–119.
———. *Foundations and Frontiers of Deliberative Governance*. Oxford, UK: Oxford University Press, 2012.
Edler, Jakob, Stefan Kuhlmann, and Ruud Smits. *Report on a Workshop Held at the Occasion of the 30th Anniversary of the Fraunhofer Institute for Systems and Innovation Research (ISI)*. Karlsruhe, Germany, 2003. http://academia.edu/2902629/New_Governance_for_Innovation._The_Need_for_Horizontal_and_Systemic_Policy_Coordination.
Eggers, William D., and Stephen Goldsmith. *Governing by Network: The New Shape of the Public Sector*. Washington, D.C.: Brookings Institution Press, 2004.
Elazar, Daniel J. *American Federalism: A View from the States*. New York, NY: Crowell, 1966.
Erdős, Paul and Alfréd Rényi. "On Random Graphs I." *Publ. Math*. 6 (1959): 290–297.
Esterling, Kevin M. *The Political Economy of Expertise: Information and Efficiency in American National Politics*. Ann Arbor, MI: University of Michigan Press, 2004.
EU External Action Service. "EU–US Co-Operation by Sector," 2013. http://eeas.europa.eu/us/sector_en.htm.

European Commission, Research D.G. *Towards the Seventh Framework Programme 2007–1013, Building Europe Knowledge,* 2005. http://eurosfaire.prd.fr/bibliotheque/pdf/FP7_Complete_presentation_April_2005.pdf.

EU–U.S. Science and Technology Portal. "The Framework of EU–U.S. S&T Cooperation." *BILAT-USA and Link2US, EU-U.S. Agreements,* 2009. http://archive.euussciencetechnology.eu/home/st_agreement.html.

EU–US. *COUNCIL DECISION of 30 March 2009 Concerning the Extension and Amendment of the Agreement for Scientific and Technological Cooperation Between the European Community and the Government of the United States of America.* Vol. 2009, 2009. http://ec.europa.eu/world/agreements/downloadFile.do?fullText=yes&treatyTransId=13421.

EUEC. "European Council Summit." March 17, 2008. http://euractiv.com/en/science/summit-backs-fifthfreedom-.

———. *Communication from the Commission to the European Parliament, the Council, the European Economic and Social Committee and the Committee of the Regions—Reviewing Community Innovation Policy in a Changing World,* 2009. http://eur-lex.europa.eu/smartapi/cgi/sga_doc?smartapi!celexplus!prod!DocNumber&lg=EN&type_doc=COMfinal&an_doc=2009&nu_doc=442.

———. *Report on the Analysis of U. S. Participation in the 6th and 7th Framework Programmes—Second Update,* 2010. http://archive.euussciencetechnology.eu/uploads/docs/D2_1_US_FP_Participation_secondUpdate.pdf.pdf.

———. "EU–US Trade Policy," 2013. http://ec.europa.eu/trade/policy/countries-and-regions/countries/united-states/.

EUEC–US. "BILAT-USA 2.0," 2010. http://euussciencetechnology.eu.

Euresearch. "Swiss Guide to European Research and Innovation," 2009. http://euresearch.ch/index.php?id=306.

European Commission. "Review of the Science and Technology Cooperation Between the European Community and the United States of America" (2008). http://ec.europa.eu/research/iscp/pdf/eu_us.pdf.

———. "Europe 2020," 2013. http://ec.europa.eu/europe2020/index_en.htm.

———. "Impact Assessment Report on the Future of EU–US Trade Relations, Accompanying the Document Recommendation for a Council Decision Authorising the Opening of Negotiations on a Comprehensive Trade and Investment Agreement, Called the Transatlantic Trade and Investment Partnership, between the European Union and the United States of America," 2013. http://trade.ec.europa.eu/doclib/docs/2013/march/tradoc_150759.pdf.

———. "Innovation Union: A Europe 2020 Initiative," 2013. http://ec.europa.eu/research/innovation-union/index_en.cfm.

"European Research Area." http://ec.europa.eu/research/era.

Finnemore, Martha. "Constructing Norms of Humanitarian Intervention." In *The Culture of National Security: Norms, Identity, and World Politics,* edited by Peter J. Katzenstein, 153–85. New York, NY: Columbia University Press, 1996.

———. *The Purpose of Intervention: Changing Beliefs About the Use of Force.* New York, NY: Cornell University Press, 2003.

Fischer, Andreas, Sarah Nicolet, and Pascal Sciarini. "Europeanisation of a Non-EU Country: The Case of Swiss Immigration Policy." *West European Politics* 25, no. 4 (2002): 143–170.

Fisher, Cathleen. "The Invisible Pillar of Transatlantic Cooperation: Activating Untapped Science & Technology Assets." *Scienceandiplomacy.org* 2, no. 1 (2013). http://scienceandiplomacy.org/files/the_invisible_pillar_of_transatlantic_cooperation_science__diplomacy_0.pdf.

Flyvbjerg, B. "Five Misunderstandings About Case-Study Research." *Qualitative Inquiry* 12, no. 2 (April 1, 2006): 219–245.

Foucault, Michel. *Power/Knowledge: Selected Interviews and Other Writings, 1972–1977*. New York, NY: Pantheon Books, 1980.
Francois, Joseph, Miriam Manchin, Hanna Norberg, Olga Pindyuk, and Patrick Tomberger. *Reducing Transatlantic Barriers to Trade and Investment: An Economic Assessment*. London, UK, 2013. http://trade.ec.europa.eu/doclib/docs/2013/march/tradoc_150737.pdf.
Franklin, Benjamin. "The Way to Wealth." In *The Works of Benjamin Franklin Vol. 2.*, edited by Jared Sparks, 292–103. Boston, 1758.
Frederick, Howard. "Computer Networks and the Emergence of Global Civil Society." In *Global Networks: Computers and International Communication*, edited by Linda M. Harasim. Cambridge, MA: MIT Press, 1993.
Freeman, L. C. "Centrality in Social Networks: I. Conceptual Clarification." *Social Networks* 1 (1979): 215–239.
Freeman, Linton C. "A Set of Measures of Centrality Based on Betweenness." *Sociometry* 40, no. 1 (1977): 35–41.
Fry, Douglas P. *Beyond War: The Human Potential for Peace*. 1st ed. Oxford University Press, 2007.
Fukuyama, Francis. "Social Capital." In *Culture Matters: How Values Shape Human Progress*, edited by L. E. Harrison and S. P. Huntington. New York, NY: Basic Books, 2000.
The German Marshall Foundation. "Transatlantic Trends 2012 Partners: Key Findings" (2013). http://trends.gmfus.org/files/2012/09/TT-2012-Key-Findings-Report.pdf.
The German Marshall Fund of the United States. *Framing a Transatlantic Agenda for a Global Era, Discussion Panel at the Brussels Forum: Transatlantic Challenges in a Global Era*. Brussels, Belgium, 2006. http://gmfus.org/doc/Program Brochure_inside.pdf.
Giddens, Anthony. *The Constitution of Society: Outline of the Theory of Structuration*. Cambridge, MA: Polity Press, 1984.\
———. *Modernity and Self-Identity. Self and Society in the Late Modern Age*. Cambridge, MA: Polity Press, 1991.
Gilgun, Jane F. "Theory and Case Study Research." *Current Issues in Qualitative Research* 2, no. 1–6 (2011). http://scribd.com/doc/48231895/Theory-and-Case-Study-Research.
Gill, Stephen. "Structural Change and Global Political Economy: Globalizing Elites and the Emerging World Order." In *Global Transformation: Challenges to the State System*, edited by Yoshikazu Sakamoto. Tokyo: United Nations University Press, 1994.
GMF. "The German Marshall Fund," 2009. http://gmfus.org/template/index.cfm.
Gourevitch, Peter A., Robert O. Keohane, Stephen D. Krasner, David Laitin, Wolfgang Streeck, Max-planck-institut Gesellschaftsforschung, Sidney Tarrow, and Peter J. Katzenstein. "The Political Science of Peter J. Katzenstein." *APSA* (2008): 893–899.
Government Office for Science. "Europe Looks West: A Resurgence of Pro-Atlanticism Within the EU?" *Department for Business, Innovation, and Skill at GOV.UK*, 2012. http://sigmascan.org/Live/Issue/ViewIssue/35.
Granovetter, Mark S. "The Strength of Weak Ties." *American Journal of Sociology* 78, no. 6 (1973): 1360–1380.
"Graphviz—Graph Visualization Software," 2009. http://graphviz.org.
Green Cowles, Maria, James Caporaso, and Thomas Risse, eds. *Transforming Europe: Europeanization and Domestic Change*. 1st ed. Ithaca, NY: Cornell University Press, n.d.
Gudmundsson, Sveinn Vidar, and Christian Lechner. "Multilateral Airline Alliances: Balancing Strategic Constraints and Opportunities." *Journal of Air Transport Management* 12, no. 3 (May 2006): 153–158.

Haas, Peter. "When Does Power Listen to Truth? A Constructivist Approach to the Policy Process." *Journal of European Public Policy* 11, no. 4 (January 2004): 569–592.

Haas, Peter M. "Introduction: Epistemic Communities and International Policy Coordination." *International Organization* 46, no. 1 (May 22, 1992): 1.

Haas, P.M. "Do Regimes Matter? Epistemic Communities and Mediterranean Pollution Control." *International Organization* 43, no. 3 (Summer 1989): 377–403.

Habermas, Jürgen. *The Theory of Communicative Action.* Original t. Cambridge, MA: Polity Press, 1981.

Hafner-Burton, Emilie M., Miles Kahler, and Alexander H. Montgomery. "Network Analysis for International Relations." *International Organization* 63, no. 3 (July 15, 2009): 559.

Hall, A., and C.R. Taylor. "Political Science and the Three New Institutionalisms" *Political Studies* 44, no. 5 (1996): 936–957.

Hamilton, Daniel S, Frances G Burwell, Daniel Korski, Hugo Paemen, and Charles Ries. *Shoulder to Shoulder: Forging a Strategic U. S.–EU Partnership,* 2009. http://transatlantic.sais-jhu.edu/publications/books/us-eu_report_final.pdf.

Hanneman, Robert A., and Mark Riddle. *Introduction to Social Network Methods.* Riverside, CA: University of California, Riverside, published in digital form, 2005. http://faculty.ucr.edu/~hanneman/.

Hassel, Martin. "Resource Lean and Portable Automatic Text Summarization." Stockholm: KTH, 2007. doi: ISBN-978-917178-704-0.

Hayes, Peter. "The Role of Think Tanks in Defining Security Issues and Agendas," 2004. http://nautilus.org/wp-content/uploads/2011/12/1021_Hayes1.pdf.

Haythornthwaite, Caroline. "Social Network Analysis: An Approach and Technique for the Study of Information Exchange." *Library and Information Science Research* 342 (1996): 323–342.

Hellmann, Gunther. "Are Dialogue and Synthesis Possible in International Relations?" *International Studies Review* 5 (2003): 123–153.

Henshaw, P.F. (Lead Author), and Mark McGinley (Topic Editor). "Complex Systems." In *Encyclopedia of Earth,* edited by Cutler J. Cleveland. Washington, D.C.: Environmental Information Coalition, National Council for Science and the Environment, 2009. http://eoearth.org/view/article/151405.

Herlitschka, Sabine E. *Transatlantic Science and Technology: Opportunities for Real Cooperation Between Europe and the United States.* New York, NY: Springer, 2013.

Higgott, Richard. "The Theory and Practice of Global and Regional Governance: Accommodating American Exceptionalism and European Pluralism," GARNET Working Paper, no. 01 (2005): 1–32. www2.warwick.ac.uk/fac/soc/garnet/workingpapers/0105.pdf.

Hook, Steven W. "Ideas and Change in U.S. Foreign Aid: Inventing the Millennium Challenge Corporation." *Foreign Policy Analysis* 4, no. 2 (April 2008): 147–167.

Hörzer, Gregor. "An Introduction to Spectral Clustering." Computational Intelligence Seminar E, Institute for Theoretical Computer Science, Graz, University of Technology, 2007. http://igi.tugraz.at/lehre/seminarE/SS07/hoerzer.pdf.

Hugo, Victor. *History of a Crime (Histoire D'un Crime).* 2005 reprint. Mondial, 1852.

Huntington, Samuel P. *Political Order in Changing Societies.* New Haven, CT: Yale University Press, 1968.

Ikenberry, John G. *After Victory: Institutions, Strategic Restraint, and the Rebuilding of Order after Major Wars.* Princeton, NJ: Princeton University Press, 2001.

Inglehart, Ronald, and Pippa Norris. *Sacred and Secular: Religion and Politics Worldwide.* Cambridge, MA: Cambridge University Press, 2004.

Inglehart, Ronald, and Christian Welzel. *Modernization, Cultural Change, and Democracy: The Human Development Sequence.* Cambridge, MA: Cambridge University Press, 2005.

Jotterand, Fabrice. "The Politicization of Science and Technology: Its Implications for Nanotechnology." *The Journal of Law, Medicine & Ethics: a Journal of the American Society of Law, Medicine & Ethics* 34, no. 4 (January 2006): 658–66.

Káldor, Mary. *Global Civil Society: An Answer to War.* Cambridge, MA: Polity Press, 2003.

Kamada, Tomihisa, and Satoru Kawai. "A Simple Method for Computing General Position in Displaying Three-Dimensional Objects." *Computer Vision, Graphics, and Image Processing (CVGIP)* 41, no. 1 (1988): 43–56.

Katzenstein, Peter J., Martha Finnemore, and Alexander Wendt. *The Culture of National Security: Norms and Identity in World Politics.* Edited by Peter J. Katzenstein. New York, NY: Columbia University Press, 1996.

Kavanaugh, Andrea L., Debbie Denise Reese, John M. Carroll, and Mary Beth Rosson. "Weak Ties in Networked Communities." *The Information Society* 21, no. 2 (April 2005): 119–131.

Keck, Margaret E., and Kathryn Sikkink. *Activists Beyond Borders: Advocacy Networks in International Politics.* Ithaca, NY: Cornell University Press, 1998.

Kenis, Patrick, and Volker Schneider. "Policy Networks and Policy Analysis: Scrutinizing a New Analytical Toolbox." In *Policy Networks: Empirical Evidence and Theoretical Considerations,* edited by Bernd Marin and Renate Mayntz, 25–54. Frankfurt am Main: Campus Verlag, 1991.

Keohane, R. O. "Ironies of Sovereignty: The European Union and the United States." *JCMS: Journal of Common Market Studies* 40, no. 4 (November 2002): 743–765.

Keohane, Robert O. *After Hegemony: Cooperation and Discord in the World Political Economy.* Princeton, NJ: Princeton University Press, 1984.

———. "The Contingent Legitimacy of UN-Based Multilateralism." In *Legitimacy and Power in the Post-9/11 World.* University of Southern California, Stanford Center for Advanced Study in Behavioral Sciences, 2006.

Keohane Robert O., and Joseph S. Nye. *Power and Interdependence.* New York, NY: Longman, 2001.

Kleinberg, Jon M. "Authoritative Sources in a Hyperlinked Environment." In *SODA '98 Proceedings of the Ninth Annual ACM-SIAM Symposium on Discrete Algorithms, Journal of the ACM (JACM),* (1999): 668–677.

Knoke, David, and Song Yang. *Social Network Analysis, Quantitative Applications in the Social Sciences Series.* 2nd ed. London, UK: Sage Publications, 2008.

Krackhardt, David. "The Strength of Strong Ties: The Importance of Philos in Organizations." In *Networks and Organizations: Structure, Forms, and Action,* edited by Nitin Nohria and Robert G. Eccles, 216–239. Boston, MA: Harvard Business School Press, 1992.

Krebs, Valdis E., and June Holley. "Building Sustainable Communities through Network Building," 2002. www.orgnet.com/buildingnetworks.pdf.

Krebs, VE. "Mapping Networks of Terrorist Cells." *Connections* 24, no. 3 (2002): 43–52.

Krippendorf, K. "Cybernetics." In *International Encyclopedia of Communications, edited by E. Barnouw et al.,* 443–446. New York/Oxford: Oxford University Press, 1989.

Kuhlmann, Stefan. "Future Governance of Innovation Policy in Europe—Three Scenarios." *Research Policy* 30, no. 6 (June 2001): 953–976.

Kuklick, Bruce. *Blind Oracles: Intellectuals and War from Kennan to Kissinger.* Princeton, NJ: Princeton University Press, 2007.

Kurbalija, J., and V. Katrandjiev. "Multistakeholder Diplomacy: Challenges and Opportunities," 2006. http://scholar.google.com/scholar?hl=en&btnG=Search&q=intitle:Multistakeholder+Diplomacy:+Chanllenges+and+Opportunities#1.

Lake, David, and Wendy H. Wong. "The Politics of Networks: Interest, Power, and Human Rights Norms." In *Networked Politics: Agency, Power, and Governance,* edited by Miles Kahler. Ithaca, NY: Cornell University Press, 2009.

Lazer, D. "Regulatory Capitalism as a Networked Order: The International System as an Informational Network." *The ANNALS of the American Academy of Political and Social Science* 598, no. 1 (March 1, 2005): 52–66.

Lazer, David. "Regulatory Capitalism as a Networked Order: The International System as an Informational Network." *The ANNALS of the American Academy of Political and Social Science* 598, no. 1 (March 1, 2005): 52–66.

———. "The Challenges of Networked Governance," 2005. PowerPoint presentation, www.hks.harvard.edu/netgov/files/talks/docs/11_14_05_Seminar_lazer_networked_governance.pdf.

———. "An Introduction to Social Network Analysis," 2007. http://hks.harvard.edu/netgov/files/sna/dg.O_2007_SNA_Tutorial_DLazer.pdf.

Lazer, David, and Allan Friedman. "The Dark Side of the Small World: How Efficient Information Diffusion Drives Out Diversity and Lowers Collective Problem Solving Ability," Harvard Program on Networked Governance Working Paper No. 06–001, 2006. www.hks.harvard.edu/netgov/files/png_workingpaper_series/PNG06-001_WorkingPaper_LazerFriedman.pdf.

———. "The Tragedy of the Network." Paper presented at the annual meeting of the *American Sociological Association, Montreal Convention Center.* Montreal, Quebec, Canada, 2006. http://citation.allacademic.com/meta/p105078_index.html.

Leenders, Roger Th.A.J, Jo M.L van Engelen, and Jan Kratzer. "Virtuality, Communication, and New Product Team Creativity: A Social Network Perspective." *Journal of Engineering and Technology Management* 20, no. 1–2 (June 2003): 69–92.

Levi, Margaret. "A State of Trust." In *Trust and Governance,* edited by V. Braithwaite and M. Levi, 77–101. New York: Russel Sage Foundation, 1998.

Levinson, Nanette S. "Unexpected Allies in Global Governance Arenas? Cross-Cultural Collaborative Knowledge Processes & the Internet Governance Forum. Paper Presented at the Annual Meeting of The International Studies Association's Annual Convention." In *"Theory Vs. Policy? Connecting Scholars and Practitioners."* New Orleans: International Studies Association, 2010. www.allacademic.com/meta/p413163_index.html.

Lin, Nan. "Building a Network Theory of Social Capital." *Connections* 22, no. 1 (1999).

Lord, Kristin M., and Vaughan C. Turekian. "Time for a New Era of Science Diplomacy." *Science and Society Policy Forum,* n.d. http://sciencemag.org/content/315/5813/769.full.pdf.

Lucas, Chris. "Synergy and Complexity Science." *Complexity & Artificial Life Research Concept for Self-Organizing Systems,* CALResCo, 2006. www.calresco.org/wp/synergy.htm.

Luxburg, Ulrike. "A Tutorial on Spectral Clustering." *Statistics and Computing* 17, no. 4 (August 22, 2007): 395–416.

MacCormick, Neil. "Beyond the Sovereign State." *Modern Law Review* 56, no. 1 (January, 1993): 1–18.

McGann, James, and R. Kent Weaver. *Think Tanks and Civil Societies: Catalysts for Ideas and Action.* New Brunswick: NJ: Transaction Publishers, 2006.

McGrew, Anthony. "Transnational Democracy: Theories and Prospects." In *Democratic Theory Today: Challenges for the 21st Century,* edited by Geoffrey Stokes and April Carter, 269–294. Cambridge, UK: Polity Press, 2002.

McPherson, Miller, Smith-Lovin, Lynn, and Cook, James M. "Birds of a Feather: Homophily in Social Networks." *Annual Review of Sociology* 27 (2001): 415–444.

Meila, M., and William Pentney. "Clustering by Weighted Cuts in Directed Graphs." In *SIAM Conference on Data Mining* (*SDM*), 2007. http://citeseerx.ist.psu.edu/viewdoc/download?doi=10.1.1.80.2833&rep=rep1&type=pdf.

Mergel, Ines, and T. Langenberg. "What Makes Online Ties Sustainable? A Research Design Proposal to Analyze Online Social Networks." *Harvard Program on Networked Governance* (2006). http://hks.harvard.edu/netgov/files/png_working paper_series/PNG06–002_WorkingPaper_MergelLangenberg.pdf.

Meunier, S. "Do Transatlantic Relations Still Matter?" *Perspectives on Europe* (*Council for European Studies*) 40, no. 1 (2010). http://academiccommons.columbia.edu/download/fedora_content/download/ac:131186/CONTENT/PerspectivesOnEurope_Meunier.pdf.

Meunier, Sophie. *Trading Voices: The European Union in International Commercial Negotiations*. Princeton, NJ: Princeton University Press, 2005.

Modelski, George, and W.R. Thompson. "The Long and the Short of Global Politics in the Twenty-first Century: An Evolutionary Approach." *International Studies Review* 1, no. 2 (1999): 109–140.

Moravcsik, Andrew. "Striking a New Transatlantic Bargain." *Foreign Affairs* 82, no. 4 (2003): 74–89.

———. "Theory Synthesis in International Relations: Real Not Metaphysical." *International Studies Review* 5 (2003): 131.

Moreno, Jacob L. *Who Shall Survive?: Foundations of Sociometry, Group Psychotherapy, and Sociodrama*. Washington, D.C.: Nervous and Mental Disease Publishing Company, 1934.

Morgenthau, Hans J. *In Defense of the National Interest: A Critical Examination of American Foreign Policy*. New York, NY: Alfred A. Knopf, 1951.

Mott, William H. *Globalization: People, Perspectives, and Progress*. Westport, CT: Praeger Publishers, 2004.

Mrvar, Andrej, and Vladimir Batagelj. "Pajek Workshop." In *Sunbelt XXIX*, San Diego, March 10–15, 2009. http://pajek.imfm.si/lib/exe/fetch.php.?id=download&cache=cache&media=dl:wsxxix.

Mueller, Milton L, Brenden N. Kuerbis, and Christiane Pagé. "Democratizing Global Communication? Global Civil Society and the Campaign for Communication Rights in the Information Society." *International Journal of Communication* 1 (2007): 267–296.

Mueller, Milton, Andreas Schmidt, and Brenden Kuerbis. "Internet Security and Networked Governance in International Relations." *International Studies Review* 15, no. 1 (March 10, 2013): 86–104.

Natarajan, Mangai. "Understanding the Structure of a Large Heroin Distribution Network: A Quantitative Analysis of Qualitative Data." *Journal of Quantitative Criminology* 22, no. 2 (June 9, 2006): 171–192.

National Academy of Sciences, National Academy of Engineering Institute of Medicine. *State Science and Technology Policy Advice: Issues, Opportunities, and Challenges: Summary of a National Convocation*. Edited by Steve Olson and Jay B. Labov. National Academies Press, 2008. http://books.google.com/books?hl=en&lr=&id=34YPVFqTW0MC&oi=fnd&pg=PR1&dq=State+Science+and+Technology+Policy+Advice:+Issues,+Opportunities,+and+Challenges:+Summary+of+a+National+Convocation&ots=A-MaygAvOX&sig=2MISrXCc6F6QKoVdFJAvPEdSEiw.

National Intelligence Council. *Global Trends 2030: Alternative Worlds*, 2012. http://globaltrends2030.files.wordpress.com/2012/11/global-trends-2030-november2012.pdf.

National Science Foundation. *Justification of Estimates on Appropriations, Fiscal Year 1952*. 81st Congress, n.d. www.nsf.gov/pubs/1952/b_1952_7.pdf.

Nelson, Theodor. "Computers, Creativity and the Nature of the Written Word," 1965. http://faculty.vassar.edu/mijoyce/MiscNews_Feb65.html.

Nooy, Wouter, Andrej Mrvar, and Vladimir Batagelj. *Exploratory Social Network Analysis with Pajek*. New York, NY: Cambridge University Press, 2005.

Nussbaum, Martha, and Amartya Sen. *The Quality of Life (Studies in Development Economics)*. Edited by Martha Nussbaum and Amartya Sen. New York, NY: Oxford University Press, 1993.

Nye, Joseph S. *Soft Power: The Means to Success in World Politics*. 1st ed. New York: Public Affairs, 2004.

Nye, Joseph S., and Robert O. Keohane. "Transnational Relations and World Politics: A Conclusion." *International Organization* 25, no. 3 (May 22, 1971): 721.

Obama, Barack. "Remarks by the President on the 'Educate to Innovate' Campaign and Science Teaching and Mentoring Awards." The White House, 2010. http://whitehouse.gov/the-press-office/remarks-president-educate-innovate-campaign-and-science-teaching-and-mentoring-awar.

Olson, Ronald L, Paul H. O'Neill, Michael K. Powell, Donald B. Rice, and Harold Brown. *Setting Politics Aside,* 2008. http://rand.org/content/dam/rand/pubs/corporate_pubs/2010/RAND_CP1–2008.pdf.

Opsahl, Tore. "Tore Opsahl Personal Web Log," 2010. http://toreopsahl.com/.

Opsahl, Tore, Vittoria Colizza, Pietro Panzarasa, and J. J. Ramasco. "Prominence and Control: The Weighted Rich-Club Effect." *Physical Review Letters* (2008): 1–4.

OSTP. "The Office of Science and Technology Policy, Executive Office of the President," 2009. http://ostp.gov/cs/about_ostp/history.

OSTP Press Release, Office of Science and Technology, 2004. http://ostina.org/index2.php? option=com_ content&.

Padgett, J. F., and C. K. Ansell. "Robust Action and the Rise of the Medici, 1400–1434." *American Journal of Sociology* 98, no. 6 (1993): 1259–1319.

Park, H. W. "Hyperlink Network Analysis: A New Method for the Study of Social Structure on the Web." *Connections* 25, no. 1 (2003): 49–61.

Parmar, Inderjeet. "American Foundations and the Development of International Knowledge Networks." *Global Networks* 1 (2002): 13–30.

Pasteur, Louis. "Quotationspage.com." http://quotationspage.com/quote/27258.html.

Peters, B. Guy. *Institutional Theory in Political Science. The "New Institutionalism."* London, UK: Pinter, 1999.

Peterson, John. *Europe and America: The Prospects for Partnership*. 1st ed. Cheltenham, UK: Edward Elgar Publishing Limited, 1993.

Peterson, John, and Rebecca Steffenson. "Transatlantic Institutions: Can Partnership Be Engineered?" *The British Journal of Politics & International Relations* 11 (2009): 25–45.

Pettit, Philip. *Republicanism: A Theory of Freedom and Government*. Oxford, UK: Oxford University Press, 1997.

Pfeffer, Jeffrey, and Gerald R. Salancik. *The External Control of Organizations: A Resource Dependence Perspective*. New York, NY: Harper and Row, 1978.

Pielke, Roger A. "Accepting Politics in Science." *Washington Post,* January 10, 2005. http://washingtonpost.com/wp-dyn/articles/A61928–2005Jan9.html.

Pollack, Mark A. "The New Transatlantic Agenda at Ten: Reflections on an Experiment in International Governance." *JCMS: Journal of Common Market Studies* 43, no. 5 (December 2005): 899–919.

Pollack, Mark A., and Gregory C. Shaffer. *Transatlantic Governance in the Global Economy*. Edited by Mark A. Pollack and Gregory C. Shaffer. Lanham, MD: Rowman and Littlefield Publishers, Inc., 2001.

Putnam, Robert D. *Making Democracy Work: Civic Traditions in Modern Italy*. Princeton, NJ: Princeton University Press, 1993.

———. *Bowling Alone: The Collapse and Revival of American Community.* 1st ed. New York, NY: Simon & Schuster, 2000.
———. "Diplomacy and Domestic Politics: the Logic of Two-Level Games." *International Organization* 42, no. 3 (1988): 427–460.
Quinlan, J.P. *Drifting Apart Or Growing Together?: The Primacy of the Transatlantic Economy.* Washington, D.C.: Center for Transatlantic Relations, 2003. http://kms2.isn.ethz.ch/serviceengine/Files/RESSpecNet/46948/ipublicationdocument_singledocument/47F34B9C-04BA-4411-8738-D31867721737/en/2003_drifting+apart.pdf.
Reinicke, Wolfgang H., Francis Deng, Jan Martin Witte, Thorsten Benner, Beth Whitaker, and John Gersham. *Critical Choices. The United Nations, Networks, and the Future of Global Governance.* Edited by Wolfgang H. Reinicke, Francis Deng, Jan Martin Witte, Thorsten Benner, Beth Whitaker, and John Gersham. Ottawa, Canada: International Development Research Center Books, 2000.
Risse, Thomas. "Social Constructivism and European Integration." In *European Integration Theory,* edited by Antje Wiener and Thomas Diez, 159–176. Oxford, UK: Oxford University Press, 2004.
———. "Social Constructivism Meets Globalization." In *Globalization Theory: Approaches and Controversies,* edited by Anthony McGrew and David Held. Cambridge, UK: Polity Press, 2007.
———. "The Crisis of the Transatlantic Security Community." In *Multilateralism and Security Institutions in an Era of Globalization,* edited by Dimitris Bourantonis, Ifantis Kostas, and Tsakonas Panayotis, 78–100. New York, NY: Routledge, 2007.
Risse-Kappen, Thomas. *Cooperation Among Democracies: The European Influence on U.S. Foreign Policy.* Princeton, NJ: Princeton University Press, 1997.
Rogers, E.M. *Diffusion of Innovations.* 5th ed. New York, NY: Free Press, 2003.
Rosenau, James N. *Turbulence in World Politics.* Princeton, NJ: Princeton University Press, 1990.
The Royal Society & AAAS. *New Frontiers in Science Diplomacy,* 2010. www.aaas.org/sites/default/files/New_Frontiers.pdf.
Saward, Michael. *The Terms of Democracy.* Cambridge, MA: Polity Press, 1998.
Sbragia, Alberta M. "Thinking About the European Future: The Uses of Comparison." In *Euro-Politics. Institutions and Policymaking in the "New" European Community,* edited by Alberta M. Sbragia. Washington, D.C.: The Brookings Institution, 1992.
———. "The European Community: a Balancing Act." *Publius: The Journal of Federalism* 23, no. 3 (1993): 23–38.
Schneider, Mark, and John Scholz. "Building Consensual Institutions: Networks and the National Estuary Program." *American Journal of Political Science.* 47, no. 1 (January 2003): 143–158.
Schmidt, Vivien. "Reconciling Ideas and Institutions through Discursive Institutionalism." in *Ideas.*
and Politics in Social Science Research, edited by Daniel Béland and Robert H. Cox, Oxford: Oxford University Press, 2011.
Scott, John. *Social Network Analysis: A Handbook.* 1st ed. Newberry Park, CA: Sage Publications Ltd., 1991.
———. *Social Network Analysis: A Handbook.* 2nd ed. Thousand Oaks, CA: Sage Publications Ltd., 2000.
Shaw, Marvin E. "Group Structure and the Behavior of Individuals in Small Groups." *The Journal of Psychology* 38, no. 1 (July 1954): 139–149.
Simmel, Georg. *The Sociology of Georg Simmel.* New York, NY: Free Press, 1950.
Skolnikoff, Eugene B. *The Elusive Transformation: Science, Technology, and the Evolution of International Politics.* Princeton, NJ: Princeton University Press, 1993.

Slaughter, Anne-Marie. *A New World Order.* Princeton, NJ: Princeton University Press, 2004.

Snyder, R.C., C.F. Hermann, and H.D. Lasswell. "A Global Monitoring System: Appraising the Effects of Government on Human Dignity." *International Studies Quarterly* 20, no. 2 (1976): 221–260.

Song, M. "Who Are the Influentials? A Cross-State Social Network Analysis of the Reading Policy Domain." *Educational Administration Quarterly* 41, no. 1 (February 1, 2005): 7–48.

Sporns, O., G. Tononi, and G.M. Edelman. "Theoretical Neuroanatomy: Relating Anatomical and Functional Connectivity in Graphs and Cortical Connection Matrices." *Cerebral Cortex* 10, no. 2 (February 2000): 127–41.

Steffenson, Rebecca. *Managing EU–US Relations: Actors, Institutions and the New Transatlantic Agenda.* Manchester, UK: Manchester University Press, 2005.

Steinbach, Michael, Levent Ertoz, and Vipin Kumar. "The Challenges of Clustering Highly Dimensional Data." in *New Directions in Statistical Physics: Econophysics, Bioinformatics, and Pattern Recognition,* edited by Luc T. Ville. Berlin, Germany: Springer, 2004.

Stine, Deborah D. "Science and Technology Policymaking: A Primer," Congressional Research Service Report, 2009. http://fas.org/sgp/crs/misc/RL34454.pdf.

Stone, Diane. "Think Tank Transnationalisation and Non-Profit Analysis, Advice and Advocacy." *Global Society* 14, no. 2 (April 2000): 153–172.

———. "Knowledge in the Global Agora: Production, Dissemination and Consumption." In *Reshaping Globalization: Multilateral Dialogues and New Policy Initiatives,* edited by Andrea Krizsán, 41–62. Budapest, Hungary: Central European University Press, 2003. www2.warwick.ac.uk/fac/soc/ pais/staff/stone/.

———. "Knowledge Networks and Global Policy." In *Global Knowledge Networks and International Development,* edited by Diane Stone and Simon Maxwell. New York, NY: Routledge, 2004.

———. "Knowledge Networks and Global Policy." In *Global Knowledge Networks and International Development,* edited by D. Stone and S. Maxwell. 1st ed. New York, NY: Routledge, 2005.

Stone, Diane, and Andrew Denham. *Think Tank Traditions, Policy Research and the Politics of Idea.* Manchester, UK: Manchester University Press, 2004.

Strange, Susan. "Toward a Theory of Transnational Empire." In *Global Changes and Theoretical Challenges: Approaches to World Politics for the 1990's,* edited by Ernst-Otto Czempiel and James N. Rosenau. Lexington, MA: Lexington Books, 1989.

The Streit Council for the Union of Democracies. "Transatlantic Cooperation," 2009. http://streitcouncil.org/index.php?page=transatlantic-cooperation.

Szent-Györgyi, Albert. *The Crazy Ape.* 1st ed. New York: Philosophical Library, 1970.

Tan, Pang-Ning, Michael Steinbach, and Vipin Kumar. "Data Mining Cluster Analysis: Basic Concepts and Algorithms," 2004. www-users.cs.umn.edu/~kumar/dmbook/dmslides/chap8_basic_cluster_analysis.pdf.

Tetzlaff, Rainer. "International Organizations (World Bank, IMF, EU) as Catalyst of Democratic Values, Rule of Law and Human Rights—Successes and Limits." Denver, CO, 2006. http://partners.civiced.org/paw/tools/people_download.php?%0Agroup=event&id=193.

Thelwall, M. "A Web Crawler Design for Data Mining." *Journal of Information Science* 27, no. 5 (October 1, 2001): 319–325.

Thompson, Grahame F. *Between Hierarchies and Markets: The Logic and Limits of Network Forms of Organization.* 1st ed. Oxford, UK: Oxford University Press, 2003.

"TransAtlantic Business Dialogue." http://tabd.com/.

"Transatlantic Information Exchange System (TIES)." http://tiesweb.org/about_ties/history.htm.

Trudeau, Richard J. *Introduction to Graph Theory.* Mineola, NY: Dover Publications, 1994.

Turekian, Vaughan C. "Building a National Science Diplomacy System." *Science & Diplomacy* 1, no. 4 (2012). http://sciencediplomacy.org/files/building_a_national_science_diplomacy_system_science__diplomacy.pdf.

USDS. "Fact Sheet: The New Transatlantic Agenda." *U.S. Department of State Dispatch, 10517693* 6, no. 49 (1995). http://dosfan.lib.uic.edu/ERC/briefing/dispatch/1995/html/Dispatchv6no49.html.

Uzzi, Brian, and Michael Schwartz. "Book Review of 'Holy Theory:' The Social Structure of Competition (1992) by Ronald S. Burt." *Contemporary Sociology* 22 (1993): 155–157.

Uzzi, Brian, and J. Spiro. "Collaboration and Creativity: The Small World Problem1." *American Journal of Sociology* 111, no. 2 (2005): 447–504.

Van Dijk, Jan. *The Network Society: Social Aspect of New Media.* London, Thousand Oaks, New Delhi: Sage Publications Ltd., 1999.

Vasconcelos, Álvaro de, and Marcin Zaborowski, eds. "The Obama Moment: European and American Perspectives." *Intereconomics.* European Union Institute for Security Studies, January 29, 2009. http://iss.europa.eu/uploads/media/The_Obama_Moment__web_A4.pdf.

Volgy, Thomas J., and Alison Bailin. *International Politics and State Strength.* Boulder, CO: Lynne Rienner Publishers Inc., 2003.

Walton, Whitney, and Mark Rennella. "Planned Serendipity: American Travelers and the Transatlantic Voyage in the Nineteenth and Twentieth Centuries." *Journal of Social History* 2 (2004). http://muse.jhu.edu/journals/journal_of_social_history/v038/38.2rennella.html.

Waltz, Kenneth N. *Man, the State, and War: A Theoretical Analysis.* New York, NY: Columbia University Press, 1979.

Wartofsky, M.W. "Technology, Power, and Truth: Political and Epistemological Reflections on the Fourth Revolution." In *Democracy in the Technological Society,* edited by L. Winner. Dordrecht: Kluwer, 1992.

Wasserman, Stanley, and Katherine Faust. *Social Network Analysis. Methods and Applications.* Cambridge, MA: Cambridge University Press, 1994.

Weare, Christopher, W.E. Loges, and N. Oztas. "Email Effects on the Structure of Local Associations: A Social Network Analysis" *Social Science Quarterly* 88, no. 1 (2007): 222–243.

Wendt, Alexander. "Anarchy Is What States Make of It: The Social Construction of Power Politics." *International Organization* 46, no. 2 (1992): 391–425. http://jstor.org/stable/2706858?origin=JSTOR-pdf.

Wong, Wendy H. *Internal Affairs: How the Structure of NGOs Transforms Human Rights.* 1st ed. Ithaca, NY: Cornell University Press, 2012.

Yang, Yu-Bin, Ni Li, and Yao Zhang. "Networked Data Mining Based on Social Network Visualizations." *Journal of Software* 19, no. 8 (October 22, 2008): 1980–1994.

Yin, Robert K. *Case Study Research.* Thousand Oaks, CA: Sage Publications Ltd., 2003.

Ziman, John. *Real Science: What It Is, and What It Means.* New York, NY: Cambridge University Press, 2002.

Index

www.ingramcontent.com/pod-product-compliance
Lightning Source LLC
Chambersburg PA
CBHW071147050326
40689CB00011B/2007
* 9 7 8 1 1 3 8 6 9 6 4 1 9 *